HOTEL & MOTEL LOSS PREVENTION
A Management Perspective

Harvey Burstein
Northeastern University

Prentice
Hall

Upper Saddle River, New Jersey 07458

Library of Congress Cataloging-in-Publication Data

Burstein, Harvey.

Hotel & Motel loss prevention : a management perspective / Harvey Burstein.

p.   cm.

Includes index.

ISBN 0-13-010909-6

1. Hotels—Security measures.   I. Title.

TX911.3.S4 B86 2001

647.94'068'4—dc21

00–039205

Publisher: Dave Garza
Production Editor: Marianne Hutchinson
Production Liaison: Barbara Martine Cappuccio
Director of Manufacturing and Production: Bruce Johnson
Managing Editor: Mary Carnis
Manufacturing Manager: Ed O'Dougherty
Art Director: Marianne Frasco
Cover Design Coordinator: Miguel Ortiz
Marketing Manager: Ryan DeGrote
Editorial Assistant: Susan Kegler
Interior Design and Composition: Pine Tree Composition
Printing and Binding: R.R. Donnelley & Sons

Prentice-Hall International (UK) Limited, *London*
Prentice-Hall of Australia Pty. Limited, *Sydney*
Prentice-Hall Canada Inc., *Toronto*
Prentice-Hall Hispanoamericana, S. A., *Mexico*
Prentice-Hall of India Private Limited, *New Delhi*
Prentice-Hall of Japan, Inc., *Tokyo*
Prentice-Hall Singapore Pte. Ltd.
Editora Prentice-Hall do Brasil, Ltda., *Rio de Janeiro*

10 9 8 7 6 5 4 3 2 1

ISBN   0-13-010909-6

This book is dedicated to my many friends in the lodging industry with whom I've had the pleasure and privilege of working over the years and from whom I've learned so much.

CONTENTS

FOREWORD

The evolution of hotel security, from stagecoach inns where doors had no locks to individual roadside cabins and motels with outside corridors, to high-rise city and resort hotels with sophisticated electronic locks, automatic fire safety systems, television surveillance cameras, and computerized inventories, has been a journey of 150 years. Today, at the advent of the 21st century, the complexity of operating a hotel is equivalent to managing a city, and the general manager's position is comparable to the office of mayor. A city, however, while protective of its citizens, is a government monopoly and remains impersonal in its actions, while a well-run hotel has a friendly, professional, and secure atmosphere encompassing its guests, staff, and the physical assets, both fixed and inventoried.

This book consists of a detailed, hands-on explanation of each department and the role it plays in overall security. It will provide essential knowledge for those who presently have the responsibility for hotel operations as well as for those men and women who are studying to become the managers of tomorrow. During my 50-year career in the hotel business, ranging from bellman and barman to general manager and president, and finally as the owner of independent and franchised hotel properties in Boston, Connecticut, and Florida, it has been my good fortune to work with a talented and friendly staff serving guests from around the world and around the corner who appreciate our efforts. There are also, unfortunately, those people who would try to defeat our goals by illegal or immoral means, given the opportunity.

It is an axiom that 80 percent of guests and employees are honest when appropriate deterrents are in place. However, 10 percent will always try to find ways to circumvent these safeguards, and 10 percent would be honest irrespective of any lack of security. We will read here how to create a comfortable atmosphere of standards that will make a hotel and its many facets a safe home to travelers, while protecting the employees and the assets of the stockholders.

Just as each employee in a hotel is a reflection of the hospitality of that property, this book is an explanation of the part that each staff member in his department plays in a secure operation.

We may not often consider that security involves every department—from the front of the house: management, sales, reservations, front office, telephone, restaurant, banquet staff, concierges, and bell staff, to the back of the house: kitchen and storeroom personnel, housekeeping, engineering, accounting, human resources, management offices, and the security staff themselves. This book provides a road map for the part that each department plays in the overall operation.

During my tenure as national president of the American Hotel and Motel Association, with over 10,000 membership properties, and previously as president of the Boston and Massachusetts Lodging Associations, I've had the privilege of knowing the author, Harvey Burstein, in his many capacities in the industry. His personal experience in hotels, education, and national societies makes this book a security bible that will be indispensable as you go forward as hoteliers to operate the best hotels securely and professionally.

Good luck in your work and your lifelong education, destined to make a good hotel better and a better hotel an ousdanding, distinctive, and profitable hostelry.

Roger A. Saunders

PREFACE

This book is not the first written on the subject of hotel security. However, the others, including some of my own, have tended to focus mainly on the roles of security directors and their staffs rather than on those of hotel management personnel and hotel employees in general. My own experiences in the industry have led me to conclude that this gap needs to be filled if future generations of hotel managers, and the properties by which they are employed, are to enjoy the optimum benefits of effective loss-prevention programs.

A large part of the problem, even at properties priding themselves on their current security practices, stems from those owners and general managers who still do not really understand what security, in the broadest sense of the word, can contribute to a property's profits and reputation. They are inclined to think of security as a limited, narrowly defined function whose sole responsibility is to prevent crime. This misconception may well persist indefinitely, to the lodging industry's detriment, unless students in hotel management programs are exposed to new ideas about what security really is and what it should be doing at any property.

With that thought in mind, I have undertaken to write this text for the uninitiated, hoping that it will serve a useful purpose. This book is designed to help students understand that policing and security are not the same and that there are differences between crime prevention and loss prevention.

One cannot ignore the importance of preventing crime. When crimes occur at any property, the impact may range from filing an insurance claim through litigation to adverse publicity and a decline in occupancy. Realistically, however, to operate profitably neither can the importance of general loss-prevention measures be minimized. Anything that prevents losses, or at least helps reduce their dollar value, is fundamental to good management. Coincidentally, many measures designed to prevent losses can be instituted with or without formally organized security departments, often at little expense. It is this awareness that I hope to create by exposing hotel management students, for whom this text is intended, to new ideas of which they previously may not have been aware.

In concluding I must thank Albert J. Pucciarelli, Chief Legal Officer, General Counsel and Secretary of Inter-Continental Hotels, and Jeffrey Saunders of Saunders Hotels, for providing me with photographs to help dress up the book, and Roger Saunders, a past president of the American Hotel & Motel Association, for so graciously having agreed to write a fore-word. I would be remiss if I failed to thank MJ Linney of El Paso Community College, whose early review was both appreciated and helpful, as well as those at Prentice Hall with whom I have had the pleasure of working, espe-cially Neil Marquardt. Equally important, in any work of this kind there may be occasional errors despite the author's best efforts and those of the editor and production staff. However, let it be understood that all errors of omission or commission are mine and mine alone.

ABOUT THE AUTHOR

Harvey Burstein, David B. Schulman Professor of Security at Northeastern University's College of Criminal Justice, is a graduate of the Creighton University School of Law, a former special agent of the Federal Bureau of Investigation, and Chief, Foreign and Domestic Investigations, Surveys, and Physical Security, U.S. Department of State. Since leaving federal service Mr. Burstein has practiced law, been a security management consultant for various Fortune 500 companies, and worked as a corporate security director.

As a consultant he has been retained by the American Hotel & Motel Association, Inter-Continental Hotels, the Chicago Ritz Carlton Hotel, Marcus Hotels, the Saunders Hotels Company, Inc., and Sage Hotels and Lodges; he has also served on the AH&MA's Security, Safety, and Fire Prevention Committee. Mr. Burstein has been the corporate security director for Sheraton Hotels and a visiting faculty member at Cornell University's School of Hotel Administration. In addition, he has addressed meetings of the AH&MA, Quality Inns, Westin Hotels, the Georgia, Iowa, Missouri, and Caribbean Hotel & Motel Associations, the Club Managers of America, and the National Restaurant Association.

The author of nine books on various aspects of security management and investigations, Mr. Burstein also was asked to write the chapter on security for the third edition of G. H. Lattin's *Modern Hotel and Motel Management*. He currently is a member of the editorial advisory board of Hotel/Motel Security and Safety Management.

CHAPTER 1

INTRODUCTION: HOTEL MANAGEMENT AND LOSS PREVENTION

Hotel security is not something new in the lodging industry. It has been evolving over an extended period of time and is still in an evolutionary stage. The same is true of its acceptance and meaningful application by hotel management, processes that are by no means complete. The delay is largely due to management's inability to distinguish between security as a concept and security as a function, and this confusion leads to a misunderstanding of what security is really all about.

In the lodging industry's relatively early days, it was not unusual to find men in plainclothes employed as "house detectives." Their primary responsibilities included acting as peacekeepers in the bars and preventing—or at least trying to control—prostitution in more upscale properties.

However, as more and more travelers used hotels, particularly in big cities, properties employing either their own security personnel or relying on local police departments also became increasingly concerned with preventing crimes, especially room burglaries, that could affect guest relations. As an example, in 1906 Detective Sergeant Joseph Faurot of the New York City Police Department, while on duty at the Waldorf-Astoria Hotel, became suspicious of a man he saw in the hallway on a guest room floor. The man was wearing formal attire—but no shoes. After taking the man into custody, Faurot learned that he was wanted in England for numerous burglaries.[1] The limited focus on security, such as it was in those days, was guest oriented; that security could or should play a role in protecting hotel assets was not given much thought, despite the industry's unique nature.

LODGING, A SERVICE INDUSTRY

One might well ask, just what contributes to the hospitality industry's uniqueness? First, it is a service industry; of course there are others, such as retailers and medical centers. All have security concerns, only some of which they share in common; others are distinctly different. As we shall see, neither retail stores nor hospitals are confronted with the same variety of challenges as are hotels.

Nevertheless, let us first look at what these three service industries have in common. All must rely on the public's acceptance and use of their services for their very survival. Thus, as a practical matter, the very public that is being served—whether guests, customers, and patients (and their visitors)—represents a threat of possible loss, regardless of the nature of the loss itself. Then there is the reality that in order to provide services to the public, all the industries need staff. Thus service industry employers are additionally exposed to the possibility of losses and risks that originate with employees. Employers' susceptibility in terms of losses from theft or other misappropriation is heightened by virtue of the fact that any number of their assets are things that can be used by persons either for themselves or for their homes.

In other words, unlike manufacturers, whose direct exposure to the general public is virtually nonexistent, hotels, retailers, and hospitals are confronted with the need to protect themselves from losses that can be attributed to two different quarters. On one hand is the public and on the other are employees, both groups potential sources of loss, which, if transformed from potential to real, can prove costly in many ways.

Of the three cited service industries, the greatest similarity is found between hotels and medical centers. Even so, a number of differences remain. Hotels and hospitals, unlike most retail stores and other publicly related activities, are open, operating, and staffed twenty-four hours a day, every day of the year. In and of itself this feature certainly increases their exposure to risks; and where risks exist, some loss is almost inevitable.

Once one goes beyond the similarity in their hours of operation, features that distinguish hotels from hospitals become self-evident. For instance, many hospital patients are immobile. Even the movement of those who are ambulatory, as well as that of their visitors, can be and is controlled. Hotels cannot restrict the comings and goings either of guests or of those who are merely attending functions or enjoying the services of the property's food and beverage outlets. Realistically, there are also limits on how much control can be exercised over people who are visiting guests. This very freedom of movement can add to a property's risk of losses in any number of ways.

As a rule, hospital patients, before being admitted, are urged to not bring money or other valuables with them but to leave them at home. Hotels most assuredly cannot do this with guests. At best they can offer, but not compel, the use of safe-deposit boxes, which may be located in the front office area or available in individual guest rooms. However, whether they use them or not, guests still expect both their persons and their property to be protected. The fact that posted copies of the *Innkeepers' Law* in every room can be a defense in cases litigated following the alleged theft of guests' valuables does not prevent a guest from filing suit. Even persons who are not registered but who use a hotel's facilities for a function, casual drink in a bar, or meal in an outlet expect to be protected. As an industry completely dependent upon the public, these are not unjustified or insignificant expectations.

REPUTATION AS AN ASSET

The foregoing considerations do not pose the only challenges for innkeepers. One of the greatest, and most important, is the need to protect a property's reputation. No business or institution likes bad publicity. However, the im-

Chapter 1   Introduction: Hotel Management and Loss Prevention

3

pact tends to have its greatest effect on service industries because of their relationship with and reliance on the general public.

With retailers the results of bad publicity often tend to be relatively short-lived. This is especially true if the adverse comments are spread by word of mouth rather than by newspaper stories or radio or television newscasts. Bad publicity can stem from rudeness or inattention on the part of a salesperson, misleading advertising, the poor quality of merchandise, or an unfortunate encounter with a security officer. Nevertheless, members of the buying public will not necessarily impute the bad publicity affecting one store to all the others in that operation. In addition, the temporary damage to reputation may be overcome with sales promotions, or the store may benefit from the fact that it carries certain brands that are unavailable from competitors.

Certainly bad publicity for a hospital can cause a great deal of consternation on the part of patients and their families without necessarily causing any marked reduction in its use. If a hospital's accreditation is unaffected, a patient's physician has staff privileges and a good relationship with the patient, the service providing treatment or care is not involved, and the facility is convenient for visits from family and friends, any concerns may be short-lived. Moreover, a patient may have relatively little choice of facilities should treatment require hospitalization.

In contrast, hotels subjected to bad publicity may suffer long-term and in time may find that their customer or guest base has eroded. True, they can offer promotions, but unlike retailers their hoped-for audience is more widespread geographically. Since most properties in any given class offer the same amenities, they cannot advertise brands or services as unavailable from competitors. Neither do they have the advantages, however few, that can help medical centers overcome a negative image. Hotels have a great deal of competition whether in terms of location, rates, or amenities. Travelers rarely have but one choice of hotel. In fact, their greatest difficulty may lie in choosing one hotel from among many.

Unhappy guests must be a cause for concern, but the causes of their dissatisfaction may be due to any number of reasons other than having been the victims of a crime. Regardless, that does not alter the fact that whatever the reason for their unhappiness, expressing themselves to business associates, family, or friends, even though by word of mouth, may prompt any or all of these people to avoid a particular property. If they, in turn, tell others, the impact obviously can be much more far-reaching.

Another distinguishing characteristic of hotels that cannot be ignored is the possible effect of adverse publicity for one hotel on others that, at least in the public's mind, are part of the same chain. The public is not inclined to think of a hospital as part of a chain, and it frequently thinks of a retail store as being local even if it is part of a chain, but the same cannot be said of hotels. Instead, with hotels it is more likely that bad publicity for one property will have an impact on others using that same name, and the result will be lower occupancy rates.

Most travelers, both the experienced and the inexperienced, tend to choose a hotel primarily on the basis of reputation. Either they have had a good experience, or they have heard good things about a particular property. The average guest neither knows nor cares about license or franchise agreements; it is name recognition that attracts them to a property. To that person it is immaterial whether a Westin, Hyatt, Sheraton, Hilton, Marriott, Ritz Carlton, Inter-Continental, Holiday Inn, and so on is owned and operated or managed by a chain or whether it merely is authorized to use the name. Bad publicity for any one can affect others that, to the public, are part of the same operation.

Therefore, to say that it is evident that a property's reputation and guest concerns are of paramount importance to inn-keepers overlooks the fact that any number of incidents can arise and affect both, without the involvement of any criminality. It is in the realm of activities that go beyond guest protection and reputation that hotel management gives short shrift to a possible role for security.

MANAGEMENT'S ROLE IN SECURITY

The problem may be one of perception, attitude, or both, but in any case it is one for which a solution is badly needed. Management personnel must learn or relearn a number of things. Among the questions that they need to answer are the following:

Just what is security?
On what should the security emphasis be placed?
Do all properties need a constituted security department, or can protection be achieved in other ways?
What is—or should be—management's role in security?

Just What Is Security?

To put it simply, from a management perspective in any business, hotels included, security is—or should be—the protection and conservation of all assets, both tangible and intangible. Certainly, an organization's real estate and most of its personal property are tangible. Its reputation, and information in other than hard copy, are intangible, but assets nonetheless. In other words, effective security consists of effective loss prevention, not merely crime prevention. To achieve this goal, inn-keepers have to take into consideration the roles of physical security, all aspects of hotel operations and staffing, guests, and risk management. They have to understand security-related legal issues and make decisions with regard to whether or not security departments are necessary for their properties.

The Security Emphasis

Accepting the proper definition of security suggests where the emphasis must be placed. It cannot be on crime prevention alone, despite its importance. Instead, the emphasis has to be on all forms of *loss prevention*. Significant losses can occur from causes other than crimes. Furthermore, loss prevention is the only truly cost-effective way of dealing with a wide range of concerns that can have an adverse impact on operations, reputations, and profitability. While it would be ideal to prevent all forms of loss, it is important to recognize that some losses are inevitable. In those cases, it is no less important to make every effort to keep the dollar value and the effect on operations of such losses to a minimum.

Can There Be Protection without a Security Department?

There is neither a single nor a simple answer. Under certain conditions it may be possible to provide an acceptable level of protection without the need for a formally established security department. Perhaps protection can be provided by a combination of some form of security training for all members of the staff and the selected use of certain types of high technology equipment. However, it would be unwise to jump to a conclusion, one way or the other, without fully considering the many factors that should be taken into account as part of the decision-making process. Certainly a property's size cannot be ignored. Neither can its location, history, use, and the types of guests and other customers that it attracts. A tendency to consider security needs only in terms of physical protection, such as locks and possibly the supplemental use of technology, to the complete exclusion of any personnel for protection may prove to be shortsighted.

When this is the prevalent attitude, it ignores the need for an essential ingredient. It must be understood that regardless of whatever physical security measures are in place, with or without a security department, it is of the utmost importance for there to be one member of the hotel's management team to whom the responsibility for loss prevention is assigned. Without a focal point for all security-related matters, risks and potentially costly problems will continue to exist.

In addition to the idea that a member of management must be directly involved with security or loss prevention, the fact that asset protection is both a management responsibility and management function must be acknowledged. At the beginning of this chapter, security was referred to as both a concept and as a function; at this juncture the distinction between them is clarified.

Conceptually speaking, it behooves lodging industry management to recognize that important as guest protection is, to optimally protect all of a hotel's many assets, its reputation included, security has to be proactive. The emphasis has to be on prevention, not mere deterrence. Prevention and deterrence are not the same. Webster's *New World Dictionary* defines *prevent* as "to keep from happening; make impossible by prior action; hinder;" *deter* is "to keep (a person) from doing something through fear, anxiety, doubt, etc.; discourage."

As we already have noted, certainly from an historical perspective the inclination has been to associate security with deterrence. This is no less true of hotel management personnel who are more inclined to think of security as a form of policing than as part of management. Where they do have security departments, they often are isolated from the rest of the property's operations. They are thought of as the hotel's private police force and the security director as the chief of police. Under these conditions the approach to loss

Grand Hotel Inter-Continental—Paris

prevention is little different from that to crime prevention. The idea is that highly visible personnel and the speedy identification, detection, apprehension, and punishment of wrongdoers will discourage wrongdoing by others. In contrast, the concept of security as part of an effective loss-prevention program mandates that it be integrated into all aspects of operations.

Let us now consider the subject of security from a functional viewpoint, that is as loss prevention and asset protection. Here a definition of the word *function* is helpful. The one most applicable for our purpose is "a special duty or performance required of a person in the course of work or activity." Therefore, to have a meaningful asset protection program, with or without a security department, it becomes necessary for every member of a property's management team to understand that loss prevention is a function that must be assumed by each and every employee—and especially by management.

However, as we already have noted, for optimum effect one member of the team has to be designated as the focal point. That person is given the task of developing the loss-prevention program, implementing it, and ensuring compliance. Logically, this is the security director's role where a department exists and asset protection is his or her full-time job. But where there is neither a department nor a full-time security director, as might be the case with a small property, one member of management must certainly be held accountable for the program's development, implementation, and oversight.

The most effective loss-prevention programs, whether or not they have full-time security directors, are the result of a combination of factors, all of which will be discussed in later chapters. However, among them one finds a need for both security and operating policies and procedures that are meaningful and realistic. Of course, even the best policies and procedures are worthless if they are not properly implemented. For that, line managers and supervisors must be directly involved. By the same token, onetime implementation without oversight to ensure continuing compliance serves only to minimize their effectiveness. Therefore, whatever measures are undertaken to prevent losses, everyone on the management team—general mangers and all their department heads—must do more than actively participate in the program; they must lead by example. Without their leadership and involvement, the risk of failure will far exceed the chance for success.

With or without a security department, concept and function have to be seen as interdependent and combined if the optimal benefits are to be realized. A successful loss-prevention initiative requires security's integration into all phases of operations. This means that security's role has to be extended beyond the mere performance of such tasks as making occasional patrol rounds, installing and monitoring physical security equipment, checking employee identification, examining items that they may be carrying from the premises, and dealing with noisy lounge patrons or guests who allege that they have been victimized. To the extent that security may be able to prevent or at least minimize losses in all departments, it should be involved.

Perhaps this wider security role can be best understood by looking at a university-sponsored, three-day seminar in 1992 on lodging industry security. Despite a minimal registration fee and a program scheduled for one day a week so as to avoid lengthy absences from work, ten general managers from a relatively small regional chain were reluctant to permit their security managers to attend. Ultimately, their corporate security director convinced them that the program was worthwhile.

Certainly security's more traditional role in dealing with guest-related concerns, patrols, crime prevention, and cooperation with public safety departments was discussed at length in the seminar. However, the many ways in which security could make a meaningful contribution by helping other departments, such as human resources, housekeeping, engineering, food and beverages, risk management, sales, credit, and the front office, also were examined. The focus was on a role for security that was designed to either prevent losses in general or to at least help reduce the scope and magnitude of those that might be considered inevitable.

When the seminar was over, the attendees returned to their properties and told their general managers what they had learned. They discussed what they now saw as proper functions for security and asked for permission to initiate an integrated approach to both problem solving and loss prevention. Permission was granted. Shortly thereafter, the small chain's corporate security director wrote the seminar's sponsor to report that the formerly reluctant general managers had unanimously agreed that the seminar was indeed a good investment. They said that for the first time their respective security managers were doing the job of preventing losses and protecting their properties' assets not only in new and much improved ways, but also in ways that the general managers felt were more consistent with sound management.

SUMMARY

Like many other aspects of hotel management, security's role has been one of evolution over time, a process not yet completed. It has gone from virtually no protection to crime prevention, with the emphasis on guest protection. Whatever attention has been given to the protection of a property's assets has been limited.

Lodging is considered a service industry, along with such activities as retailing and medical centers. As a service industry, where public use and acceptance are essential to survival, let alone profitability, guest needs and concerns must be attended to, thus mandating the presence of staff for that purpose. Consequently, hotels find themselves doubly exposed to a variety of incidents that may result in losses. However, the undeniable importance of guest protection is no excuse for failure to attend to the protection and conservation of a property's assets, including its reputation. All-inclusive protection and conservation is precisely what security is or should be all about.

In order to properly attend to the task of asset protection, hotel management must appreciate security not only as a concept but also a function with which it must become actively involved. A member of the hotel's management team must be given the responsibility for program development, implementation, and oversight. Loss prevention, not merely crime prevention, must be emphasized regardless of whether or not there is ample justification for the establishment of a security department as such.

REVIEW QUESTIONS

1. What was security's early role in the lodging industry?
2. How are hotels similar to retail stores and medical centers?
3. What causes service industries to have a double exposure to possible security problems?
4. What is there about hotel, retail, and hospital assets that makes them more susceptible to theft then assets of other types of businesses?
5. Despite the commonalities found among the lodging and retail industries and medical centers, what distinguishes hotels from the others?
6. How can security problems affect a property's (or chain's) reputation?
7. Explain the difference in focus between policing and security.
8. What is the difference between deterrence and prevention?
9. From a business perspective, on what should the security emphasis be placed?
10. Why is it important for one member of a hotel's management team to be given the responsibility for loss prevention?

ENDNOTES

1. Jurgen Thorwald, *The Marks of Cain* (London: Thames & Hudson, 1965), p. 129.

CHAPTER 2

THE ROLE OF PHYSICAL SECURITY

Physical security is a significant part of protection and prevention, but just as security itself is still in an evolutionary stage, the same can be said of physical security's role. Even security professionals, accustomed to thinking of physical security primarily in terms of hardware, now realize that new and ongoing developments in the field of technology, as well as an increasing awareness of environmental factors, mean the wider use of an increasing variety of tools.

At one time physical security measures consisted primarily of various types of alarm systems and key-operated or combination locks. However, changes with respect to both began to occur with the advent of the 1960s. Locks and alarms were becoming more sophisticated, and technology was becoming more adaptable and available. It also was becoming less expensive to buy and install. In addition, those concerned with security began to see more clearly the existence of a logical relationship between protection and certain physical environment considerations.

To appreciate what needs protection, from a lodging industry perspective, one first needs to understand what is covered under the umbrella of physical security. Only then is it possible to focus on the subject's various components. In other words, while it is virtually impossible to have an effective loss-prevention program without physical security, a great deal more is involved than merely buying and using hardware and security-related technology.

Before we examine at length the multiple subtopics that are now logically considered part of physical security, we should enumerate and briefly explain each. But even before that, we need to look at the role of hotel executives and general managers in relation to physical security.

Not every hotel executive—and certainly not the average general manager—has to deal very often with the construction of new properties. In fact, some never do. On the other hand, there is a strong probability that hotel management personnel will find themselves involved with major alterations and renovations of existing properties. When decisions are made to build new properties or significantly alter the appearance of existing ones, architects and engineers are employed and relied upon by hotel executives and general managers. Unfortunately, not all the selected architects and engineers may have prior experience in hotel construction.

Despite their lack of experience, some tend to merely solicit the approval of the hotel's representatives rather than to actively ask for their meaningful input. Architects and engineers are inclined to focus on aesthetics and, presumably, operating efficiency, giving little thought to anything more than what they consider to be standard physical security measures—namely, locks, peepholes in guest-room doors, and whatever might be specifically required either by law or the hotel company's insurance carrier.

Too many rationalize that physical security, aesthetics, and operating efficiency are incompatible.

As a practical matter it is not unusual for a hotel chain to give the responsibility for overseeing the timely completion and opening of a new property to that hotel's general manager designate, despite his or her lack of training in architecture or engineering. It certainly is not uncommon for general managers to be involved with major alterations and renovations. In any event, whether in new construction or major alterations and renovations, it is naive to ignore the fact that a hotel's design and layout can have an impact on its vulnerability to all types of losses.

FEASIBILITY STUDIES

When new construction is contemplated, especially of properties that will be owned by a chain operation or in which it will have an equity interest, a feasibility study will usually be part of the decision-making process. Unhappily, such a study seldom includes any reference to physical security–related factors.

As noted in Chapter 1, it may or may not be possible to operate without an established security department, but the protection of assets, staff, and guests and the prevention of losses is impossible without adequate physical security. In this respect, to ask whether or not an installation is doable is not enough; the feasibility of maintaining and operating systems is equally important. Furthermore, decisions about the incorporation of physical security may, under certain conditions, influence decisions about the need for a full-time security organization. Even in the case of a minimal rather than an optimal use of physical security, employing at least some security personnel may be unavoidable.

From the standpoint of a market for a new hotel, for example, labor pool availability, government-offered incentives, resources, and financing may result in the selection of a site in an area that is in the process of becoming fully developed. From a construction and operating perspective, the project is feasible, but there may be significant security-related issues. By no means should the security considerations be the prime determinant in the decision-making process, but the realities of protecting the property and preventing losses need to be recognized.

Certainly being able to effectively use physical security, even though it may require a sizable initial expense, is more cost effective than having to rely completely on security personnel. However, if problems would be encountered in properly installing equipment or in maintaining it because of distance from resources, such as trained or skilled mechanics, or a spare parts inventory, attempting to use anything more than minimal physical security may be unwise. In other words, the availability of equipment should not be confused with the larger issue of feasibility with respect to its use.

Additional concerns arise if technology, as part of physical security for a property, involves an installation in a foreign country. Then it is not simply a question of facing either import duties or the types of possible problems mentioned in the preceding paragraph; the government may prohibit the use of some forms of technology.

For instance, in one case a consultant evaluating security abroad for a hotel chain pointed out to the general manager that using two-way radios not only would allow for a reduction in the security department's size but it also would increase its operating efficiency. The general manager liked the idea but told the consultant that the government prohibited the private ownership and operation of two-way radio systems, even though, in this instance, the government itself had a financial interest in the property and had designated one of its police officials as the hotel's security director.

To illustrate another possible obstacle although a camera for photo identification badges is not a physical security item, a property in a country ruled by a dictator could not comply with corporate policy vis-a-vis uniform badges for all chain personnel. Why? The one particular camera then in use for that purpose was not allowed to be used by any organization outside the government itself.

PRODUCT SELECTION

Recognizing that physical security is an important factor in protecting assets, employees, and guests and that it should be taken into account whenever any form of construction is involved is one thing; how to use it is another. Due to the proliferation of products now available, care must be exercised in choosing those that will best serve a property's interests.

The specifications for either the construction of a new property or the major alteration of an existing one should include appropriate sections for physical security and safety systems. They should incorporate the details for both security and fire safety systems and should specify where they are to be used. For example, what kinds of security alarms are needed? Is a central station or proprietary silent alarm preferred for the protection of cashiers or possibly the controller's office in case of an attempted robbery? What about a proprietary silent alarm so that the executive office's receptionist can summon help if confronted by an unruly guest or employee? Since security's objective is loss prevention, specifications should also provide for temperature or heat-detection alarms for freezers and coolers.

While building codes, federal and state safety standards, and even insurance company requirements will play a major role in the development of specifications for fire safety systems, this does not mean that the hotel owner is devoid of options. For instance, if a property has a centralized computer room rather than a distributed computer system, will an emergency power cutoff be sufficient in case of fire, or should a halon installation be considered? Fire sprinkler systems (and sprinkler alarms) undoubtedly will be required throughout the inn. In all likelihood smoke detection alarms will be installed in guest and function rooms. However, should they also be installed in all back-of-the-house areas? And what about the need for some form of heat detection?

Illustrative of the fact that in some cases there are options, a look at those available relative to smoke and heat detection for back-of-the-house operations if justified. Deciding on the best course of action to be followed will be preceded by a question that innkeepers need to answer just as they would in arriving at any business decision: What is the most cost-effective way to deal with the issue?

This very question presented itself to the vice president and general manager designate of a property under construction in a major Midwestern city. Should the entire back-of-the-house area have smoke and heat detectors (and alarms)? The answer was *no*. Instead, allowing for the fact that all areas would be sprinklered, they would be installed only in certain specific places based on the following criteria:

1. Only those rooms or areas designated as storage space would be considered.

2. Any storage space would have to contain assets that could burn with relative ease as a result of such things as spontaneous combustion, lack of circulating air, or accumulated dust.

3. The stored assets would have to be of a kind that could not be easily replaced within twenty-four hours in case of fire or water damage.

Of course, alarm and detection systems are not the only physical security items for which specifications need to be written. They also have to be written for emergency lighting systems (a battery-powered or backup generator on site) and any time-lapse or closed-circuit television cameras, monitors, and videotape recording systems that are to be used. Specifications for locks for access to storage or guest rooms, which may well be different, have to be included, as do peephole and chain lock requirements for guest room doors.

For instance, will guest room door locks be part of an electronic or computerized system, or will they be key operated? If the latter, will they be spring or dead locks, and will the lock cores be of the easily changeable kind or not? Will there be electronic or computerized locks and card readers, or standard mortise locks on storeroom and floor linen closet doors? Will the door to liquor stores have a time-recording lock to add to security?

These multiple options need to be carefully considered as part of the product selection process. In choosing security or safety-related products, the choice should never be based solely on a product's novelty or the fact that another hotel uses it. However, neither should a product be rejected simply because it is new. Cost alone should not be the basis for a decision; there is much truth to the saying that one gets only what one pays for. To determine which are the best products for a particular property, all significant factors have to be weighed.

First and foremost, for what purpose is any one item to be used? Then, of those available, which one is best suited to a particular hotel's specific needs? Of course cost will be a factor, but so will the vendor's and manufacturer's reputations for service and reliability. It is also important in selecting products to try to anticipate the possible impact that the selection and use of any one item would have on labor and guest relations. For instance, would a closed-circuit television camera in the food preparation area effectively deter theft, or would it create a labor relations problem because employees feel their work habits are being monitored? Would a number of highly visible cameras on guest floors make guests feel safer, or would they assume that the cameras are there because the hotel has serious security problems? One last word regarding product selection: It should be the buyer, not the vendor, who decides how much is needed. Let us now examine the role of physical security.

NEW CONSTRUCTION OR MAJOR ALTERATIONS

It is in connection with projects of this magnitude that physical security should first be taken into account. Failure to do so can have an impact on both the subject of protection per se and construction costs. Consequently, as a practical matter, input on physical security should begin with the first available set of plans and specifications. Assuredly it is easier and less expensive to make changes on paper than it is to make them once actual construction is under way or has been completed. It also is important to remember that design and layout, not just hardware or the application of technology, are a part of physical security. There are risks if physical security, including design and layout, is not considered at this early stage.

One risk has to do with the failure to incorporate adequate physical security during construction. If this happens, once those who either own or are managing the property realize the deficiency, they would be confronted with having to choose between gambling on future security or incurring what should have been an avoidable expense. To gamble that nothing will happen and so doing nothing to correct this failure is shortsighted. On the other hand, choosing to take corrective action and make the called-for changes by retrofitting can prove to be more expensive than the work would have been if properly done from the project's inception. These points are illustrated by the following three hotels.

The first example involves a luxury hotel that was to be built on an inner-city site as part of a new, seventy-two-story high-rise complex. The traditional lobby was to be on the twelfth floor, with the hotel occupying floors twelve through thirty-two. However, most of its storerooms, the butcher shop, the preliminary food preparation area, housekeeping, engineering, the laundry, and guest parking were to be located below grade. The floors below twelve would consist of retail and office space; above thirty-two would be residences unrelated to the hotel. Adding to the project's complexity, the hotel's owners and operators were not the same as those concerned with the rest of the building.

The vice president and general manager designate, an experienced hotelier who was given the responsibility for overseeing the hotel phase of the project, immediately retained the services of an experienced security management consultant familiar with the lodging industry and involved him with the project from its inception. His early access to the drawings and specifications enabled him to (a) incorporate and recommend physical security and safety systems for the new property before actual construction began, (b) coordinate the installation of the hotel's security and safety systems' cable and wiring with that of the rest of the building, and (c) make allowance for future expansion of those systems in ways that would involve only minimal expense and little disruption to the property's operation. To ensure that his client's requirements would be met, he also attended monthly job meetings throughout the entire construction period.

The second situation involves a hotel chain that entered into a contract to manage a newly built, very busy, commercial hotel, following its completion, in a major European capitol. The property was part of a major urban renewal project that included a new office building adjacent to the hotel. Since construction was complete, the chain's corporate security director had no chance to participate in, let alone comment on, the property's design and layout.

A major concern, from a guest protection point of view, was the ease with which unauthorized persons could get to guest room floors. Compounding the problem was the fact that in addition to its eight passenger elevators, an escalator provided access to two floors with function rooms.

Multiple doors allowed people to access the ground floor directly from the street and use either the elevators or escalator with little risk of detection.

The property could not be faulted from an aesthetic perspective, but its designers failed to consider the risks posed by such easy, uncontrolled access. The front desk faced a double door leading to a drive-through for taxis and other automobiles. While this door was a convenience for arriving and departing guests, from a loss-prevention viewpoint the design and layout represented a risk. With the passenger elevators located directly behind the front desk, yet completely out of sight, and the escalators on the other side of the elevator bay, front-desk personnel could not possibly exercise even minimal control over access to the function and guest room floors via the elevators and escalator.

The third example involves a comparable situation in another European property, where, after construction was completed, management was assumed by a chain. In this instance more was involved than a failure to consider security; it was equally apparent that those responsible for the hotel's design had not sought any input from persons familiar with hotel operations.

The second cited case illustrated how a design deficiency had an adverse impact on access control; now we look at how a design problem affected the protection of a hotel's assets, its reputation included. Two of the more significant deficiencies involved the oversize space allocated for the kitchen and a failure to provide secure storage space for certain hotel assets and guest luggage.

Without exaggeration, upon the project's completion the size of the kitchen was equal to or greater than that of the property's main ballroom. Taking advantage of all this room, the designers elected to spread out the serving stations to such an extent that the dining room's reputation suffered. For example, in some instances the distances were so great that if a party of two or more diners ordered selections of both hot and cold menu items, their servings were neither as hot nor as cold as they should have been and as the diners expected.

At the same time, despite the kitchen's overabundance of space, the designers made no allowance for the secure storage of the hotel's high-quality flatware, sugar bowls, creamers, wine coolers, and champagne buckets. True, room service was available twenty-four hours a day, yet a reasonable number of these items, based on forecasts, could have been set out for that purpose without such complete exposure. This, however, was not done. Instead, the entire inventory's accessibility virtually encouraged employee theft. The food and beverage director's concerns about these deficiencies prompted him to seek funding so that corrective action could be taken.

In addition, this property's guests consisted mainly of business travelers and tourists. In fact, tour group business was actively sought. It frequently happened that the checkout time was earlier than guests' scheduled departures, yet guests, both tourists and business people, often wanted to do some last-minute shopping before leaving for the airport or train terminals. Understandably, not wanting to carry their bags with them, they chose to avail themselves of the hotel's offer to store luggage pending departure. There ostensibly was a storeroom in which guests could safely leave their bags; in truth the space could accommodate only about a dozen pieces. Excess luggage was relegated to "storage" in the hallway leading to the secure space. Unfortunately, this exposed guests' bags to the risk of loss.

Another aspect of physical security that often gets less attention than it deserves in new construction is that of safe-deposit boxes. Standard practice is to include them in new construction. But their relationship to a property's physical security needs and its possible liability for losses is not always fully appreciated. The purpose of safe-deposit boxes is to enable a hotel to safeguard some of its own assets, as well as provide guests with safe storage for their valuables.

Innkeepers' laws limit liability when a guest who did not use a safe-deposit box alleges that a loss of personal property occurred while the guest was registered. In the interest of good guest relations, for years one would find tent cards and other reminders encouraging guests to store valuables in a hotel's safe-deposit boxes, a practice that still continues.

In reality, urging guests to use the hotel's safe-deposit boxes was, and in some cases still is, a bit of a gamble on a property's part. Realistically, the number of safe-deposit boxes actually installed represents but a small percentage of the total number of rooms. And, as we already have noted, some are reserved for the hotel's use. Suppose the number of boxes for a 450-room property was equal to 10 percent of its rooms. Suppose, too, that at any point in time 20 percent of its guests wanted safe-deposit boxes. This would mean that the valuables of forty-five guests were vulnerable. Consider the obviously negative impact on the hotel and its reputation in the event that one of those guests suffered a loss. Realizing that such an event is not beyond the realm of possibility, more and more hotels have elected to install some form of safe storage facility in the guest rooms themselves.

The foregoing are some of the factors that need to be taken into account when considering projects involving new construction or major alterations. From the first planning stages of a project, considering questions of design and layout can help prevent embarrassing or damaging incidents from occurring once new construction or major alterations have been completed. The goal is the incorporation of reasonable physical security measures to help ensure the protection of hotel assets, reputation included, and certainly of guests and their property in the most efficient and cost-effective way.

DESIGN AND LAYOUT

The examples illustrating some of the pitfalls that can be encountered whenever new construction or major alterations are involved also show how important it is to consider physical security from the inception of any such projects. However, they are not the only concerns with which innkeepers have to deal. Many other design and layout factors need to be considered.

Many people, including some security managers, assume that physical security's primary role is to control access. Access control, whether to the hotel itself, its storerooms, the back of the house, its various outlets, or function and other rooms intended for guest use, is important. Nevertheless, since security's overall objective is to protect and conserve an inn's assets, provide for the reasonable protection of its guests and staff, and prevent losses, not just crimes, there are other and equally important considerations. To the extent that physical security contributes to that stated objective, a property's design and layout can be a significant factor.

Hotel managers, who understand and appreciate the importance of loss prevention, as well as of asset and guest protection, know that design and layout problems are not confined to new projects. They also are of concern in existing properties. The primary difference, as we already have said, is that these issues can be disposed of fairly easily and economically during the design phase of new construction or major alterations, whereas that is not true of fully operational hotels. In the latter, design and layout may have a bearing on both the nature of the physical security measures needed and a decision as to whether or not a full-time security department is necessary.

Where does the physical security–design interface begin? The logical answer to the question is, at the hotel's property line. That line will be determined by the location and nature of the hotel. For example, for most urban hotels the property line will begin at the four exterior walls. In some cases it may extend to include an adjoining garage. Suburban hotels probably will have some form of guest parking, perhaps some landscaping, and possibly an outdoor swimming pool, all within their property lines. The property lines of resort hotels most likely will encompass the amenities of suburban hotels, plus tennis courts, perhaps one or more golf courses, indoor and outdoor swimming pools, and possibly even a beach. However, regardless of the type of hotel, its physical security should begin at its property line.

Obviously, the inn's location will affect any decisions as to what kind of physical security is most appropriate in terms of property line or perimeter protection. As a rule, urban properties need not be concerned about trespassers outside the building or aesthetics in choosing what is best for access control purposes. Suburban and resort properties have to be mindful of both. For instance, urban hotels can control access by limiting the number of street-level doors through which the public can enter; emergency exits can be secured from within by installing approved fire locks. The latter come in various designs and materials that are inoffensive to the eye yet help secure the inn's perimeter.

Suburban and resort hotels are not that fortunate. First, the amount of land to be protected can be so expensive that a complete enclosure may be either impractical or prohibitive in terms of cost. Second, if any enclosure is to be used, consideration of both aesthetics and possible maintenance costs tends to limit the choices. While unadorned chain link fences or those with barbed or razor wire on top may be acceptable for a manufacturing plant, they are not acceptable for a hotel. Using plain chain link fencing adorned with plants or flowers for aesthetic reasons calls for maintenance and adds to the cost. Shrubs of sufficient height and thickness are attractive, but they also have to be maintained. An attractive and suitable alternative, requiring virtually no maintenance, is architectural masonry.

Reducing the risk of trespass to land is not the only factor to be considered when thinking about whether or not to enclose real estate. Another risk, depending on location and surrounding property, may be one of a legal nature that ultimately could affect the title to the real estate. For instance, if any persons enjoy the *uninterrupted* use of a right-of-way over any part of the land for a period of time prescribed by the laws of the state in which the inn is situated, they would acquire what is called a prescriptive right to its use. That, in turn, could result in a cloud on the title to that land in the event that at some later time the owner wanted to sell it.

Let us now turn our attention to the matter of controlling access to the hotel itself. Physical security comes into play in connection with access to both the building and certain operations within the building. Not only are there parts of any hotel to which guests or other members of the general public are denied access, but there are even some to which certain categories of employees are not admitted.

A logical starting point is access to the building itself. Preferably there should be an employees' entrance/exit through which all members of the staff pass. Some general managers may authorize exceptions, a subject that will be discussed in greater detail in Chapter 3, but in any event, it is desirable that this monitored, street-level doorway not be next to the shipping-receiving dock, or any dumpster or other container used for garbage or trash disposal in which hotel assets might be concealed by errant employees.

There obviously must be doors through which the public can enter either as registered guests or attendees at functions. Unfortunately, there often is a tendency to permit access through multiple rather than one or two street-level doors. If this leniency were raised as a security deficiency, the defense would argue that limited access would be an inconvenience. This is not necessarily true. It is what people become accustomed to that they perceive to be convenient. It is only if they have become used to something and then it changes do they consider it inconvenient. True, there are any number of guests who always stay at the same hotels who, on subsequent visits, might find such a change an inconvenience. By the same token, to the vast majority of guests who are making a first visit to a property, such a limitation probably would not even be noticed.

Consequently, there is no valid reason why those doors at street level, installed primarily to satisfy fire safety and building codes and insurance company requirements that call for emergency exits, should also be available for general ingress to the property. Therefore, it is in the best interests of the hotel and its guests that the number of ways in which people can enter the property be limited and that all other street-level doors be secured with approved fire locks.

Another design and layout concern, where two or more different solutions will have to be considered, involves those hotels that are adjacent to parking garages that have one or more transfer floors that lead directly from parking to guest or function room floors. These situations represent a dual threat. One is posed by persons who are neither registered guests nor present for a function. They see the easy access to and from guest or function rooms as a way to commit burglaries, and perhaps even assaults, and to escape with minimal risk of detection. The other threat comes from those few occasional registered guests who, when ready to depart, will go directly from their rooms to their automobiles, skip the cashier, and leave without paying their bills.

Three other design and layout matters that have security overtones concern the location of certain lobby functions and storerooms, and the design of some guest room floors. Unlike the previously cited newly constructed property, whose lobby was on the twelfth floor, most lobbies are located at street level. It is here that guests register upon arrival and clear their accounts with the cashier when they leave. Unfortunately, in some properties the cashiering station's location may increase the risk of loss by virtue of its close proximity to the hotel's main entrance.

It is naive to rationalize that since most guests use credit cards to pay their bills, the need to have a lot of hard currency on hand is limited and precautions are unnecessary. Credit cards may have affected, but they have not eliminated, cashiers' needs to have money with which to cash guests' travelers' or other checks or to exchange foreign for local currency. Neither is it that uncommon for cashiering stations to be the point from which outlets' "banks" are distributed and to which they are returned, thus increasing the amount of cash on hand at certain times. Consequently, although front desk cashiers should not be stationed in inconvenient or out-of-the-way locations,

Hotel Intercontinental—Miami

neither should they be the function closest to the street and an escape route in case of a robbery.

In designing and laying out hotel receiving and stores areas, efforts should be made to minimize the distance that has to be traversed between receiving docks and storerooms. This arrangement can help reduce losses in three ways. First, the less distance between receiving and stores, the more easily and quickly goods received can be moved to their designated storerooms, thus limiting their exposure to possible theft. Second, perishables received can be quickly moved to coolers or freezers, reducing the risk of spoilage. Third, being able to move receivables quickly into their proper storerooms further reduces the risk of shortcuts being taken in filling requisitions, especially for foodstuffs, by picking from among newly delivered items rather than those already in stores.

One might not readily associate the subject of guest protection with that of design and layout, but deficiencies in the latter can certainly affect the former. These concerns are distinguishable from the broader subject of physical security, yet to be considered in this chapter. Suffice it to say at this point that the effectiveness of much of the physical security provided by hotels is largely dependent on its proper use by the very guests for whose benefit it has been installed.

However, guest room floor design is another matter; it is strictly within the province of hotel owners and their architects. No right-minded innkeeper can guarantee that only guests and hotel staff will have access to guest room floors. Put another way, burglars, muggers, and rapists may also be able to get to those floors, and the ease of difficulty that they have in committing their crimes can be influenced by design and layout factors. Doors to guest rooms that are deeply recessed instead of being almost flush with corridor walls are a boon to the criminal and a potential hazard for guests. These recessed spaces rarely add significantly to an inn's aesthetics or guest privacy; they do provide concealment for those waiting for a chance to burglarize a room or surprise and assault a guest or member of the hotel staff.

USING TECHNOLOGY

So far we have focused attention on the need to incorporate physical security features in connection with new construction or major alteration projects. We have looked at the impact that design and layout can have on loss prevention, and we have discussed when and under what circumstances physical security systems, technology included, should be considered. As a result, one might ask, why does the use of technology warrant further attention?

One reason to pursue the subject is that technology's use is not confined only to new construction or major alteration projects. Another is that it can be a significant factor in determining whether or not a property, either new or existing, needs or will need a full-time security department. If it does, technology can have a bearing on the department's size. For example, assume that there is a need for a full-time security department, and among management's concerns is the need to monitor guest parking facilities. The question is, how many security officers will be required to adequately protect the inn, guest parking included? Using closed-circuit television can be more effective and less expensive than employing security personnel to patrol the parking facility on a full-time basis, thus helping to reduce the total number of officers required.

Then, too, when properly used, technology offers benefits that more standardized security hardware cannot. One example would be to replace a key-operated mortise lock, perhaps supplemented with a hasp and combination padlock, on the liquor storeroom with either a time-recording lock or a card reader that is part of a computerized or electronic access control system.

The key-operated lock, with or without the combination padlock, can keep unauthorized persons out, but there is no provision for accountability. There is no way to identify who, among those authorized, entered the storeroom, when they went in, or how long they stayed. Neither is there any mechanism to ensure that a requisition was filled out to cover what was taken. A time-recording lock or card reader would provide data to help identify who entered and when and how long they stayed. That information would be the basis for follow-up—that is, checking whether a requisition had been filled out.

Before proceeding, however, one point needs to be made, and another that has been made bears repeating. As for the first, it is important to remember that despite what technology can contribute to security, other hardware items that can help protect assets (and guests) and prevent losses should not be ignored; they are part of physical security.

The point that deserves repetition deals with product selection. Whether in choosing technology or any other form of physical security for asset or guest protection, there are pitfalls to be avoided. Selecting what is needed and will best serve the hotel's interests is a role for those responsible for the property's management, including its profits and losses. Consequently, they, not the security or safety equipment vendors, must be the ones to choose. In doing so the managers should avoid being persuaded to buy a product simply because it is the newest thing on the market or because a competitor has bought it. No less important, they should not reject a product *only* because it is new; and they also need to avoid being oversold. Looking carefully at the different aspects of loss prevention, we can see that certain specific issues need to be addressed:

1. What is to be protected?
2. Of what should that protection consist?
3. What is the most cost-effective way to provide that protection?

WHAT IS TO BE PROTECTED?

The answer to the question of what is to be protected is an easy one: assets, guests, and staff. The extent to which they should be protected is only somewhat more difficult to determine since different situations call for different levels of security. Good managers, while agreeing that all assets should be protected, also know that physical security can be used only where tangibles are involved. Furthermore, logic tells them that requiring a uniform standard of protection for all assets is impractical.

For instance, housekeeping's inventory of small bottles of shampoo or sewing kits for guest rooms (likely to be taken as souvenirs) does not call for the same degree of security needed to protect linen supplies. Then, sometimes protecting assets against loss goes beyond secure storage; there is an accountability or usage component, as illustrated in citing the advantage of using technology rather than standard hardware to protect liquor stores.

Insofar as guest protection is concerned, certain limitations have to be recognized. No matter how anxious innkeepers are to protect guests, and without minimizing the importance of their protection, it is important to remember that hotels are required only to take *reasonable* measures for that purpose; they are not guarantors of guest security.

OF WHAT IS PROTECTION TO CONSIST?

There is neither a single nor a simple answer to this question. Where assets are involved, the extent of protection will vary in relation to value and the impact of loss, no matter the cause, on the inn's operations. Generally speaking, a combination of standard hardware and technology can be used. The same is true for protecting guests, but with a caveat. Here, regardless of what technology or hardware hotels provide for the security and safety of guests, in reality no purpose will be served unless guests use properly whatever is made available for their protection.

Key-operated locks can be used to secure all the property's doors, but the question is whether or not they will provide the desired level of protection. For instance, if they are the locks of choice, should they be spring locks or deadbolts, and should they have changeable cores or not? If card readers are used instead, should they be used throughout the hotel or only to control access and provide data for guest rooms and certain back-of-the-house operations?

We have already acknowledged that government-mandated safety standards will set forth the minimum acceptable installation of sprinkler systems and fire extinguishers; local building codes and insurance company requirements also will be factors. Nevertheless, should innkeepers consider any additional measures? As an example, it might be worth while to install some type of heat-detection system in coolers or other storage rooms where unexpected temperature increases can cause spoilage. Accidental kitchen fires can be costly in a number of ways. Consequently, regardless of code or other requirements, of the various fire suppression systems on the market, which one would be best for this particular inn?

Other security measures used for loss prevention that should be considered are a property's location in relation to the area's public safety agencies. The concerns of hotels in cities are different from those in suburban or relatively undeveloped areas. As an example, police can respond faster to a robbery in midtown New York City than they could to a robbery at a resort property where one or two sheriff's deputies have to cover a large sector of a few hundred square miles in which the inn is located. Furthermore, a city fire department has firefighting apparatus that allows it to respond in ways that a volunteer department cannot.

In other words, a hotel's needs, based on its size, location, and the nature of its activities and clientele, should be carefully studied. Then there should be an equally careful study of the many products available that would appear to be capable of satisfying those needs. Only after this has been done should purchasing and installation decisions be made.

COST-EFFECTIVE WAYS TO PROVIDE PROTECTION

While there admittedly is no single or simple answer to the question of what should protection consist, deciding on what constitutes the most cost-effective way to provide security is by far the most difficult. Making that determination requires careful analysis of each individual situation so decisions can be made on their merits.

In this respect two points need to be made. First, in order to realize optimum benefits when making this analysis, thought must be given to "each individual situation" within the hotel rather than to the hotel as an entity. The inn's configuration, which will include its design and layout, also have to be looked at closely. Second, applying a cost-effective approach to loss prevention should not be equated with simply buying the least expensive items on the market. There is much truth to the saying that one gets only what one pays for; in the long run the cheapest items may prove to be the most costly.

The greatest difficulty in deciding on the most cost effective equipment lies with the numerous choices. For some hotel operations there are so few products or vendors that management's options are very limited. This is not the case where security is concerned. First, in all physical security considerations, not merely those of hotels, any attempt to be specific is virtually impossible because of the plethora of security hardware now on the market and the speed with which new products are developed and made available. Second, and especially true of the lodging industry, each individual property's unique requirements limit the application of sweeping generalizations; and as for industry standards, they are nonexistent.

Therefore, perhaps the best and fairest way to offer guidance is simply by illustrating some of the many available options and the different kinds of equipment that can be adapted for various purposes. However, before proceeding some basic principles have to be both understood and accepted.

Those who believe that simply by using some form of physical security all assets can be protected and all losses can be prevented are wrong. This is a misleading and unrealistic premise. Furthermore, in using physical security it is important to remember that levels of protection can and should vary. The criteria for determining levels should be based on the value of the assets involved and the impact on operations if they are lost, regardless of what may cause the loss.

Let us first look at the value factor. A number of hotel assets are expendables. But that does not mean that they need no protection at all. The truth is that even expendables may have different values. In addition, some contribute directly to profits while others do not.

For instance, food and beverages are expendables, as are small bottles of shampoo and sewing kits in guest rooms. An important difference is that food and beverages served to guests represent income. Part of that income is profit; part goes to replenish supplies. As a result, losses due to theft or spoilage have an unavoidable impact on profits. On the other hand, shampoo and sewing kits for guests' use and convenience make no direct contribution to income or profits; they are considered "paid for" in the room's price. Consequently, if guests take them as souvenirs, their replacement costs are covered and written off as good guest relations. Nevertheless, if they have to be replaced because they were stolen or taken in excessive numbers by guests, there is an impact on profit, even if only a small one. It is evident that both classes of assets need protection, yet their different values make it clear that one calls for a higher level of security than does the other.

Therefore, a hotel's tangible assets throughout the property need to be protected against loss. Although it is immaterial whether they are in storerooms, the back of the house, guest or function rooms, public areas, or food and beverage outlets, their location has to be taken into account when looking for cost-effective ways to prevent their losses.

These several factors, and the widespread concern for loss prevention, suggest looking at access control as a logical starting point. However, in addressing the subject one needs to take a broad rather than a limited view. This means examining access control needs not only externally—from the perspective of the hotel's perimeter—but also internally. Put another way, one focus is on the overall protection of the inn itself; the other on the protection of the hotel's various components.

On the subject of perimeter protection, earlier in this chapter we discussed the importance of limiting the number of street-level doors through which people can enter. Of course, these doors usually fall into three classes. Some are used as emergency exits, some serve general public use, and others are used by employees only.

Emergency exits are required, but they do not have to be usable as entrances to the hotel. Most are equipped with panic hardware, or "crash bars" so that there can be unimpeded exit from the inn if necessary. Some innkeepers also have these doors alarmed, either on a door-by-door basis or connected to a central panel monitored in a security office.

Theoretically, panic hardware on these doors, with or without alarms, should satisfy access control needs, but does it? Panic hardware will not prevent a person from using an emergency door to leave the hotel or from opening it to let someone in. Even if the door is alarmed and security officers are on the job, by the time they respond it may well be too late to prevent a room burglar or assailant from exiting or to stop an accomplice from letting one in.

Approved fire locks with self-contained alarms can be considered as viable alternatives to panic hardware. They are no more hindrance to emergency departures than the latter, but they also can be unlocked with keys if there is a legitimate but nonemergency reason for doing so. If, no matter what access control measures are in place, the use of emergency exits for unauthorized departures or entries occurs with any frequency, either time-lapse cameras set to operate only on door openings or closed-circuit television can be installed.

In this respect, properties with full-time, fully staffed security departments and personnel who already monitor alarm systems would find closed-circuit television cost effective. Despite the initial investment, good-quality cameras and monitors should not need a lot of maintenance; their cost can be amortized over time for tax purposes, and additional personnel would not be required. On the other hand, it is not unusual for small properties to use front-desk personnel or night managers, or auditors for security or to hire one or two security officers to work only during certain hours or on certain days. Time-lapse cameras would be cost effective for such properties. Since the cameras would photograph only on door openings, film costs would not be great, there would be no need for constant monitoring, and if there is reason to believe that access control has been compromised, the film could then be removed and developed.

While time-lapse cameras can be cost effective for smaller properties, their advantages for larger ones should not be overlooked. A case in point is the construction of a new luxury hotel, part of a seventy-two story building project, cited earlier in this chapter. Housekeeping, its storerooms, butcher shop, and preliminary food preparation were below street level; so was the building's garage. Of necessity, there was an emergency exit from the functional areas to the garage. Its need was unquestioned. However, it also offered a chance for the removal to, temporary storage in, and later recovery of assets from the garage. Physical security was used to provide a cost-effective way to prevent possible losses at this level. The emergency door was equipped with a fire lock. In addition, a time-lapse camera, placed on a building column line opposite the emergency door, was set to take pictures only on door openings.

Doors for general public use can pose different problems. A question that needs to be asked is whether they can be subjected to any form of access control. Certainly the vulnerability of hotels to after-hours robberies cannot be ignored. A possibility is limiting access to but one entryway during certain nighttime hours. If guest room access is card-reader controlled, guests' cards could be programmed for that door's use during the restricted hours. This control is cost effective since it builds on the system already in place. A viable and cost-effective alternative for reducing the risk of unauthorized access at other properties would be an electric lock, controlled at the front desk, used in conjunction with an intercommunication system between the door and the desk.

Occasionally one finds an inn that has no specific entrance for employees, but most do out of the realization that their comings and goings need to be controlled and monitored. This restriction does not mean that most hotel employees cannot be trusted. It merely acknowledges the fact that some, given the opportunity, might steal both time, which equals money, and tangible assets. Unfortunately, physical security equipment alone cannot offer management cost-effective ways of dealing with these concerns. With or without time clocks or other mechanical means to check staff in and out, hotels of any appreciable size can lessen the risk of loss by supplementing hardware with the physical presence of either time keepers or security officers.

While protecting assets, guests, and employees involves controlling access to the hotel proper, of equal importance is the need to control access to diverse parts of the inn, such as the executive offices, kitchen, storerooms, laundry, boiler room, and swimming pool if there is one. Unfortunately, the overwhelming fear of liability, with its genesis in crime—by no means to be ignored—often detracts from the need to control access to these functions as well.

For properties that have elected to use electronic or computerized systems, those systems can certainly be adopted as access-control mechanisms for these various areas. They can be programmed to limit access not only to particular persons and hours but also to specific days of the week. Furthermore, they can enhance management's accountability procedures through their ability to identify card users. Hotels with indoor swimming pools can even use cards issued to guests for access to their rooms as a way to limit access to pool areas to only those hours when lifeguards are on duty.

Resort properties with outdoor pools or oceanfront or lakefront locations are faced with a more difficult task since walls and doors for access control purposes are nonexistent. However, this openness and the "reasonable care" standard do not mean that the risk to guest safety and the litigation that can follow if it is ignored are of no consequence. During daylight hours lifeguards can be employed, but what about those times when—at least in theory—swimming is not allowed?

Realistically, there is little that resort properties with oceanfront or lakefront locations can do to prevent beach access. If security officers are employed, beaches can be patrolled, but cost aside, their constant presence might be objectionable to some guests. Although some after-hours protection is available for outdoor pools, there are practical limits to what can be done. Combining thick and high enough shrubs or architectural masonry with gates can enclose pool areas and help limit access, but the inn's best interest would be better protected by also installing closed circuit television that is monitored by security personnel.

For all practical purposes, hotels using electronic or computerized access control systems have a single standard approach. Due to the inherent nature of hotel operations, however, the same cannot be said of key-operated systems if there is to be effective loss prevention. For example, executive offices may be "officially" closed after hours, weekends, and holidays, yet at least some managerial personnel still need access, especially if one or more major functions are scheduled. Nevertheless, by limiting the issue of executive office keys to only those who legitimately might need access to the executive offices, general managers can maintain control.

Kitchens, as well as food and beverage outlets, may or may not necessarily need controlled access, but arrangements have to be made to protect those items that lend themselves to theft or breakage; and certainly limits must be imposed in terms of who has access to storerooms, coolers, and bar stock in lounges. Secure storage should be provided for flatware, linens, china, and glassware. If the inn offers guests extended or twenty-four-hour room service, limiting access to its own supplies is preferable to allowing unlimited access to items needed to service the outlets. Cost-effective protection requires accountability for the issue of and control over the keys to each of these facilities. The same restriction applies to protecting bar stock already in outlets.

Food and beverage storerooms and coolers are another matter. Whether they are used for dry stores, perishables, or beverages is immaterial; both accountability for as well as control over access should be considered. A cost-effective way to satisfy both needs is to equip the doors with time-recording locks, discussed earlier in this chapter. Security, concerned with loss prevention, would include installing heat detectors for all coolers in which perishables are kept and for storerooms containing wine, liquor, and other alcoholic beverages.

Laundries and boilers rooms are usually considered open space, yet laundry supplies as well as engineering supplies, tools, and associated equipment should be protected. Of particular importance to engineering at hotels with key-operated locks is the need to protect not only tools and equipment used to make keys but also blank key stock. But for the hotel's locksmith, the easiest and most cost-effective way is to use deadlocks, limit the issue of keys to only those laundry and engineering employees who have a legitimate need for access to their respective storage facilities, and have strict account-ability for those keys. The locksmith's role is another example of a function that needs not only controls for access to the room in which key making equipment and key blanks are kept, but also for accountability. Again, a time-recording lock would provide management with both.

In addition to the foregoing, certain assets are kept on guest room floors other than in the rooms themselves, mainly floor housekeeping supplies. If the inn uses an electronic or computerized card reader system, obviously it is best to extend it to the locks on linen closet doors as well. If key-operated locks are in use, housekeepers' master keys should be adequate, with em-phasis on accountability for the issue and recovery of keys.

Examples of some other measures that can cost-effectively protect the inn's offices, as well as rooms in which tangible assets are stored, are key-operated lock types, "pick plates," and hinge protection. For instance, while not always done in practice, in theory lock sets should be replaced whenever a key is reported lost or stolen or when there is reason to believe that a lock-ing mechanism has been compromised. These repairs can be expensive, es-pecially if changes have to be made with any frequency. However, protection can be improved and labor and material costs reduced if lock sets have easily removable and changeable cores that also can be made compatible with housekeeping and engineering section or floor master keys.

Another inexpensive physical security item that can help prevent losses attributable to unauthorized access to all spaces, guest rooms included, is the "pick plate." As a general rule, key-operated locks, whether in hotels, private homes, or offices, tend to be spring locks rather than deadlocks. With the for-mer, the lock bolt automatically slips, or "springs" into place to secure a door once it is closed. The bolt itself has a beveled or slightly rounded edge; a key is needed only to unlock the door. The deadlock bolt has angular edges, and a key must be used to both lock and unlock it.

Both types of lock mechanisms have their advantages and disadvan-tages, but in some respects spring locks are better for hotel use. However, they also are much easier to manipulate or slip back for allowing access with-out a key; a credit card or thin piece of plastic can be used instead. Combat-ting the problem inexpensively involves attaching a "pick plate" to the outside of any door that has a spring lock. Each plate consists of a metal strip, which need not be aesthetically offensive, that extends about two inches above and below the lock set itself, thus making it much harder for someone to slip the bolt and open the door.

Doors with locks are nevertheless vulnerable to unauthorized access if their hinges are on the outside. Hinge pins can be taken out so that doors can be removed, then replaced and the hinge pins put back. Simply drilling a small hole through one or two of the hinges and inserting a needle like pin is an inexpensive way to upgrade protection for that room's contents.

OTHER PHYSICAL SECURITY MEASURES

By no means do the various items described thus far constitute the only equipment available for protection. Once again, however, their adoption should be based on the specific needs of specific properties and of the particular functions within a hotel. For instance, while various biometric systems, including eye-retina, fingerprint, and voice identification, are now available, there is no real justification for their use by the lodging industry, with the possible exception of cash-counting and retention rooms at hotels that also offer guests casino gambling.

Within the United States, as a rule, building codes and insurance company requirements call for hotels to be sprinklered, and sprinkler systems have sprinkler alarms. In many cases smoke detection systems, which are a form of alarm, are also required. Earlier in this chapter the need and justification for heat detectors in select coolers and storage areas was discussed. But to assume that these are the only alarms worth considering is a mistake. Some needs can be satisfied by an alarm itself; others may call for an alarm in concert with other equipment.

Alarms for executive offices' receptionists are not exactly commonplace despite the receptionists' relative isolation. Although the risk may be a relatively minor one, a disgruntled guest or employee in the executive office demanding to see the general manager may be threatening to a receptionist who has no discreet way to call for help. Shouting or reaching for a telephone is impractical; it may only make the complainant more agitated. A silent alarm that can be discreetly activated to summon help deserves consideration. Activation should inform the security office, if there is one, of a need for help. Otherwise, it should let either the front desk or someone else in the executive office area know that help is needed. True, the risk of a similar confrontation at the front desk also exists, but the likely presence in the lobby of other members of the hotel staff, and even of some guests, decreases the level of the apparent threat and lessens the need for a comparable alarm.

That credit card use by guests has meant less cash on hand for cashiers and in controllers' offices does not necessarily eliminate the threat of robbery; having some cash at each of these locations is unavoidable. Some form of physical security should be provided for both personnel and money. Cashiers and controllers' offices should have silent alarms that can be discreetly operated in case of robbery. Again, if there is a security office functioning around the clock, an audiovisual signal should alert on-duty personnel so that the police can be notified. Absent a security office, the alarms should go directly to the nearest police station, if the authorities are agreeable to such an arrangement, or to a central station alarm company that can then call the police.

Supplemental measures should also be considered for the protection of each of these functions. Unless certain employees need frequent and regular after-hours access to the controller's office, an intrusion or burglar alarm should be installed that uses the same response procedure noted in the preceding paragraph. If there is occasional need for their access, the few, select, authorized persons can be instructed in how to deactivate and reactivate the system.

Since cashiers are on duty constantly, an intrusion alarm is useless. An effective supplement to their alarm installations would be closed-circuit television cameras placed behind and above cashiers and directed toward those with whom they are dealing. They should have peephole lenses and should be connected to videocassette recorders whether or not security personnel are employed by the inn. In case of robbery the video tapes can be invaluable not only in helping to identify and catch the robber(s) but also as evidence at time of trial. If there is a constantly manned security office, cashiering activity can be monitored and the police called if anything suspicious involving third parties seems to be happening, or an internal investigation can be initiated if an individual cashier's honesty is in question.

SUMMARY

The intense focus on providing service and accommodating the public, without which no hotel can survive, is understandable; so is concern for aesthetics and hoped-for operating efficiency. However, minimizing what physical security can contribute to service and public accommodation, or assuming that it is incompatible with an inn's appearance and operating efficiency, can prove costly. The key questions revolve around when and how physical security deserves to be considered.

Certain physical security measures, especially those involving the use of the latest technology, cannot completely eliminate the need for security personnel, but they may be important in determining a security department's size. However, before embarking on a program that leans heavily on high-tech security systems, it is imperative to ensure not only that the equipment is available (or even permissible in certain countries) in any given location but also that there is a local service in case repairs are ever needed. Therefore, security feasibility studies should precede physical security buying decisions.

In turn, a buying decision should not be based only on a product's newness or cost but rather on which one will best serve the hotel's particular needs. Requesting proposals from vendors is to be expected, but those responsible for the inn's protection and overall management, not the suppliers, should be the ones who make the actual determination. This rule holds true whether the proposed purchase is for an existing property or one that has yet to be built.

If new construction or major alterations are involved, the hotel's physical security needs should be considered from the project's inception. This is the most logical and cost-effective way to provide protection through the medium of physical security. It allows for the incorporation of appropriate hardware and high technology throughout construction, as well as for adjustments in terms of design and layout. The physical environment created by the latter can either help or hinder the loss-prevention effort as it applies to assets, guests, and employees.

From an asset protection viewpoint it is important to understand that while all assets need protection, not all are of equal value. Therefore, the relationship between the value of assets and the level of protection to be provided will dictate the nature of the protection. Once these determinations have been made, the objective is to ensure their protection by choosing the most cost-effective measures from among the many products available. It may be entirely possible to satisfy some, if not all, of the inn's physical security needs by installing standardized hardware, a less expensive approach. On the other hand, under certain conditions the most cost-effective way to prevent losses and protect guests, employees, and assets in the long run may be to employ one or more forms of high-technology systems.

REVIEW QUESTIONS

1. What is meant by the term "physical security"?

2. Explain the relationship between a security feasibility study and physical security.

3. Who chooses physical security products, those who are responsible for the hotel's protection or security equipment suppliers?

4. At what point in time should physical security be considered relative to new construction or major alteration projects?

5. Are physical security measures necessarily incompatible with aesthetic and operating efficiency?

6. How are design, layout, and physical security related?

7. Should the installation of physical security measures be considered for existing properties or limited to new construction projects?

Chapter 2   The Role of Physical Security

35

8. What is the relationship, if any, between the use of technology and a security department's size?

9. If physical security is to be used to protect assets, to what kinds of assets should it be extended?

10. Which is more important in choosing physical security products, their cost effectiveness for that particular hotel or the mere fact that other properties use them?

Security Feasibility Checklist

1. Name of city, state, and/or country of proposed site.

2. The proposed property's setting will be in an urban _____ or a suburban _____ area. If urban, central city or outlying part?

3. Are local, full-time police and fire services available?

4. If so, what are their reputations with respect to integrity, professionalism, status of equipment, and cooperation with private businesses?

5. How far are the nearest police and fire stations from the proposed site? What is the average response time if either service is needed?

6. What is the average number of police officers and fire fighters on duty per shift at those stations?

7. How often are police patrols made of the area in which the property is or would be located?

8. If local, full-time police and fire services are not available, by whom are such services provided?

9. If the fire department is composed of volunteers, what is the extent of their training, and by whom is it provided? What is the status of their equipment, and is it capable of handling all kinds of fires regardless of cause?

10. Criminal Activity:
    (a) Is the local crime rate high, average, or low for the type of community?
    (b) Is the source of this information reliable?
    (c) What kinds of crimes are most prevalent?
    (d) How does the crime rate for the proposed site's neighborhood compare with the rest of the community's?

11. Are central-station alarm services available?
    (a) If so, how many companies provide such services?
    (b) What are their reputations with regard to the types of equipment used, reliability, service, and the maintenance of their systems?

12. If contract security services are available, by how many agencies are they offered?
    (a) Are the agencies local or national companies? If local, who is the owner?
    (b) What are their reputations in terms of integrity, reliability, training, and the caliber of experience and response time on the part of local management?

13. How do the prevailing rates for contract security officers compare with what the hotel would pay proprietary officers?

14. Should the hotel prefer to hire its own staff, is there a labor pool in the area from which to recruit qualified people?

15. Do most other properties in the area use proprietary or contract agency personnel?

16. When built, what will the property have in the way of security, fire alarm, and fire suppression systems?

17. If closed-circuit television, two-way radios, electronic or computerized access controls, or other high-technology equipment will be used for security, are there reputable, skilled service companies in the area to help maintain or repair the equipment?

18. Is it permissible or illegal for private employers to make inquiry about an applicant's or an employee's arrest and/or conviction records?

Additional Considerations for International Properties

1. Is security and related equipment available locally, or does it have to be imported?

2. If imported, are the duties high, moderate, or low?

3. In either event, are competent installers and maintenance personnel readily available?

4. Are there any prohibitions against the use of fire locks on doors whose use would normally be limited to emergency evacuations?

5. Does the government impose restrictions on the issuing of photo identification badges by private employers to employees or on the types of equipment used to make them?

6. Does the government either restrict or prohibit the use of closed-circuit television or two-way radios by private companies?

7. If the hotel will be locally owned but operated under the terms of a management contract, will the hotel select the security director, or will one be imposed by the owner?

CHAPTER 3

LOSS PREVENTION AND HOTEL OPERATIONS

During the late 1960s the American Hotel & Motel Association, recognizing the industry's increasing concern with loss prevention, engaged the services of a security management consultant whose job it was to offer its members generally useful advice. Despite this first step to provide meaningful, albeit limited, security assistance to those actively engaged in hotel management, programs designed to educate the industry's future leaders, paid little attention, if any, to the subject.

Signs of change appeared in 1977. Gerald W. Lattin, then at Florida International University, wrote in his preface to *Modern Hotel and Motel Management:* "This third edition contains a comprehensive section on security, which has become a vital concern to all hotel and motel sections."[1] Not long thereafter John E. H. Sherry, Professor of Hotel Law at Cornell University's School of Hotel Administration, joined the relative handful of lodging industry people who saw not only that security was becoming a matter of increasing importance and concern but also that it often failed to get the attention that it deserved from both industry practitioners and the academic community.

The subject of security was not so much ignored by innkeepers and lodging industry educators as it was misunderstood. Their focus concentrated on guest protection and subordinated the need to protect assets. Then, and even to a large extent today, lodging industry security was and is driven by the fear of lawsuits and bad publicity. This concern is understandable. If guests suffer losses, are injured, or even killed on occasion, litigation and unwanted publicity are almost unavoidable. Adverse publicity, even if only by word of mouth, can have a negative impact on occupancy. If a hotel is found liable for damages, its insurance policy may or may not cover attorney's fees and court costs, and the deductible amount is an out-of-pocket loss. Thus, necessarily absorbed costs due to litigation, plus a drop in occupancy, will reduce profits; but losses involving guest-related incidents are not the only ways in which profits can suffer.

The lodging industry is highly competitive in terms of rates and amenities for guests. Besides the traditional shoe-shine cloths, small sewing kits, bottles of shampoo, and use of television sets, some hotels now provide in-room safe-deposit boxes, coffee makers, cold beverages, hair dryers, terrycloth bathrobes, larger desks, better lighting, and ports for laptop computers. Periodically, hotels are refurbished in order to improve their images. Some even offer guests free continental breakfasts, and some do not charge for children under a certain age. All of these amenities cost money, but to stay in business both old and new properties constantly strive to make themselves more attractive to the traveling public.

From a financial perspective, experienced managers at least have a reasonably good idea as to what these amenities will cost, and they prepare their budgets accordingly. However, one cannot budget realistically for the unexpected or inexcusable loss of assets. It is in this regard that the need for an effective security or loss-prevention program has to be considered. It is also important to understand that to accept this premise in no way diminishes or detracts from the importance of serving guests. To the contrary, integrating security into all phases of a hotel's operations can actually enhance the inn's ability to better serve its guests, largely because its properly protected assets are available for that purpose.

Before looking at additional ways in which a greater role for security can benefit operations, one needs to understand what is meant by security's "integration." Security has to be taken out of isolation and made an integral part of the entire operation. It should not be thought of as private policing whose sole duty is to prevent crime. From a business viewpoint security equals loss prevention; therefore, it is also concerned with preventing waste, accidents, mistakes and employees' unethical behavior. It aims to be helpful to other departments without usurping their duties and responsibilities. However, general managers must let all department heads, especially at hotels with full-time security directors, know that security's integration is not a substitute for discharging their individual responsibilities.

While hotels measure their success in terms of occupancy, in the final analysis they, like all businesses, succeed or fail on the basis of profits made in relation to goals set. Due to the competitive nature of the business, simply increasing room rates to compensate for reduced profit margins can lead to pricing oneself out of business. Compensating by reducing services can be no less of a disaster. However, being able to prevent losses or to minimize the dollar value of those that are inevitable can help active, well-managed properties be profitable and sustain themselves.

A point made in Chapter 1 and earlier in this chapter is that from a management perspective security equals loss prevention. In Chapter 1 we also took note of the fact that, depending on circumstances, a formally constituted security department may not be necessary for every hotel, although at a minimum there must be one member of the management team to whom the security responsibility is assigned.

In addition, however, for optimally effective loss prevention, regardless of a property's size or location, sound operating systems and procedures are essential, and line management must be closely involved in the security program. These two factors, even at inns with security managers and security departments, can be more critical to the prevention of losses than the size of the security department or its budget.

Undoubtedly, some who read much of what follows will argue that while the ideas and suggestions for preventing losses are logical, they are not necessarily new, and they already are in place. Consequently, they even may ask why the material is included. The answer is that experience has shown that in too many cases there is a significant gap between recognition and implementation; too much is taken for granted. Put another way, much of what follows may be "in place" at any number of properties in theory rather than in practice. As a result, loss prevention, operating systems and procedures, line management involvement, and the interdependency of virtually all aspects of hotel management have to be understood.

THE ROLE OF THE HUMAN RESOURCES DEPARTMENT

Most losses resulting from workplace incidents can be traced to the way in which someone did or did not do something. Even the breakdown or failure of a piece of equipment may be due to its improper use or maintenance. Consequently, in looking for the underlying cause of any loss that can be attributed to a person, three things need to be examined. One is the care given to hiring that individual, another is the training provided, and the third is the way in which that person is supervised.

These principles apply to all businesses, but they are of special importance to hotels. In Chapter 1, lodging, like retailing, was described as a service industry. All service industries require employee-public contact, but the kinds of contact differ. In retailing, sales person–customer contacts do not last long, perhaps not more than a few minutes, whether customers buy or not. Neither is it likely that on subsequent visits the same salesperson will wait on the same customer. Nor as a rule do salespersons have direct access to customers' property.

In contrast, hotels offer a wide range of services where employee-guest contacts are unavoidable, in many cases for more than a matter of minutes. These contacts can occur either during the relatively short time it takes to order and be served a meal or drink, or during the course of a stay that may be for one night, several days, or even weeks. Repeat contact between some guests and certain members of the staff is not unusual. In addition, certain employees, such as members of the bell and housekeeping staffs and possibly even room service or engineering personnel, not only have some access to guest rooms and thus to guests' property, but they also may have that access at times when guests are not present. The consequences can be disastrous.

A couple of illustrations here may be useful. Suppose a guest calls the front desk to complain that something is missing from his or her room. Whether or not the claim is valid the first thought likely to enter the guest's mind, and possibly management's, is the presumption that a housekeeper is guilty of theft. In the interest of good guest relations, the guest's allegation of a loss will not be questioned.

The hotel will initiate an inquiry of its own or will report the loss to the police. While the loss, if real, may be the result of the guest's own negligence or behavior, at its inception the investigation most likely will focus on the housekeeper or other employees who conceivably might have been in the guest's room. A thorough, objective investigation will determine to what extent, if any, there was employee involvement. This does not alter the fact that one of the first steps in the inquiry will be a review of the personnel files of those employees who might have had access to the guest's room.

In another situation, a female guest alleges that she was assaulted in her room by a male member of the hotel staff. The matter is referred to the police, there is an arrest, and in a trial the employee is found guilty. The hotel is the recipient of unwanted and unneeded bad publicity. The victim also files a civil suit for damages, adding to the inn's image problem. The police investigation discovers that the assailant has a prior record of assaults. When plaintiff's attorney examines his personnel file during the civil action's pretrial discovery process, it shows that he was subjected to only a very cursory screening before he was hired. This prompts the adding of a count for negligent hiring to the complaint.

Preemployment Screening

Both examples show the possibility that any number of events conceivably could prompt a review of personnel files and highlight the importance of properly screening applicants for employment. However, to begin and end a discussion of the hiring process by merely saying there should be careful preemployment screening is to oversimplify a complex topic.

Problems with hiring are likely to happen not because of the need to comply with equal employment opportunity legislation or the Americans with Disabilities Act but rather because of management's attitude, the nature of a particular hotel's business, or a combination of the two. Each of these factors needs to be considered.

Large chains have system-wide operating policies and procedures, but general managers set the overall tone for the management of their particular properties—this certainly is true of independent hotels. Whether part of a chain or an independent, goals are set. As with any business, success or failure depends on the amount of profit made in relation to the projected objectives.

One expects capable businesspeople to look constantly for ways to boost profits. In some cases they try to increase sales; in others to economize on operating expenses. The danger lies in the fact that some of the economies chosen are false. On their face they would seem to increase profits; in reality they may well do the opposite.

A comparison between two different businesses, one a manufacturing plant and the other a hotel, helps illustrate this point. If the economy slows down, deferring much-needed painting in a plant and replacement of worn carpet in the manager's office for one year will not have any real impact on productivity. To defer painting and carpet replacement in a hotel, however, even for only one year, may significantly affect an inn's reputation, resulting in fewer room nights sold and an obvious reduction in profitability.

However, this is not the only kind of false economy that can affect a hotel. From a loss-prevention viewpoint, losses of one sort or another also can occur if preemployment screening is either inadequate or nonexistent. The same can be true if there is a failure to properly train employees, particularly if, as will be discussed in Chapter 7, they are full-time security personnel at a property that has a security department.

Part of the problem can be attributed to the misconceived idea that an employee's pay is a good indicator of his or her value to the employer. This misconception, plus, the fact that many lodging industry employees are paid only the legally required hourly minimum, or perhaps slightly more, can cause both general and human resources managers to rationalize that it would be a waste of time and money to look into the backgrounds of relatively low-level employees before they are hired. This ignores the reality of hotel work, where interaction among people occurs routinely. Virtually all lodging industry employees have access to assets, and many have contact with guests or their possessions; none work in isolation. Nevertheless, the focus tends to be on what jobs pay, not on the extent to which employees have access to hotel assets or to guests and their property.

For instance, members of the bell and housekeeping staffs are among those paid on an hourly basis; suppose that none have been adequately screened. Compare the savings in wages with the cost of a judgment for damages and its impact on an inn's reputation when a bellman with a record of convictions for assault rapes a guest, who then sues the hotel. What is the cost of replacing bed linens and towels stolen by a housekeeper with a history of convictions for theft compared with that of a reasonably careful screening process?

Recognizing that virtually all of the United States and some foreign governments have criminal history statutes prohibiting or greatly limiting access by private persons or corporations to individuals' criminal histories, and that applicants with criminal records might not list them on applications, does not excuse either a failure to screen or a lax screening process. The primary responsibility for minimizing the risk of hiring unqualified or incompetent persons rests with the human resources department. Despite whatever legal limitations may be imposed upon their efforts, they nevertheless should be alert for what might be considered telltale signs of future problems, and there is no reason why lawful avenues of inquiry should not be pursued. What are some of the signs for which they should look, and some of the things they can do?

The most logical place to start is with a careful examination of the completed application itself to ensure that all questions have been answered and all periods of time have been accounted for. Unanswered questions or unexplained gaps in time should not be ignored; applicants should be questioned and blanks filled in.

For example, in one case a seemingly reliable housekeeper failed to report for work for three days; repeated efforts to contact her were unsuccessful. It was rumored that she had been arrested for larceny, so the human resources manager called the police and learned that the charge was stealing a leather jacket from a retail store. When he pulled the housekeeper's file to note this, he also decided to review it. First he looked at the application. While there was no answer at all to the lawful question about any prior felony convictions, neither was there any explanation for a three-year gap in time. He also noticed that despite this particular housekeeper's seeming reliability, from time to time she had reported linen and other supply shortages. Asked about them, she invariably said they must have been caused by guests who took the items from her cart while she was servicing rooms. When the detective handling the larceny case came to the hotel for background information on the housekeeper, the human resources manager learned that the unexplained three-year gap on the application had been spent at a state correctional facility; the housekeeper had an earlier conviction for stealing from a previous employer.

In this illustration the applicant did not admit to any felony convictions, and state law prevented the hotel from accessing her criminal history. However, the human resources representative who conducted the initial interview either ignored the gap in time or failed to ask for an explanation. True, if asked for an explanation the applicant might have lied, but at least a reasonable effort would have been made to get an answer to what should have been a troubling question.

Of course, careful preemployment screening is not designed for the sole purpose of minimizing the risk of hiring persons who might be inclined to commit crimes. It is also a mechanism for the employment of the most reliable and best-qualified applicants. Despite the fact that honest answers from former employers, supported by evidence, are not fraught with the dangers that some have been led to believe, the accepted practice on the part of most is more or less limited to confirming dates of employment, position held, and wages paid. Since in many cases the human resources department responds to questions from prospective employers the same way, the tendency is to accept the confirming data and not ask anything more.

However, one additional question should always be asked of former employers. Unfortunately, it often is not. Would they consider the person eligible for reemployment? As a rule, if an individual has left an earlier job on good terms, the employer most likely will say "yes" without any hesitation. Only in relatively rare cases will the answer be "no," and even more rarely will it be followed by any explanation. On the other hand, if the answer is "yes," but hesitant, it might signify some concern on the part of the former employer. Perhaps the employee was a basically good worker who nevertheless seemed to disappear when certain tasks had to be performed. Such hesitation should not automatically disqualify the applicant; it should suggest a need for a more in-depth inquiry by human resources before making a job offer. In the long run the additional time and effort involved can prove to be far less expensive, and perhaps even less embarrassing, than hiring someone and having to fire them soon afterwards.

Other things to look for in reviewing employment applications, especially with regard to former positions held, are the reasons given for leaving, the frequency of job changes, and the pay, commuting, and work done in succeeding positions. In contacts with former employers, every effort should be made to verify the stated reason for leaving.

In a tight economy there may be valid reasons for frequent changes, lower pay, less responsibility, and greater hardship in traveling to and from work. Just having a job and an income can be critically important. However, when these things happen at a time when business is good and unemployment is down, they should raise questions in the minds of prospective employers. Most people prefer job security and do not tend to move to new positions unless the latter are perceived as a marked improvement over what they are leaving behind. Since frequent employee turnover means additional expense in the form of advertising, recruiting, and training, in normal times care should be exercised in looking at applicants whose histories suggest their inability or unwillingness to stay with one employer for any length of time.

Despite the fact that most applications for employment ask for personal references, who may well offer useful information, the persons listed are often not contacted by human resources. The tendency is to rationalize that applicants will not list as personal references people whose comments will be other than favorable. This ignores the possibility that a person may say something about the prospective employee that he or she considers favorable, yet to the astute human resources representative it suggests a need for caution before an actual hiring decision is made.

To illustrate this point, suppose an opening exists for a chief engineer; since the inn is in constant operation, one of the criteria for the position is reliability. Several people apply, and on the basis of the applications and initial interviews all seem qualified, but one stands out. Human resources calls the referenced people. They speak highly of the applicants, but one contacted in behalf of the leading candidate is especially praiseworthy of the latter's ongoing attempt to deal with a long-standing drinking problem. To the advocate this is a real plus, but from a human resources and hotel management point of view, this disclosure calls for further consideration before a job offer is made. They need to think about hiring this applicant in relation to the possible risk of his not being able to do the job if an emergency arises.

It is not unusual for some job seekers to first apply for positions by submitting résumés. They may result in a prospective employer's invitation to an interview. Upon arriving for that purpose, applicants usually will also be asked to complete a standard application. However impressive a résumé, not only should a standard application be completed, but it also should be reviewed for any discrepancies that may appear between it and the originally submitted résumé.

Some positions may require academic qualifications, and some applicants for those positions may submit transcripts of grades with their résumés or applications. It is easy to be impressed, and perhaps even misled, by an applicant's seeming efficiency and knack for organization. Nevertheless, human resources interviewers should inform applicants that policy precludes acceptance of grades directly from prospective employees and instead requires that they be sent directly from the school to the inn.

What can happen if this is not done? Some years ago a graduate student at a prestigious university wanted to make some money. This prompted him to steal a ream of transcript forms from the registrar's office, have a duplicate of the school seal made, and offer "official" transcripts to job seekers for a fee based on the grades they wanted shown. Occasional news items about people practicing medicine (including surgery), law (including trial work at an appellate level), and nursing without degrees or licenses make it obvious that it would be wise to assume that this deception could happen in the lodging industry as well.

Another important aspect of preemployment screening is a need for physical examinations for viable applicants. Neither human resources nor hotel general managers may see any relation between security (or loss prevention) and this step in the hiring process, yet one with three possible ramifications, all of which can prove costly, does exist. However, before discussing the risk of not requiring such examinations, it should be understood that compliance with the Americans with Disabilities Act and physical examinations are neither in conflict nor mutually exclusive.

One of these risks involves the hiring of a person with a preexisting ailment or condition that is unknown to the employer. At some point in time the ailment or condition is aggravated, and the employee cannot work for a period of time. A workmen's compensation claim is filed, but absent any record of the preexisting condition, the costs are charged to the current employer. This is an unforeseen expense that might well have been avoided.

Another concern is an applicant's possible addiction. We already have discussed how addiction can affect reliability, but it can contribute to losses in other ways. It may well increase the likelihood of the addicted person's being injured on the job due to carelessness or negligence. Then, too, if this type of employee finds it hard to live on what he or she is paid and at the same time satisfy a drug or alcohol habit, that person may end up stealing from either the hotel or its guests. One should not ignore the possible damage to the inn's reputation in addition to the tangible losses suffered in such cases.

The third risk that can certainly result in adverse publicity, plus possible losses caused by settling claims, arises when a person with a contagious illness is hired, especially for a job involving serving food or beverages to guests. True, giving physical examinations to viable applicants will cost money. However, in deciding on what to do, one is well advised to weigh that expense against what the cost might be if any of these risks become realities.

Preemployment screening, therefore, is a legitimate security concern since it is a major step in the overall loss-prevention and risk-reduction effort. At the same time, a careful reading of the foregoing discussions makes it clear that primarily it is a human resources rather than a security function. A conscientious human resources staff is essential for the program's success, and responsibility for implementation is the human resources manager's. Close scrutiny of the ideas for improved screening also makes it abundantly clear that implementation involves relatively little time, effort, or actual expense, yet failure can prove to be embarrassing at best and costly at worst.

Part-Time and Seasonal Employees

Certain categories of hotels, such as those that cater to functions or resort properties with seasonal increases in business, are confronted with yet another issue insofar as preemployment screening is concerned. They have a need for part-time or seasonal employees. Even those general and human resources managers who are agreeable to careful screening of applicants for full-time jobs might dismiss the idea of extending the program to part-time or seasonal staff due to the difficulty in predicting their staffing needs in these areas.

It is hard to accept an argument based on the inability to predict, however, since forecasting is an essential part of good hotel management. Consequently, why cannot the same effort be applied to forecasting staffing needs? Insofar as cost is concerned, we already have seen that reasonable preemployment screening measures actually involve very little in the way of real expense. Denying that part-time or seasonal employees can be guilty of embarrassing or costly conduct is imprudent.

The question is, is the risk of loss posed by them great enough to justify expending any amount of time and effort to screen them? In answering this, remember that security's concern is with prevention of loss, not just crime. Thus the answer is that their behavior could result in even greater losses than those attributable to full-time employees since, for the duration of their employment, their opportunities for any form of misbehavior are the same.

There are reasons for this extra risk. Part-time or seasonal staff are inclined to see themselves as transients, without either roots or any sense of employment stability. Consequently, they feel no loyalty to a temporary employer, are less concerned with accountability, and tend to rationalize that unless their poor performance or misconduct is blatant it will not even be discovered until after they have departed. Put another way, attitude as a factor in losses cannot be ignored. Is there a possible solution to the problem?

It would seem that since cost is no excuse for failing to screen, but part-time or seasonal staff attitudes can be problematic in trying to minimize both risks and losses, innkeepers need to think of ways in which to overcome the mind-set of this category of employees. However, since the needs under each subset of staff are different, let us consider them separately, beginning with part-timers.

Part-time staff will most likely come from among permanent residents of the community in which the hotel is located. Some will not want to work full-time; others hope that by taking part-time jobs they will be considered for full-time employment when vacancies occur. Instead of waiting for a particular need to arise, consideration can be given to recruiting and screening people in advance, according to their job preferences or aspirations, as a group from which to draw personnel for future events or functions. Ensuring them of either part-time employment or consideration for full-time work when openings occur can help eliminate the transient feeling and create the sense of loyalty that is so important to any organization. This approach serves several purposes. It justifies preemployment screening, overcomes the attitude problem, facilitates the transfer of a part-time employee to a full-time job, improves accountability, and minimizes the risk of loss in every category covered under the security umbrella.

The conditions surrounding the hiring of seasonal staff can be different. Although in operation throughout the year, many properties with seasonal highs tend to be resorts. Some may offer golf, tennis, outdoor swimming pools or beaches, or a combination thereof; others may offer skiing, ice skating, and indoor pools and saunas. Resorts attract a certain class of guests, many of whom are affluent people who can afford to take the time and spend the money to travel and enjoy themselves.

To offer the high level of service their guests expect and thus maintain their reputations and customer bases, inns of this type find it necessary to employ additional staff during their peak seasons. The search may range from merely advertising in local papers to actively recruiting beyond a given locale; unlike part-time employees, all seasonal applicants may not necessarily live in the area. Some may be students who see a chance to both earn some money and find time to relax.

However, another possible source should not be ignored. Some applicants for seasonal employment are professional thieves. Relying on lax or nonexistent screening, they search for these jobs because of the unique opportunities to steal from guests and inns. Consequently, the presence of affluent guests and the inadequate or nonexistent preemployment screening of truly transient temporary staff is a combination that increases the risk of losses.

Once either guests or a hotel suffers a loss that is attributable to a member of the staff, the impact is the same whether that employee is full-time, part-time, or seasonal; but if the incident prompts the filing of either a lawsuit or insurance claim, the preemployment screening process may become relevant. This rebuts the notion that screening is an avoidable expense, a fallacy we discuss more fully in Chapter 6.

Some might argue that even if expense is not a factor, the nature of seasonal hiring prevents a reasonable screening process. *Not true.* As we said before, forecasting is so much a part of hotel management that there is no reason why it should not apply to staffing, including seasonal employment. General and human resources managers with a need to hire seasonal staff know approximately when their seasons begin and end, and they know about how many temporary employees they will require. Therefore, the ability to screen them actually depends on planning rather than numbers.

Instead of waiting until just before the season's arrival, the number of temporary employees should be forecast well in advance; whatever method is used to recruit should begin. Although applications should be accepted when advertising begins, the advertisements themselves should give the projected starting date for those who will be hired. Thus, without misleading applicants, background information can be made available to human resources in advance, providing ample time for making the same inquiries as for any prospective employees. Once the screening has been completed and a decision to hire an applicant has been made, the person can be given a firm reporting date.

While it is true that making background inquiries of all prospective employees will require the expenditure of some time and effort, and in that sense is an expense, the benefits that can accrue outweigh the minimal costs involved. For instance, staff turnover is also expensive, the cost of which increases in proportion to the rate of that turnover. It may be necessary to advertise; then replacements have to be interviewed, trained, and most likely uniformed. To the extent that sound preemployment screening programs can help minimize the risk of hiring dishonest or incompetent staff, thus reducing the turnover rate, they add to rather than subtract from profits. They also can make a further contribution to profits by helping reduce the risk of possible lawsuits and insurance claims, both of which almost always cause embarrassment and damage to reputation regardless of the outcome.

Identification

Although a majority of hotel employees are uniformed, they report for work in their own clothes. Personal recognition by a timekeeper or security officer should not be considered as sufficient justification for admission via the employees' entrance. Photo identification badges should be issued to all employees, whether full-time, part-time, or seasonal, and required to be shown as a condition for admission to the property. Personal recognition can be risky since, for example, there is no assurance that a timekeeper or security officer would know that a person seeking to enter had in fact been terminated the day before.

The badges should be color-coded to indicate not only the departments to which employees are assigned but also any limits imposed upon them in terms of movement within the property. To illustrate, receiving personnel or laundry workers have no need for total access; housekeepers and bell staff do. The issuance of photo identification badges does not mean that all members of the staff should be required to wear them at work, but in some cases they should since despite the number of uniformed personnel, uniforms alone are insufficient for identification purposes.

Badges are especially important for those employees with whom guests may have contact under conditions that conceivably could cause some discomfort. What assurance, for example, do guests have that someone who knocks on the door and says they are from housekeeping or engineering is telling the truth? Duplication of many housekeeping or engineering uniforms would not be too difficult or expensive. The photo identification badge serves as confirmation.

Even for those whose uniforms are more distinctive, such as front desk personnel, bell staff, room service, and yes, even security officers, and whose duplication would be more difficult and costly, name tags can serve a dual purpose. As a form of identification they can add to guests' comfort and sense of personal safety. They also can be a plus in terms of staff courtesy. Employees, knowing they can be identified by name rather than merely by job, are less inclined to be rude or inconsiderate.

Orientation and Training

Orientation and training of new employees, offered by the human resources department, are important to the development of any sound loss-prevention and labor-management program. This is the time when new hires should learn their employers' ground rules with respect to both how they do their jobs and how they conduct themselves at work. Despite this, too often new hires are introduced to their jobs at relatively brief sessions when they fill out tax withholding forms, are told about such things as when they get paid, what their fringe benefits are, and when they can take breaks and for how long. Security and safety, integral parts of effective loss prevention, may not even be mentioned in passing.

Nevertheless, if asked what they do in the way of orientation and training for new employees, any number of human resources managers will answer, "We hire only experienced people, so we don't need to do any." General managers who endorse, or at the very least tolerate, this attitude will find that it can prove costly in terms of both loss prevention and good labor relations.

All new hires, regardless of experience or other qualifications, should be given an extensive orientation not only with respect to the inn's design and layout, but also with regard to its policies and procedures in general, and those dealing with employee conduct in particular. During these sessions they need to be told what is expected of them in terms of performance and behavior, and what they can expect in return from management if either or both are unsatisfactory. For instance, among security issues to be discussed are the ground rules for possible locker or parcel inspections and employee theft or substance addiction.

Properly oriented employees are less likely to be subjected to criticism and disciplinary action than those who are not. Inadequately or improperly oriented new employees can feel that they are being unfairly blamed for something that they did or did not do if no one ever told them what was or was not permissible. Instead of being thought of as a waste of time, well-planned and organized new employee orientation and training programs should be considered a good investment.

For example, a new bartender is hired; being experienced, he or she gets no orientation or training. Not having been made aware of the new employer's rules, after starting work he or she is seen free-pouring liquor and offering a customer a drink "on the house." The bartender is criticized for following practices allowed at his previous job. Under the circumstances, the criticism is resented and results in a less than harmonious relationship between subordinate and supervisor. It may even prompt union intercession in the employee's behalf.

True, free-pouring liquor and free drinks represent a loss and reduced profit margins; but if the bartender is fired or quits, there is the expense of hiring a replacement. If nothing else, the lack of instruction at the outset adversely affects labor-management relations. The risk of such an incident could have been avoided, or at least minimized, through the simple and inexpensive expedient of an orientation for all new employees, regardless of their experience.

When orientation and training are offered to new hires, attention must be paid to those who will present the program. Sponsorship, and much of what has to be done, rightly are human resources functions, but topical presentations should not be limited to members of that department; other department heads should also participate. Furthermore, since truly effective loss prevention is impossible without security's integration into all aspects of operations, it is important that the person responsible for security, even if there is no full-time security department, present the loss-prevention part of the program.

Discipline and Termination

From a loss-prevention point of view, discipline and termination pose two different concerns. Admittedly, some disciplinary and termination decisions are related to security issues, while others are not. Under the circumstances, one might be willing to recognize a role for security, even if grudgingly, when security-related issues are the basis for disciplinary action. By the same token, one also might question the justification for security's concern when other forms of such action are involved, termination included. We shall consider each type separately.

Before we do, however, it is critically important for all members of the inn's management staff to understand two separate and distinct things. First, regardless of the reason for any disciplinary action, it is impossible to anticipate how the involved employee will react. Resentment can result in acts of vandalism. Worse still, and illustrative of this point, a *New York Times* article in the February 14, 1994, edition took note of the fact that in September 1993 a U.S. government agency (the National Institute for Occupational Safety and Health) called workplace homicides "a serious public health problem"; moreover, U.S. Department of Labor statistics for 1992 indicated that homicides were responsible for 17 percent of all occupational deaths.[2] Second, the ultimate decisions regarding action to be taken should be made only by employees' supervisors or managers in conjunction with human resources personnel, regardless of the reason for discipline or termination. The person responsible for security should not be involved with the process, for reasons to be explained.

To enlarge upon this topic, suppose there is a violation of security policies and procedures, which normally would include any criminal activity. An employee is a suspect. Most such cases, unless a major crime has been committed, will be investigated and dealt with internally, usually by the security director or manager or the person responsible for security. However, the inquiry itself must be conducted, and the resulting action taken, in ways that will add to rather than detract from the overall loss-prevention effort.

Suspicions or allegations are one thing; proof of guilt is another. Therefore, the loss-prevention program will be helped or hindered in large part based on the staff's perception of how investigations are conducted and disciplinary or termination decisions are made. True or false, if employees think that those conducting inquiries are not only biased but also are acting as investigators, judges, and jurors, the loss-prevention program may do more than suffer; it may fail.

As a result, no investigation should be initiated with presumptions of guilt or innocence. All inquiries undertaken by security must be completely objective and limited to fact-finding. Once completed, all the facts should be presented in an objectively written report to the individual's manager, who, with guidance from human resources, will decide on the action to be taken. Investigators, whether the security director or anyone else connected with the security function, should not participate in the decision-making process.

Of course, we already have acknowledged that not all disciplinary actions or terminations are based on security-related matters. There can be many other reasons for such actions, among them insubordination, incompetence, and excessive absenteeism. Nevertheless, whenever any employee is disciplined or fired, regardless of the reason, an employer places itself at risk. Trying to avoid, or at least minimize, those risks is very much of a security concern. The obvious questions are, of what do such risks consist, and how can they be preempted in whole or in part?

No matter how resentful or unhappy they may be, most people who are disciplined or terminated tend to accept their punishment or firing. But this is not necessarily true of everyone. It is how the exceptions will react that is of real concern. Two risks have already been mentioned: acts of vandalism and workplace violence. In addition, they may go out of their way to damage the employer's reputation or steal property. Regardless of the vengeful means, in the final analysis a loss is incurred. Furthermore, the number of persons involved is irrelevant; risks can exist whether one individual or a sizeable group has been disciplined or fired.

The first line of defense in trying to keep risks from becoming realities is close cooperation between human resources and security. Before any employees are disciplined or fired, their respective managers and human resources representatives should review the individuals' respective personnel files to see if they contain any information that might suggest that there is cause for concern. If so, security should be alerted before any meeting takes place with the involved employee. This delay will permit security to take whatever steps may be appropriate to forestall a problem before any further action is taken.

Then, too, the way in which affected employees are told what is about to happen can be critical. The aim is to defuse a situation that might prompt a violent reaction. If those who deliver the bad tidings seem to be doing it by rote, possibly even enjoying this display of authority, without any explanation or sign of concern or empathy, the level of risk can increase. On the other hand, the risk level can decrease if those same persons make a genuine effort to show understanding and to explain why a certain action is being taken. Empathizing with someone who is obviously going through a trying time, regardless of the justification for the discipline or firing, costs an employer nothing but may save it a lot.

From a loss-prevention perspective, certain things have to be considered if the ultimate disciplinary decision, namely the termination of employment, is made. They include accountability for and the recovery of assets that may have been issued to that person, how they are to leave the hotel yet have a chance to recover their personal property, and suitable ways to deny them future access to the inn.

The vast majority of lodging industry employees wear some kind of uniform, usually issued by housekeeping and laundered or dry-cleaned by the hotel's laundry. Many are issued name tags and, increasingly, photo identification cards. Some employees, engineering personnel for example, also may be issued other assets, such as tools. Whether they are uniforms, equipment, name tags, photo identification cards, keys, or anything else, the fact remains that items issued by the hotel are assets. If they are not recovered from employees departing voluntarily or involuntarily, the cost of replacement must be borne by the inn. Rationalizing that on an item-by-item basis replacement costs may be fairly small ignores the reality that the cumulative amount can be sizeable and that failure to recover even the most inexpensive item, such as a name tag or identification card, may allow a former employee to reenter the premises unimpeded.

While the goal of eliminating losses or risks in these areas is a worthy one, it is unrealistic. The practical approach is based on minimizing losses and allied risks. For this there must be an effective asset recovery program. That, in turn, presupposes effective accountability on the part of issuing departments. Specifically, they must maintain accurate records of all assets issued to individual employees for whom they are responsible; finally they have to ensure that these assets are recovered from those persons leaving the hotel's employ. For instance, the chief engineer should keep records of all tools and equipment signed out to engineering department personnel. Housekeeping should know not only to whom uniforms have been issued, but of what they consist.

Since issuing departments can and should be expected to know precisely what assets they have issued, they must be the ones to ensure the recovery of those assets. They should be required to sign off for the recovery of those assets before departing employees are finally processed by human resources. At exit interviews, human resources, before signing off on whatever pay may be due those employees, should be responsible for recovering only the assets it has issued. That department cannot and should not be expected to know precisely what others may have issued.

Not unexpectedly, employees usually keep some personal property at the workplace. The nature of that property often depends on the person's position. Members of the housekeeping, bell, laundry, and engineering staffs may have nothing more at work than what they keep in their lockers, principally clothes worn to and from the hotel. Members of management or persons working in offices may have considerably more. Leaving a job, except for persons who voluntarily resign, can be a traumatic experience, and one that should be taken into account when terminations are involuntary.

Uniformed personnel, told they are being let go, should be given a form to be completed by the individual departments from whom they received any hotel property and then should be accompanied to their locker rooms so they can change into their own clothes; however, they should not be embarrassed by having the person accompanying them present while they make that change. That same person then should go with them to the appropriate departments to return the inn's assets. The last stop should be human resources, where the asset recovery form is turned in and an exit interview is conducted. Upon completion they should not be allowed to remain on the premises but should be promptly escorted to the employees' entrance/exit.

Termination may be an even more traumatic experience for management personnel or office workers, who most likely will not have assigned lockers. Nevertheless, persons who work in offices, whether managers or not, usually have access to some of the employer's assets, and it would be wrong to assume that because of the nature of their jobs they automatically pose less of a risk than other employees. Assets to which they may have access can range from little more than an in-house telephone directory to sensitive proprietary information, keys, or other valuable assets. Although many of these things will be in their offices or desks, except for the locker sequence that same procedure should be followed with them for the recovery of whatever assets they may have been issued.

In addition to the embarrassment of being fired, the recovery of their own property from their offices can pose a problem. In these circumstances, and as part of the exit interview, thought should be given to telling them that it would be best for everyone, themselves included, if arrangements were made for them to return after their normal working hours for the express purpose of cleaning out their offices or desks; then, after collecting such things as their coats, purses, or briefcases, they too should be escorted off the premises. Once arrangements are made for their return to clean out offices or desks, they should be accompanied by a member of the management staff to make certain that none of the inn's property is taken.

Afterwards, it is obvious that regardless of the jobs they held, any terminated employees who return as guests must be treated as such. However, this is not where the risk lies. Instead it stems from what we recognized earlier,—namely, one can neither realistically anticipate how any terminated employee will react to being let go, nor can one forecast for how long that person may harbor resentment. Consequently, despite the impossibility of reading the mind of a former employee returning as a guest, an element of risk remains, and every effort should be made to prevent such a person from entering via the employees' entrance.

Two things must be done to prevent unauthorized reentry. First, it is imperative that whatever was issued to an employee as a form of hotel identification be recovered at the time of that person's termination. Second, those responsible for controlling access, whether members of a security department or timekeepers, must be promptly made aware of terminations and the identities of those to whom entry is to be denied. In addition to names, they should be given copies of photo identification badges, if available, or physical descriptions, but under no circumstances should they be given information about the reasons for termination, especially if the latter was for cause. Furthermore, if management has any reason at all to believe that a former employee has a propensity for violence, those who control access to the property should be be alerted to that fact. They also should be told that if that particular individual tries to enter and is or threatens to become a problem, the police are to be called.

PURCHASING, RECEIVING, STORING, AND MOVING ASSETS INTERNALLY

The vast majority of losses are attributable to the behavior of people. This fact only heightens the importance of cooperation between loss-prevention personnel and the human resources staff. After all, employees can both cause and help prevent losses. The care with which they are chosen, trained, and supervised can have a significant impact on the security/loss-prevention program. However, another significant factor in the loss of tangible assets is the degree to which, and to whom, they are exposed. We already have noted that many of the tangible assets found in hotels consist of things that can be used in one's home. As a result, it would be naive to deny that their exposure during their reception, storage, and transfer only adds to their vulnerability; but even before anything is received, it has to be bought, and the purchasing function is another part of operations that can contribute to losses.

Purchasing

No one person or business organization is completely self-contained. Any number of items, whether used in homes or by institutions, retailers, manufacturers, or hotels, must be acquired from outside sources. Therefore, purchasing can be described as a universal activity in which individuals, as well as large and small business organizations, engage. However, it is also true that of the many business functions in both the private and public sectors, people employed as buyers are among the most susceptible to becoming involved in activities that if not outright unlawful, at the very least are a conflict of interest. In either case, unless it is closely monitored, the purchasing function can become not only a source of loss but also one of embarrassment.

Inventories and accountability may alert management to known or suspected losses, but those controls do not necessarily prevent losses from occurring if buyers solicit or accept kickbacks from certain suppliers. Furthermore, unless payments to buyers are outlandish they may never even arouse suspicion, yet in reality employers rather than suppliers actually absorb the cost of those bribes. Consequently, losses can occur, albeit indirectly, even before purchases are delivered.

Such losses can be of particular concern to the lodging industry, where the relationship between reputation and the services provided to guests depends largely on the quality of a hotel's tangible assets. That quality can be compromised by buyers who, in return for bribes solicited or willingly accepted, buy things, both expendable and nonexpendable, that do not measure up to a hotel's advertised standards. Such shortfalls can damage a hotel's reputation and, in turn, its profit margins.

The possibility that neither quality nor reputation will necessarily suffer if buyers accept kickbacks from suppliers does not alter the fact that their employers will still suffer losses. To simply rely on the fact that commercial bribery is a crime in any given jurisdiction, or to assume that the participants will be apprehended, is not realistic. Even if the offender is successfully prosecuted, there is little likelihood that the victim will be compensated since if a fine is levied against the defendant, it goes to the state.

One objective of effective security or loss-prevention programs is to prevent losses that can result from unethical as well as criminal behavior; at the very least, accepting kickbacks is unethical. Thus security's concern with purchasing practices is essential. However, even though as a practical matter it is impossible to prevent all possible losses that can be traced to bribes, failure to institute meaningful measures that can help reduce the problem's scope and magnitude is inexcusable.

We have taken note of the insidious nature of the kickback problem by pointing out that unlike any number of other employees' activities, where telltale signs may at least raise questions in management's mind about their behavior, cautious recipients of bribes may go undetected. If and when they are discovered, it is often due to a very noticeable change in their lifestyle, or perhaps their greed has reached a point where even the suppliers who have benefited from the relationship elect to complain to their employers, anonymously or openly.

Strangely enough, there are times when existing kickback schemes may be known to, or at least suspected by, competing suppliers even before an employer's suspicions are aroused. If so, in addition to any monetary loss suffered, the potential for damage to reputation exists, at least among the area's reputable vendors. To them it signifies one of two things: Either the inn is a willing participant in an unlawful activity, or its general manager is incompetent or uncaring. That neither assumption may be correct does not alter their perception.

For a conscientious, concerned general manager, contact with these same reputable vendors could prove to be an invaluable source of information with respect to any existing questionable arrangements between members of the purchasing department and current suppliers. There are two possible courses of action. One, rely on information from third parties. On the rarest of occasions, knowledgeable or suspicious competitors may report what they know or suspect via an anonymous written or telephone message; however, this is the exception rather than the rule. Two, become proactive in minimizing the risk of bribery.

Obviously, even anonymous information from third parties should be welcome and thoroughly investigated; proactivity involves three steps. First, buying goods or services should be, to the greatest extent possible, based on competitive bids submitted by reputable vendors. Second, the general or executive assistant or resident manager, or perhaps the controller as an alternate, should periodically review all purchase orders to see if (a) buying patterns suggest that certain vendors seem to be favored, or (b) other reputable suppliers simply do not submit bids. Third, vendors in the latter category then should be contacted to see if there is a reason for their not bidding.

Since getting anonymous information admittedly is unlikely, this method for uncovering kickback schemes obviously cannot be relied upon. At the same time, concerned managers cannot afford to wait and hope that any disgruntled suppliers will voluntarily and openly voice their suspicions. If this is the case, can anything be done? The answer is *yes*.

Calls to reputable companies with which the hotel is doing little or no business are worthwhile. Although the recipients of such calls might not initiate contact with the caller, they may welcome being contacted and asked why they seldom do business with the hotel. Their answers may imply a problem with buyers; for example, if they have tried repeatedly without success and have given up, that would suggest that perhaps someone in purchasing is involved with a kickback scheme. Certainly, this information should justify a much closer examination of the purchasing department's operations. If a problem exists it can be dealt with. Obviously, nothing can be done about a problem whose existence is unknown and whose impact on profitability can continue indefinitely.

Being proactive in combating the kickback problem should not be construed to mean that no buyers can be trusted; in fact, the vast majority can be. Instead, it takes into account the need to identify and terminate those who are dishonest, and it helps the honest ones stay that way. Initiating a program to deal with the problem of kickbacks being either solicited or accepted, plus making it a matter of hotel policy known to all employees, serves two purposes. One, it minimizes the risk of losses through this medium. Two, making the policy known to everyone is less disruptive to good labor relations than waiting until something wrong is suspected and then initiating an investigation that focuses on a particular individual or group.

Receiving

Goods purchased have to be delivered and received. Although neither cost controllers or other receiving personnel are susceptible to kickbacks, they nevertheless are vulnerable in ways that can prove costly to the inn. Innkeepers cannot oversee, let alone control, how things are done at their suppliers' places of business or by suppliers' employees, yet it is there that losses can occur.

Some losses are attributable to vendors who are less than honest, however rare they may be, or to quantity or quality problems with the products of even the most honest ones. Other losses may be caused by collusion between delivery people and receiving employees. Still others may be the result of carelessness or laziness on the part of cost controllers or those working with them in the receiving process. Thus, the way in which goods are delivered and received can be another source of loss. It would be naive to say that these risks are minimal since it is the cost controller's job to see that what is delivered is what was ordered.

Totally eliminating losses or risks is impossible, but their reduction is not. Initially, three things can be done with respect to the receiving function. First, much depends on the work done by cost controllers, so they must be carefully chosen. Second, they must be given meaningful written procedures for the receipt and verification of all purchases, and their compliance with those procedures has to be assured. Third, there must be supervision of everyone involved with the receiving process.

Despite any cost controller's qualifications, it is important to provide that person with procedures setting forth how deliveries are to be received, verified, and moved into the appropriate storerooms. Many purchases are made by weight, but unless there is a blatant discrepancy, it is doubtful that a shortage will be visually detected. As a result, unless each delivered unit is weighed, shortages can occur; they can also add up in terms of cost. Consequently, if weight is not checked for each purchase made on that basis, the loss stems from paying for goods not delivered. In the case of foodstuffs, the extent of the loss is compounded by the fact that what is not available for use cannot be sold; therefore, food service profits can be eroded even more.

The quality of what is bought and delivered also can contribute to losses. Remember, although a major asset of any property is its reputation, standards may vary where quality is concerned. To illustrate, one does not expect to find the same thickness of towels and quality of china and flatware in a five-star hotel as in the average motel. Nevertheless, within each of the several categories by which hotels are ranked, their reputations hinge largely on what their guests see as acceptable within their own perceived standards. Therefore, to accept a delivery that does not measure up to the inn's standard can mean not only a tarnished reputation but also a loss for having paid more for something of a lesser quality.

The loss can be even greater, and conceivably more embarrassing, if acceptance of a lesser quality involves foodstuffs. As an example, perishables or seafood whose freshness does not measure up to standard may cause some guests to become ill. If their sickness, traced to food served in one of the hotel's outlets, is relatively minor, most likely the meal would be free for everyone at that table even if only one person was affected. For a more severe illness, but one not necessarily requiring hospitalization, a decision to "compliment" the room would probably be in order. Regardless of whether meals or even the room itself are "comped," there is an obvious loss of income in addition to the impact on the hotel's reputation. Then, too, depending on the nature and severity of the illness and the number of people involved, the possibility that this event could become a news media item cannot be ignored. The resulting damage to reputation from this could be either short- or long-term.

Minimizing the risk of losses from short deliveries, possible collusion, and quality control problems suggests a need for and adherence to practical but not needlessly burdensome procedures. Several things can be done in this regard:

1. No deliveries should be accepted or signed for until all items have been unloaded onto the receiving dock.
2. Whether receiving is done by cost controllers or other employees hired for that purpose, they should
   (a) have copies of purchase orders and ensure that delivery tickets contain the hotel's purchase order number;
   (b) not sign delivery tickets until they have been compared with the purchase order, and all purchases made by weight or quantity have in fact been weighed or counted, and the actual weights or counts have been noted on both the vendor's and hotel's copies of the tickets; and
   (c) make certain that delivery persons are not allowed to enter the hotel beyond the receiving dock.

Quantity and quality aside, additional losses can occur during the receipt of breakable items. With purchases of this sort delivered in cartons, the steps previously outlined can be taken, but there is a difference between signing for a specific number of boxes and acknowledging the condition of their contents. Although the volume of deliveries at any one time may make it impractical to open and examine every item for breakage, it also can be costly to simply acknowledge receipt without some provision for recourse if breakage is subsequently discovered.

Broken items have to be replaced, and replacements cost money; but filing a claim after the damage has been discovered can prove to be an exercise in futility. Upon getting a claim in these cases, both vendors and their carriers undoubtedly would resist any payment. They would contend that any damage must have happened after the hotel accepted the merchandise; therefore, it must bear the loss.

The standard receiving procedure should be followed when items of this kind are delivered—but with two differences. One, acknowledging their receipt should be conditioned upon the hotel's right to examine the contents within a reasonable and specified number of days and to file a claim for any damage discovered. Two, deliveries in this category should be temporarily set aside in the receiving area and inspected within the specified time; any claims for damage should be promptly filed.

To have procedures in place is one thing; making certain that they are followed is another. However, it is also important to ensure compliance in ways that will not alienate or otherwise jeopardize good labor relations. Toward that end it is helpful to let cost controllers or receiving personnel know that from time to time they can expect certain members of the hotel staff, such as the general, executive assistant, or resident managers, food and beverage director, executive and sous chefs, purchasing and stores managers, and controller, to make unannounced visits to the receiving area.

When those visits are made, deliveries should be randomly sampled for the express purpose of confirming, as is within the particular visitor's competence, the weight, quantity, and quality of goods not yet moved from receiving to stores. These visits serve a dual purpose. By providing the oversight needed to ensure compliance with receiving procedures, they help reduce the risk of loss in the process, and they signify management's intention to maintain high standards in all operations.

Stores

Once goods have been received, the accepted practice is to move them either into designated storerooms or to the functional areas for which they were bought. For instance, such things as cereals would go into dry stores, dairy products into coolers, while towels might go directly to housekeeping. From a loss-prevention viewpoint, a key consideration is the time that elapses between their arrival and acceptance and their removal from the receiving dock. Undeniably, goods received but not yet moved into stores or to their destined operating areas are vulnerable on several counts.

First, as stated earlier, many hotel assets are items that can be used in almost every home. Second, a significant percentage of the goods received with the greatest frequency are foodstuffs; many are perishable, subject to spoilage. Third, sometimes delivery schedules and "labor-saving" techniques followed by some employees also can add to losses. In any event, the longer items are exposed, the greater the risk of their being stolen or becoming spoiled. In either case the result is a loss. Consequently, all goods received should be transferred to their proper destinations as soon as possible after delivery and verification in accordance with the hotel's receiving procedures.

A case in point was an island resort property, most of whose supplies, especially foodstuffs, had to be shipped in. Losses due to both theft and spoilage occurred. Three things contributed to the problem:

1. Since most vendors made their deliveries at roughly the same time, the volume was such that invariably there was a backlog of goods to be moved into stores.

2. The hotel did not have a "first-in-first out" (FIFO) policy in place with regard to any of its expendable assets, foodstuffs or otherwise.

3. Without such a policy, and because of the volume of goods received, receiving personnel filled requisitions from the kitchen from among items on the receiving dock rather than taking things from stores and moving newly arrived goods into stores.

Despite the fact that the inn was the customer with whom vendors wanted to do business, the purchasing manager conceded that he had never thought of discussing the possibility of staggered delivery times and transportation schedules with any of them in an effort to alleviate the backlog problem. Following up on this idea, he learned that transportation to the island was so frequent that deliveries could be staggered without creating any hardship for the vendors. New delivery schedules, mutually agreeable to suppliers and the property, were implemented; receiving backlogs were eliminated, and the hotel benefited.

Still to be dealt with was the matter of moving deliveries into stores. "FIFO" had rarely been discussed by the management staff, and then only as a mechanism for moving things into and out of stores. Its relationship to loss prevention, costs, and profits had not been considered. However, once that relationship was clearly understood, a "first in—first out" policy applicable to all expendable assets was adopted. The responsibility for ensuring implementation and compliance was given to the cost controller and stores manager.

Internal Transfers of Assets

The practice of moving deliveries to storerooms may be implemented in various ways, but there is less difference in the ways in which assets are transferred from stores to operating departments; department heads generally submit written requisitions to the stores manager. Since risks comparable to those found in the vendor-to-hotel delivery system exist here, some of the same standards apply but on a somewhat different scale. Internal transfers also are distinguishable in that if losses do occur during the internal movement of assets, only employees are involved.

As a first step, accountability for requisition forms is important. If the "paper" used to control the movement of assets cannot be accounted for, how can one account for the assets themselves? Requisitions should be prenumbered and issued by the controller to department heads in blocks of numbers. A record of the numbers issued to each department should be retained in the controller's office. Department heads should be instructed to safeguard the forms.

Ideally, all requisitions from stores should be signed by department heads. However, with hotels and motels operating around the clock, every day of the year, such a requirement would be unrealistic since there inevitably will be times when they are not available. Nevertheless, controls can be maintained by appointing backups for all department heads who, in a department head's absence, would be authorized to sign requisitions.

Employees designated as backups should be approved in writing by either the general or executive assistant (or resident) manager. Parenthetically, a backup for the stores manager, similarly designated and approved, is equally important. Copies of the signatures of persons authorized to sign requisitions should be on file in a safe place in the stores manager's office and used for authentication purposes if questions arise.

Requisitions should be in triplicate, used sequentially, and completed in every detail, including not only what is being requisitioned but also the date and department head's (or authorized backup's) signature. Two completed copies should go to the stores manager; one should be kept by the department. Of the two sent to stores, one should accompany delivery of the goods to the requisitioning department.

When delivered to the requisitioning department, the department's copy should be pulled and compared with the copy from stores. If the order has been properly filled, the latter should be signed as a receipt; if there are discrepancies, they should be noted thereon by the person signing for the delivery. Both receipted and departmental copies should be kept on file until they have been audited.

Audits help account for all requisitions by number, determine whether or not there are any discrepancies that warrant investigation, and ensure that requisitions have been properly completed and signed only by authorized persons. Their timing should be determined by the controller's office, but an effort should be made to conduct them at intervals of about thirty days. This practice helps reduce the risk of loss by reaffirming the importance of controls and accountability in relation to the internal movement of assets; it also allows inquiries to be undertaken within a reasonable time after suspect discrepancies have been noted.

ASSET ACCOUNTABILITY

Effective loss-prevention programs must be concerned with controls and accountability that go beyond dealings with vendors and moving assets from stores to operating departments. The need to be able to account and fix responsibility for the protection of assets once they have reached those departments is of the utmost importance. Of necessity this accountability will involve employees in both management and other positions.

We have emphasized the fact that good security is loss prevention, not merely crime prevention; it is concerned not only with preventing crimes but also with preventing other misconduct that can prove costly. Carelessness, mistakes, accidents, and unethical behavior are no less important considerations.

In discussing the human resources role in loss prevention, we said that employees can both cause problems that lead to losses and help prevent them. Good controls and accountability make it easier to identify employees and fix responsibility when their behavior results in losses. Meaningful operating systems can also make them less inclined to misbehave than if they feel they can act with impunity. Consequently, accounting and being able to fix responsibility for assets has to be viewed from the point of view of key operating departments.

Food and Beverages Operations

No meaningful discussion of loss prevention relative to food and beverages can be limited to actual foodstuffs and liquids sold. Neither can it be confined to this chapter's earlier discussion of how losses can occur in connection with purchasing, receiving, and the movement and storage of assets, particularly foodstuffs where spoilage is a factor. How food and beverages are served can also contribute to losses, as illustrated in the kitchen layout problem cited in Chapter 2, as can the ways in which the items used for that purpose are handled.

From the standpoint of service in relation to loss prevention/security as used throughout the text, how can losses be incurred? Largely by failing to properly train and supervise the wait staff to make certain that all guests are treated both courteously and equally. An actual incident helps illustrate this.

Two guests were seated at adjacent tables by a maitre d'hotel; both would be served by the same person. One, known to the waitress, was asked if he wanted something to drink before dinner, given a choice of salad dressings, and without having to ask, was served extra butter and sour cream for a baked potato. After finishing his main course, he was asked if he would like dessert, an after-dinner drink, or anything else. The waitress made certain that his coffee cup was always full. The other guest, unknown to the waitress, was not asked about drinks before or after dinner or offered dessert. Neither was he given a choice of salad dressings nor asked if he would like butter or sour cream for his baked potato. He had to ask for coffee refills.

To say the second guest could show his or her displeasure by leaving either the no tip or a minimal one misses the point insofar as the hotel itself is concerned. It overlooks two things. First, the second guest's obviously disparate treatment could not help but adversely affect the inn's reputation. That, in itself, could translate into a loss of repeat business from this guest as well as a loss of new business from those to whom he might tell his story. It also represented a possible and more immediate loss of income; the waitress ignored a chance to "sell" the guest a cocktail or aperitif, an after-dinner drink, or dessert, any or all of which would have generated additional income for the outlet.

Service-related losses can also occur in lounges. Unless acting in accordance with the inn's accepted practices, bartenders who free-pour liquor instead of measuring it, give regular customers or "big tippers" an occasional free drink, or permit or even encourage guests to "run a tab" instead of making a polite but deliberate effort to collect for each drink served, are or can be responsible for losses.

Great as the risk of loss is from these sources, it pales by comparison with what can be lost if bartenders are not trained how to manage lounge customers with a tendency to consume more alcohol than they can handle. Such customers can become noisy, boisterous, and offensive to others in the lounge; at times they can also become belligerent. Their behavior can do more than affect the hotel's reputation it can also cause other guests to leave before they intended to, thus reducing the outlet's potential sales.

Another consequence, however, is even more important than the possible loss of revenue. If untrained or inadequately supervised bartenders continue to serve a guest whose behavior is already questionable, and if that guest's actions subsequently cause death or injury to themselves or others due to their condition, more is at stake than the possible loss of revenue. In addition to the likelihood of adverse publicity and the accompanying loss of reputation, the inn risks a possible lawsuit, payment of damages, and loss of license. In the United States and many other countries, laws, often cited as "Dram Shop Acts," hold establishments liable for continuing to serve seemingly inebriated persons alcohol if that service was the proximate cause of an incident that thereafter was caused by that person and that resulted in death or injury.

Thus, despite varying levels of risk, service-related losses in all phases of food and beverage operations are of concern because of their possible impact on both reputation and income. With respect to accountability and responsibility, it is true that the wait staff and bartenders must be held accountable for how they do their jobs, but the ultimate responsibility for preventing damage to reputation and possible losses stemming from service-related issues rests with outlet managers.

Of course, service is not the only source of loss in food and beverage operations. We already have discussed the importance of written requisitions in drawing supplies. In discussing receiving, stores, and the internal movement of assets, we said spoilage can occur if foodstuffs, primarily perishables, are not processed on a first in–first out basis. Spoilage equals waste; waste equals loss. Serious as this can be, other potential sources of loss exist unless steps are taken to further reduce risks linked to carelessness, theft, and inadequate supervision.

Dishwashers' carelessness can mean excessive breakage of china and glassware, as well as the accidental disposal of flatware into garbage. The quality of the china and flatware used is immaterial; the fact that anything broken or improperly disposed of must be replaced is not. While proper training and supervision can help reduce losses in both categories, additional steps can help to further reduce the risk of flatware ending up with garbage.

One is to have garbage periodically inspected by food service management, or even by security personnel where there is a security department, so that items that accidentally or negligently thrown out can be recovered. This is not a pleasant job, but it sends a message to everyone involved with the process that losses due to carelessness are taken seriously, not simply written off as part of the cost of doing business.

These same random but regularly conducted garbage inspections can also help reduce losses due to the theft of foodstuffs. Our earlier discussion of loss prevention took note of the fact that one contributor to lodging industry losses is that so many tangible assets, whether expendable or not, can be used in any home. Certainly this is true of foodstuffs. Carefully wrapped items can be and have been found in garbage, put there by employees and recovered by them when leaving work. While good forecasting and good accountability are compatible, they cannot prevent stealing. Even with the best controls over waste and spoilage, strict accountability is impossible.

Important as garbage inspections are, still more is needed for an effective program to prevent the theft of foodstuffs. One is to locate the dumpster or other garbage disposal receptacle where it cannot be accessed by employees either while leaving or after having left the premises. Another, all employees leaving work should be subject to parcel inspections. However, with respect to the latter, *it is imperative that these examinations be conducted in an absolutely nondiscriminatory way.*

The manner in which room service trays or tables are recovered can either help prevent or lead to losses. Although the ways in which guests can contribute to losses will be discussed in greater detail in Chapter 4, tables or trays left in hallways can adversely affect the loss-prevention effort in terms of both reputation and the protection of certain tangible assets.

From a guest's perspective few things are as offensive or unsightly as a smelly table or tray, literally shoved into a hallway by another guest who is through with it, especially if it stays there for any length of time. In addition, tableware and expendable food items that can be reused without risk, such as packets of jam, jelly, or sweetener, can be stolen by passersby. If these losses are not totally prevented, they at least can be minimized if there is accountability and responsibility on the part of room service, housekeeping, and security. Things that room service can do are the following:

1. Place tent cards on all room service trays or tables inviting guests to call for their removal when they are through with them.

2. Accept the fact that despite the cards some guests will not call. In these cases allow a reasonable time for consumption, depending on what was ordered. Room service then can call and ask if the guest would like the tray or table removed.

3. If there is around-the-clock room service and an order is placed late at night, again allow a reasonable time for consumption, depending on the order. Then room service should go to the room since the guest probably will have put the table or tray in the hallway.

Housekeeping and security personnel also have a role to play in this regard, although it obviously is different. They cannot be held responsible for returning room service items or equipment to the kitchen, but like all the inn's employees they have a duty to actively participate in the overall loss-prevention program. If they find trays or tables in corridors, they should do two things: (1) move them to the nearest service area on the floor and (2) call room service and say where the tables or trays can be found so that the latter can recover them.

Beverage operations are vulnerable both in lounges and at functions. Bar stock has to be controlled and accounted for by management if losses are to be reduced to a minimum. The first step in the process occurs when liquor has been properly receipted for upon delivery and then is moved to stores. Bottles should be color coded or otherwise marked in ways that make them easily identifiable as hotel assets and distinguishable from other bottles that may appear on shelves or in storage cabinets in outlets. Coupled with attentive management, this procedure helps reduce losses that can occur if dishonest bartenders introduce their own bottles into bar stock and profit by selling from them.

Another method for the control and accountability of bar stock is the way in which supplies are replenished. In addition to color coding, a bottle-for-bottle exchange not only discourages the substitution of private for hotel stock, but it also further reduces the risk of bar stock being appropriated for personal use or stolen for sale. In reality, neither expense nor inconvenience is attached to the requirement that empty bottles must accompany requisitions and be turned in before full ones are issued.

Equally important is the need for good accountability, via the use of written requisitions, for who has access to liquor stores and how much time is spent in the storeroom even by authorized persons. Effective inventory control and accountability for liquor stores are impossible without written requisitions. Experienced bartenders have a feel for what they need in the way of bar stock in order to adequately serve customers; they are the ones who should fill out requisitions. However, all requisitions then should be approved by either the bar manager or the food and beverage director before going to the stores manager. Only those requisitions properly completed and approved should be filled.

The ability to forecast is part of lounge as well as food operations, and there is a relationship between forecasting and outlet inventory. At times, however, lounge business may increase unexpectedly with additional liquor needed at a time when those who would normally fill the requisition are unavailable. Under those circumstances an authorized employee who is ordinarily not involved with the transfer of bar stock may be called upon to fill the order. Nothing, however, should prevent a written requisition from being completed.

Physical security, discussed in Chapter 2, also has to be considered as an additional safeguard in helping prevent losses in beverage operations. Certainly the number of employees allowed access to liquor stores, other than the food and beverage director or the bar or stores managers, should be limited and not extended to include all bar staff. Time-recording or electronic locks, previously discussed, that show the times of entry and exit and the person's identity should protect the liquor stores. Stores personnel and any others with authorized access should be approved by the food and beverage director.

To further reduce the risk of theft of liquor stores, requisitions should be examined against the time shown as spent by anyone in the storeroom, a logical task for the controller's department. This analysis, which need not be time consuming, can be useful in several ways. For instance, suppose a printout for the liquor storeroom lock shows access; has a requisition been completed? If not, one should assume that something is probably wrong. The person who had access and failed to file a requisition then can be identified and questioned in an effort to find out what that wrong is.

Even if a requisition exists, the analysis can be enlightening. Here the issue is whether the amount of time spent filling the requisition seems to be reasonable in relation to the order's size. Let's say that the order was for one bottle each of scotch, vermouth, vodka, and bourbon. According to the lock printout, twenty minutes were spent filling it. Was that length of time reasonable or excessive in proportion to the size of the order? If it seems excessive, an impromptu inventory of the liquor storeroom might be worth considering.

The timing of food and beverage inventories can also contribute to preventing losses. The fact that these assets are consumables does not lessen their value of importance insofar as profitability is concerned. Although it is a lodging industry practice for controllers to take departmental inventories at prescribed intervals—a topic to be discussed in detail under the controller's heading—there is no reason that food and beverage directors should not take their own additional inventories.

Depending on a property's size and the quantity of supplies needed on hand for an efficient operation, it may be impractical to take complete inventories with any frequency. Nevertheless, the idea of weekly inventories (not always on the same day)—complete if possible, random if not—deserves to be considered.

It is important to remember that inventories per se do not prevent losses; they will indicate whether or not a loss has occurred, but if one has, they will not reveal the reason for the shortage. Despite this fact, taking them regularly and frequently can serve a dual purpose. First, the food and beverage director's concern for accountability is reinforced, and departmental employees are made aware of that fact. Second, if any discrepancies are found, a reasonable inquiry should be made to determine the reason. From an investigatory perspective, the shorter the time between inventories, the easier it is to try to determine how the shortage occurred.

In discussing bar service, mention was made of the risk of loss when bartenders allow customers to "run a tab" instead of paying for drinks in a timely fashion. There also is a risk of loss when restaurant or lounge customers seem to have paid their checks when in fact they have not. Getting payment from all restaurant or lounge customers requires a great deal of tact on the part of the wait staff, but this is especially true if the person claims to be a registered guest. In reality, anyone can put a room number on a check and sign it without being registered at the inn. If they are not in fact registered, once they leave the premises it is too late to do anything. The hotel then has to absorb the cost of whatever was consumed.

Consequently, although the accepted practice is for guests to note their room numbers on the check and sign their names, a way has to be found to verify the fact that the person is indeed registered. In many European and Asian hotels that use keys for guest rooms, guests are accustomed to placing them on the table when being served in any outlet. In part, doing so is a matter of convenience since, unlike key tags still used by some American hotels, the tags frequently are too large and heavy to carry in one's pocket. On the other hand, with the increasing use of electronic locks both in the United States and abroad, guests carry their card "keys" with them. As a result, guests in any outlets who enter room numbers and sign their checks should be politely asked to show their card keys. In those cases where electronic locks are not used, they should be asked to show their room keys. Adopting this simple approach does not guarantee that all losses of this kind will be eliminated, but asking for verification of guest status will markedly reduce the risk.

The Laundry

A hotel laundry has a dual obligation: One relates to the inn itself; the other, to its guests. Regarding the former, the laundry must ensure that housekeeping has whatever it needs in the way of clean linens so that guest rooms can be serviced, that food service operations are similarly supplied, and that uniformed members of the hotel staff have clean and pressed uniforms. With respect to guests, it must make certain not only that guest items sent for laundering or for cleaning and pressing are done to the guest's satisfaction and returned on time, undamaged, but also that any guest valuables inadvertently left in clothing are recovered and returned to the guest. Problems can arise in both situations.

One may wonder how a failure to implement controls over and accountability for laundry operations can have an unexpectedly far-reaching, adverse impact on an inn's various activities. What actually occurred at one property helps illustrate the point.

This was a four-star hotel, with an outdoor Olympic-size swimming pool, that catered to both business travelers and vacationers. The general manager's policy clearly stated that the laundry would neither wash nor dry-clean employees' personal items. Two exceptions were made: one for employees' uniforms; another for the general and executive assistant managers, both of whom were required to live on the premises. Nevertheless, the laundry manager, entirely on his own, elected to make a few additional exceptions.

How did this affect the hotel not only as a whole but also in terms of departmental losses? While the cost of the water, laundry, or cleaning materials used at any one time was relatively small, it did add up over time. Of greater importance was the fact that the time spent by the laundry's staff doing that work interrupted and interfered with normal operations, which, on more than one occasion, were slowed considerably. Providing clean linens and uniforms to housekeeping and food service functions was temporarily delayed, thus disrupting their work. Furthermore, this unauthorized use of the laundry's time, materials, and personnel, coupled with guests' demands for more towels and the need to satisfy their other laundry and cleaning requirements in a proper and timely way, put the staff under additional pressure.

The impact on laundry employees' morale was decidedly negative. They resented disruptions to their work for the benefit of a select few even more than being denied personal laundry and cleaning privileges. The general manager's failure to respond to a policy violation was seen as a sign of weak-

Hotel Inter-Continental–New York

ness and interpreted to mean that he most likely would tolerate or forgive misconduct by other employees. Consequently, incidents of employee misbehavior increased.

Several things can be learned from the foregoing. One is that the personal use of the hotel's laundry by employees can prove costly in more ways than the dollar value of the water, materials, and time spent washing or cleaning their belongings, although the latter expense can add up to a fairly sizeable sum. Also, once general managers set a policy, whether for the laundry or any other departments, they cannot afford to tolerate exceptions made by individual department heads. Finally, if for any reason a decision is made to allow the laundry's use for washing and dry-cleaning employees' personal items, perhaps as a fringe benefit, the hotel's needs must be satisfied first. Then, specific time limits must be imposed and adhered to with respect to the laundry's use for the benefit of employees.

When it comes to providing laundry and cleaning services for guests, the inn's perspective and the guests' may differ. While the inn understandably wants to offer the best service possible, in its relationship with guests it tends to focus on crime prevention to reduce the risk of liability from that quarter.

Chapter 3   Loss Prevention and Hotel Operations   73

As we have said before, certainly crime prevention is important. However, liability can be incurred for reasons that have nothing to do with crime, and they do not always get the attention they deserve. For purposes of loss prevention, these other possible sources of liability need to be considered.

Crime prevention, of course, is the first concern. When guests place a call for laundry or cleaning services, both collection and return are usually handled by a member of the bell staff, not infrequently in the guest's absence. This gives the employee full access to the guest's belongings. Sadly, when guests think something of theirs has disappeared, they—and all too often, the front desk—immediately suspect employee involvement. Such a reaction is unfair to the staff and prejudicial to good labor relations. It also emphasizes the need for and importance of a careful, thorough preemployment screening of applicants by human resources, as discussed earlier in this chapter.

To help protect the hotel against unwarranted claims of loss or damage, as well as to enhance its reputation, upon receipt of a guest's belongings in the laundry each item should be carefully examined. If anything on the laundry or cleaning slip submitted by the guest is missing, or any existing damage to a garment—a stain or a tear—is found, it should be brought to the laundry manager's attention and noted in detail on the guest's submission. It is naive to assume that guests never make false claims, and since the amounts claimed for damage in these instances are inclined to be relatively small and most likely not covered by insurance, hotel management may decide that payment is the quickest and easiest way to dispose of the matter. Without doubt, paying legitimate claims is important to the maintenance of reputation as well as part of the cost of doing business. To pay unjustified claims, however, represents a needless loss. In short, the best protection against false claims is to ensure not only that all garments listed by the guest are received but also to note what shortages or damages may exist on the guest's order for service.

This careful inspection of garments can also benefit the inn by conceivably adding to the lustre of its existing reputation. Certainly, if a guest inadvertently leaves something of value in a garment, and it is recovered and returned, this will enhance the reputation of both the property and its staff. In a similar situation, a guest may have overlooked something left in a pocket that could damage a garment by either discoloring or tearing it.

Finding, removing, and returning objects of value or ones that can cause damage to guests' clothing does more than show that laundry and cleaning are handled with care. It can help reduce the risk of claims for either items assumed to have been lost or stolen or for damage to clothing. Furthermore, examining guests' belongings immediately upon receipt can offer other benefits. Recovering and returning things promptly to their owners can help reduce the number of items placed in lost and found, lessen the time spent trying to identify the owners, and facilitate the inn's ultimate disposition of unclaimed property with less risk.

Housekeeping

All hotel departments and activities can contribute to or help prevent losses. This is truer of some than of others, but few are in housekeeping's unique position. All employees have access to at least some of the inn's assets, even if only on a limited basis. Some of these same employees also have access to guests' belongings, albeit in a limited way, and then most often in the guests' presence. Good examples are members of the bell staff and, on occasion, room service personnel.

Housekeeping is different. Housekeepers have access not only to hotel assets but also to guests' property, usually when guests are absent. As noted earlier in this chapter, this makes them prime suspects when guests allege that something has been stolen. In addition, the nature of the female housekeeper's job adds to her vulnerability to assault or rape.

It is because of housekeeping's unique operational function, which gives it access to assets and guests' belonging and also exposes some housekeepers to risks, that its relationship to security and loss prevention has to be considered from two different viewpoints. One focuses on protecting and conserving the inn's assets, reputation included; the other concerns the personal protection of those housekeepers who may be at risk.

Considering its special function, how can housekeeping either contribute to the loss of hotel assets or help protect them? An issue applicable to all applicants for employment, especially to housekeeping personnel, was discussed under the human resources heading: the importance of a sound preemployment screening procedure.

The fact that housekeepers have access to both hotel and guest property highlights how careful screening is in the inn's best interest. Furthermore, it can help morale by reducing the risk that an employee will be unfairly suspected when something goes awry. An additional benefit lies in its usefulness in rebutting a plaintiff's complaint alleging negligent hiring in a case where any employee's misconduct is an issue.

Recognizing that virtually all employees have access to at least some assets, housekeepers nevertheless are distinguishable from most of their coworkers in that their access is to assets that can be used in any home. The fact that guests also have access to the hotel's assets and can contribute to losses will be discussed at length in Chapter 4. Therefore, ways need to be found in which the risk of loss can be reduced and losses can be minimized without adding to operating costs or interfering with operating efficiency.

The answer lies mainly in accountability and inventory control. A logical starting point involves the issue and laundering of housekeeping uniforms. When issued uniforms, each housekeeper should sign a receipt for the number issued; the receipt then becomes a part of the individual's personnel file. Thereafter, the issue of clean uniforms should be on an exchange basis. All uniforms issued should be accounted for and turned in whenever any housekeeper no longer needs uniforms either because of termination or acceptance of a new position within the hotel.

For housekeepers to do their jobs, they must have access to guest rooms. Regardless of whether those rooms are protected by electronic locks with card-readers or by standard key-operated mortise locks, housekeepers should sign receipts for their cards or keys when they start work, and the cards or key should be returned and accounted for at the end of each shift.

Principles of accountability also must be applied to the use of housekeepers' carts, whether they are stocked directly by the housekeeping department preceding each shift or by individual housekeepers from floor linen closets. Based on occupancy and the nature of the property, carts should contain sufficient linens and cleaning supplies to service the number of rooms assigned to a particular housekeeper. For instance, resort hotels might provide guests with more towels than one would expect to find in purely commercial properties.

For purposes of accountability, the resupply of clean linens should be based on two things: the number of rooms actually to be serviced (where dirty linens go directly to the laundry), and the current occupancy forecast. On the other hand, cleaning materials should be resupplied on an exchange basis. Requiring the exchange of empty cans of soap powder or bottles of furniture polish as a condition for the issue of full ones is neither expensive nor inefficient, and it discourages the theft of such supplies for home use.

In addition, regardless of the frequency with which scheduled inventories are taken, in those cases where floor linen closets are used thought should be given to a program of unannounced, weekly, random inventories by housekeeping supervisors. However, while they also can be used at home, the small amenities provided for guest use, such as shampoo, packaged coffee, lotion, shoe-shine cloths, sewing kits, and shower caps, would be exempt from strict accountability standards. This exemption takes into consideration the cost/benefit factors. Furthermore, there can be no strict accountability since these items are used for sales promotion, and the idea that guests frequently will take them as souvenirs is accepted.

To the extent that it is feasible, the contents of housekeeping carts should be protected. This is not to suggest that they should be encased in wooden or metal cabinets that can be locked, but rather that the possibility of attaching either cloth or opaque plastic sides to conceal their contents be considered. This would serve as a deterrent to those guests, however few they may be, who are not stealing but are merely electing to help themselves to extra towels or other supplies. Certainly the need to raise and lower these sides would be less troublesome and time consuming for housekeepers than having to get additional linens or supplies from either housekeeping or floor linen closets when they encounter shortages attributable to those guests.

In our earlier discussion of room service, we took note of one way in which housekeepers can help prevent losses. There is another, much more closely related to their actual work. It involves ensuring that all of a room's contents, not just those items with which they have direct contact, are present. As part of their training, they should be told that all losses must be reported immediately to supervisors so appropriate inquiries can be initiated. For instance, it is highly improbable that housekeepers would not notice if any items of bedding, such as bedspreads, blankets, sheets, and pillow cases, were missing; the same can be said of towels and shower curtains.

Equally important to their training is the need to pay attention to other assets, of which they may be less conscious, that may be found in some properties' guest rooms. To illustrate, if there are hair dryers, are they still in the bathrooms? Are coffee makers where they should be, or does the housekeeper merely make certain that there is an adequate supply of coffee, sweetener, and creamer? Today most telephones use jacks; are the telephones in the rooms? Do housekeepers check closets to see if the terry cloth bathrobes, extra blankets, and pillows left for guest comfort and convenience are still there? What about wall hangings or other assets that can be taken; are they where they should be?

If assets in any of the foregoing categories are missing, they have to be replaced; replacements cost money. Furthermore, in all likelihood the volume of these losses will be such that they will not be covered by insurance. Even if a supply of replacements is kept on hand and an immediate outlay of cash is not required, these losses and their impact on profits are undeniable.

Guest room access remains a matter of concern despite the fact that so many properties have converted from keys to card readers as a way to control access and, in many of those cases, record usage. True, a degree of risk has been reduced, although not necessarily eliminated, where card readers are the norm, but there has been no appreciable reduction at hotels and motels that still use standard lock-and-key systems. From a loss-prevention or security perspective, there are two issues: (1) access by housekeepers and (2) requests of housekeepers for access by persons who claim to be guests.

Housekeepers, more than any other group of employees, must be able to enter guest rooms in order to service them. However, it is in the best interest of the inn, its housekeepers, and their supervisors to issue cards (or keys, where still used) that limit access to blocks of rooms instead of allowing entry to all rooms. For purposes of security, efficiency, and convenience, housekeepers should be issued a single card or key with which to enter only those rooms in the section to which they have been assigned rather than having access to an entire floor. For the same reasons, cards or keys issued to supervisors should limit access to no more than the floor or floors for which they are responsible. There is neither a logical reason nor any justification for either housekeepers or their supervisors to have access to cards (or keys) that are the equivalent of great grand or grand master keys that will allow them to enter rooms without limit.

These limitations represent a form of accountability with regard to the housekeeping staff, and they make it easier for either supervisory or security personnel to investigate allegations or suspicions of theft by employees from guest rooms. However, the problem of thefts of hotel assets or guests' belongings by so-called third parties, with an unintended assist from housekeepers, remains even with the introduction of card readers for access control to rooms.

Some burglars concentrate on hotels, but like all members of their craft who consider themselves "professionals," they strive to commit their crimes without attracting undue attention. When the standard practice at hotels was for guests and hotel staff to use keys, one method used by burglars was to dress as any guest might and wait until housekeepers were on the floor to make up rooms. Then, patting pockets as if looking for something, the burglar would approach a housekeeper, claim that he must have forgotten to pick up his key at the front desk, and ask if the housekeeper would open the door to his room in order to save him from returning to the lobby for his key. Not infrequently, the combination of knowing how important good guest relations are, and the possibility of being named "Housekeeper of the Month," were justification for unlocking the door. If the housekeeper hesitated, the burglar often added an additional incentive in the form of a cash gratuity.

The problem still persists, even where keys are no longer used. Of course, with cards and card readers burglars no longer can claim that they seem to have forgotten to pick up their keys at the front desk. Instead, they will say that they must have left their cards in the room or have misplaced them, and for reasons already given, housekeepers may be tempted to unlock a door.

Both the initial and ongoing training of housekeeping personnel, coupled with effective supervision, are needed in order to minimize the risk of successful burglaries being perpetrated in this way. Housekeepers must be made to understand that they never should open room doors simply because someone who appears to be a guest asks them to. If the person is a legitimate guest, a polite refusal, and an explanation that this is the inn's policy for the protection and benefit of its guests, can be far more important to good guest relations than acceding to an illegitimate request, having a room burglarized, and trying to deal with and placate an understandably irate guest.

An allied matter with respect to guest relations is that of housekeepers' identification. It is true that they almost invariably wear uniforms and nameplates; it also is true that more often than not they do their work when guests are out of their rooms. Nevertheless, innkeepers need to ask themselves whether the uniform and nameplate are sufficient identification at those times when guests either are in or returning to their rooms while the latter are being serviced.

In many cases housekeeping uniforms, and certainly nameplates, are neither so distinctive nor expensive to duplicate that a thief specializing in hotels might not be willing to spend money for that purpose. Furthermore, the average guest might have little occasion to even see a housekeeper. However, if a guest (especially a woman alone in her room) hears a knock at or key in the door and the announcement "maid" or "housekeeping," do the uniform and nameplate by themselves offer sufficient assurance that the person entering the room is who she or he purports to be? If they are, but the guest is unsure, any attempted verification can be embarrassing for both parties; if the person is not from housekeeping but is a burglar or possible rapist, any attempt to verify who they are may be too late.

One step that innkeepers can take, with little or no expense, that would add at least some degree of comfort and reassurance to guests was discussed earlier in this chapter. It dealt with the subject of issuing employees some form of photo identification. Issuing photo identification badges to housekeeping employees, plus requiring that they be worn at all times while on guest floors, deserves consideration. Certainly they would be helpful to guests, male or female, who happen to be in the room or who return to it when a housekeeper is either entering or working there.

The safety of the housekeeping staff while servicing rooms is another matter that needs to be addressed. It is naive to ignore the possibility that housekeepers could be assaulted while working in rooms, or to say that such a rare occurrence is no cause for serious concern. Even if it happens but once, the morale of all employees can be adversely affected, and low morale will most likely cause a noticeable decline in productivity. The seriousness of the assault may generate unwanted publicity, and the extent of the bad publicity may also result in lower occupancy even if only for a relatively short term. A combination of low employee morale, a reduction in productivity, and a decrease in occupancy all mean reduced profit margins.

Two things can help minimize the risk of such assaults taking place. Each housekeeper should carry a personalized, handheld, audio alarm that can be easily and quickly activated when necessary. Without knowing who else might be on the floor to respond to a housekeeper's need for help, the assailant would, in most cases, leave the area as quickly as possible.

In addition to alarms, the other risk-reduction measure involves the way in which room assignments for individual housekeepers are made. To the extent possible, an effort to "pair" housekeepers should be made. This arrangement would mean that for the most part they would find themselves working in rooms opposite each other at the same time, adding a degree of comfort and safety to both in knowing that help was at hand if needed.

Another aspect of housekeeping—and security—that can be problematic as well as costly concerns the uncertainty confronting both housekeeping and security personnel when "Do Not Disturb" signs are displayed on guest room doors for what would seem to be an unreasonably long time. What to do in such cases should not be left to the discretion of housekeepers and/or security officers; it should be based on the inn's policy, either as set forth by the general manager or, where appropriate, by corporate security and safety guidelines.

Whether the task of trying to develop a suitable policy on the subject will be at corporate level or rest with general managers, those responsible for doing so will find themselves on the proverbial horns of a dilemma. On one hand there is justifiable concern that prematurely entering a room may be resented and considered an invasion of a guest's privacy. On the other, too long a delay may actually contribute to the death of a sick guest. Despite the absence of any single or easy answer, innkeepers have to ask themselves whether it is better to risk the embarrassment of an entry, for which they at least can apologize and offer drinks and dinner or a night's stay "on the house," or to defer entering only to become a defendant in a lawsuit?

Bearing in mind these conflicting factors, of what should such a policy consist? Its development will be influenced by two things. First, whatever action is to be taken must be reasonable under the circumstances. Granted, deciding on what is "reasonable" is a subjective rather than an objective decision. Second is the availability of either the general or the executive assistant (or resident) manager who can be contacted for guidance as to what would seem to be the most suitable course of action to be taken based on all available information. Let us first look at an actual case as an example; then we shall consider how it might reasonably have been handled.

At turn-down a housekeeper found a "Do Not Disturb" sign on a guest's door. She did not enter, assuming that the guest really did not want to be disturbed. When it was time to make up the room the next morning, the sign was unchanged. This time, however, the housekeeper knocked on the door. Getting no response, she then tried her key but to no avail; the door had been double locked. This prompted her to discuss the matter with a security officer who felt that the "Do Not Disturb" sign should be respected.

At turn-down time that evening, approximately twenty-four hours after the sign was first seen, nothing had changed. Nevertheless, neither the housekeeper nor the security officer saw any reason for concern.

It was not until make-up time the next morning, after some thirty-six hours had passed with no change in conditions, that housekeeping and security jointly decided to call the room for the first time. When there was no response, a decision was made to enter. They broke open the double-locked door and found a comatose guest. The fire department was called and dispatched an ambulance with emergency medical technicians. The guest was taken to the nearest hospital, where he died shortly thereafter. From information provided by the deceased's family and the results of an autopsy, the medical examiner learned that the deceased suffered from an illness that he controlled with medication. The illness was one for which he should have avoided alcoholic beverages except in very small quantities; this time he had consumed some alcohol on an empty stomach and had a reaction. However, the medical examiner also concluded that the deceased's life *could have been saved if he had gotten medical attention at least twelve hours before he did.* In other words, in the medical examiner's professional opinion the guest's life could have been saved if the hotel had acted when housekeeping and security found conditions still unchanged after twenty-four hours or at the time of the second turn-down.

The news media, customarily monitoring police and fire department transmissions, picked up and reported the story, including the hotel's name and the circumstances under which the guest had been found. They—and their public—also learned that the deceased was a salesman in his mid-forties, with a wife and three school-age children, who had been a member of his employer's "million dollar club" for the past five years. This obviously was not the kind of publicity that the hotel needed or wanted.

Based on reports from the hotel's security department and the medical examiner, the widow retained the services of an attorney. Taking into consideration the deceased's personal situation, including his projected earnings, age, and anticipated life span, a multimillion-dollar lawsuit was filed against both the inn and its licensor. To avoid a lengthy trial and the risk of even more damage to its reputation, the inn agreed to an out-of-court settlement.

What, then, might be a "reasonable" policy when a "Do Not Disturb" sign hangs on a door for an extended period of time? True, what one person considers reasonable, another might consider unreasonable; yet would not the lodging industry's interest be better served if each property had a policy for dealing with comparable situations despite the fact that they rarely occur?

Nevertheless, to suggest adopting a single standard for all properties, without taking into account a particular inn's operation, would be unrealistic. There are variables to be considered. For instance, does housekeeping turn down beds in the evening or merely ensure that rooms are made up in the morning? Do housekeepers or their supervisors inspect rooms after guests have checked out to see if towels or anything else needs to be replaced? Does the inn have a full-time security staff? These factors could have a bearing on the implementation of a policy to deal with situations such as the one described.

From a security or loss-prevention viewpoint, perhaps the following suggestions would be helpful.

a. No particular action should be required if a housekeeper sees a "Do Not Disturb" sign on a door at the regularly scheduled make-up time.

b. If, upon returning to service the room some time later in the day, the sign remains, this should be called to the attention of a supervisor and security (or the person responsible for security).

c. Without doing anything to disturb the guest, consider looking at the arrival and check-in time; it might suggest a logical explanation for the sign's continued display.

d. Whether or not there is turn-down, the door should again be checked after twelve hours have passed. If the sign remains, the senior manager then on duty should be informed. He or she should consider calling the room.

e. In the absence of a response to a call, an attempt to enter the room deserves serious consideration. However, in the event that that manager feels an effort to enter at that time would be premature, the general or executive assistant (or resident) manager should be informed. If he or she agrees that entry should be deferred, the time should be noted. Otherwise, the manager then on duty, accompanied by representatives of housekeeping and security, should enter the room.

f. If there was agreement to delay an attempted entry, but conditions are unchanged after a total elapsed time of twenty-four hours, the general or executive assistant (or resident) manager's permission should be sought and the room should be entered as prescribed in the preceding paragraph.

Even if a policy that takes into account the foregoing provisions is no guarantee that something may not go awry, but in reality no policy can provide such assurance. From the innkeeper's perspective, both in developing a policy and defending against a possible lawsuit, what is important is that every reasonable effort can and will be made to provide for guests' needs, even in what can be uncertain and trying situations, without any needless or unwarranted invasion of their privacy.

Engineering

Members of the engineering staff, like housekeepers, may have access to guest rooms, though much less frequently. They too should be uniformed. Unlike housekeepers, who, depending on the type of property and the services provided, have to get into rooms at least once a day, engineering personnel need to enter only when something needs to be repaired, such as a television set or a leaky faucet. In both cases, access most often occurs when the guests are absent, but there may be times when they are present.

If, as we have said, housekeeping uniforms may not be that difficult or expensive to duplicate by would-be thieves, duplicating engineering uniforms is even easier and less costly. Stores where the commonly worn khakis, or dark blue or green shirts and pants can be bought, are easy to find. Consequently, like housekeepers, engineering department employees should be issued and required to wear photo identification badges. This requirement shows consideration for the psychological comfort of guests who may be in their rooms when there is a knock on the door and the answer to the guest's "Who's there?" is "Engineering." It also adds to the peace of mind of the inn's staff in general and of those working on guest room floors in particular.

Earlier in this chapter we discussed the importance of preemployment screening for all applicants by human resources. We noted that this screening can be a mitigating factor in complaints filed by guests or other third parties who allege that negligent hiring practices contributed to the problems they are now complaining about. However, possible litigation aside, among the questions of importance for which answers should be sought in all such inquiries are those concerning an applicant's reliability and work habits.

Nowhere is the need to inquire into these particular traits more important than in the case of applicants for the engineering department. Engineering personnel play a unique role in the round-the-clock operation of the inn. Engineering is responsible for maintaining the property's physical plant for the comfort of its guests and the benefit of those employees whose primary job it is to provide the multiple services that guests expect. Engineering duties range from such mundane jobs as the previously noted fixing of television sets or leaky faucets in guest rooms to ensuring that the hotel's heating, ventilating, and air conditioning systems work, that backup generators are regularly tested and in good working order in case of a power failure, and that there is a constant supply of hot water for guests, the laundry, and kitchen.

True, reliability in general is important since the vast majority of hotels function twenty-four hours a day throughout the year, and they expect their employees to be available to work during their prescribed hours. However, even if overtime has to be paid it is much easier to cover for an absent housekeeper, member of the wait or bell staffs, or front desk clerk, for whom licensing is not a job requirement, than it is to cover for a licensed electrician or plumber.

For instance, if the general manager is absent, the executive assistant or resident manager can fill in; the executive chef can substitute on a temporary basis for an absent food and beverage manager. However, relatively little can be done if an unreliable engineering employee does not report for work. Thus the latter, in many respects, represents a greater threat to an inn's uninterrupted operation and to its reputation than any other members of the staff. Rude employees can offend guests, but if they do, damage to the inn's reputation is not nearly as widespread as when an air conditioning system fails on a hot day or the hot water for showers runs out.

Of course, important as reliability is, it is not the only way in which engineering personnel are involved with the loss-prevention effort. In order to properly maintain a hotel, the engineering staff needs tools with which to work. Some are small or hand tools frequently used; others may be considerably larger and used less often. In some places all engineering or maintenance tools are the inn's property; in others, hand tools are owned and provided by individual "mechanics." If any are lost or stolen, regardless of ownership, not only can their absence interfere with work that has to be done, but it also involves the cost of replacement.

To reduce the risk of such losses, several things can be done. First, a secure place should be provided in which tools can be stored when not needed. For those owned by the hotel, an enclosed tool crib, with controlled access and supervised by the chief engineer, deserves consideration. If tools belong to individual employees, they should be assigned one or more lockers large enough to accommodate them; individuals should furnish their own locks.

All hotel tools, regardless of size, should be marked for identification. A combination of a colored strip and an imprinted serial number would serve this purpose. In addition, employees to whom tools are issued on a long-term basis should sign receipts in duplicate that list each individual item, including its identification number. One copy should be retained by the chief engineer, and the other should go into the employee's personnel file. Receipts for these tools should be checked against those tools turned in if an employee is terminated for any reason. If a tool is issued to an employee only for a specific task, the chief engineer should get and keep a receipt pending the return of that particular item; then the receipt should be destroyed.

From time to time engineering personnel will also need to draw certain types of supplies that are expendable. As part of the control of and accountability for assets, however, when items of this sort need replacement, the chief engineer should keep a record. This record is also helpful for reordering such supplies when inventories drop below an acceptable level. Furthermore, and to the extent that it is possible, a modified exchange policy is worth considering. In other words, when items of this sort (such as light bulbs, shower heads, telephones, etc.) have been replaced, they should be returned to the engineering office for disposition.

Virtually all properties have at least a few areas to which access is controlled through the use of locks and keys. Even those hotels with electronic systems may well have some spaces that are protected with keyed locks. Key making, as well as the issue of keys, whether for employee use only or for distribution to guests by front desk personnel in inns that do not have electronic systems, is usually considered the province of the engineering department. Consequently, to ignore engineering's ability to duplicate a hotel's keys, whether many or few, is shortsighted when formulating a loss-prevention program.

In this respect, from a security or loss-prevention perspective, more is involved than merely making keys. As we shall see, although how they are made is critically important, how they are handled afterwards also has to be taken into consideration. To begin with, blank key stock should be kept in a locked receptacle in the chief engineer's office with access thereto controlled by the chief engineer. When new or additional keys have to be made, only the number of blanks needed to fill a specific requisition should be given to the engineering employee designated and authorized to make keys. The key-making machine itself should be secured whenever it is not in use.

All requisitions for keys should be in writing and signed by the requesting department head. They should indicate whether or not the purpose is to replace lost or broken keys, and if the latter, the broken parts should accompany the requisition. Requisitions should be retained by the chief engineer and periodically reviewed to see if any department's requests for replacement keys suggests a pattern, even if only of carelessness on the part of its personnel.

Department heads should keep records, in the form of signed receipts, of keys issued to their employees on a long-term rather than a daily basis. It should be their responsibility to recover those keys if such a person's employment is terminated. Whenever an employee no longer needs to have such a key, it should be returned to the department head and forwarded, in turn, to the chief engineer for retention pending receipt of a new requisition from the department head. For effective control of and accountability for keys issued on a long-term basis, if another person is to replace the one to whom the key was first issued, under no circumstances should the latter be allowed to simply turn over the key. Instead, for the sake of record accuracy, the latter should return the key to the department head and be given the receipt that he or she signed; then the key should be reissued to and receipted for by the replacement.

In the interest of both the hotel's and guests' protection, properties that are still on a key-lock system are well advised to provide guests with keys that have only a stamped room number on them. To tag them or put the inn's name on them only invites problems and can contribute to a needless operating loss. These points are best illustrated.

In the first instance, keys that identify a hotel and room and fall into the hands of the wrong people, such as burglars who specialize in hotels, can lead to guests' losses. The applicable Innkeeper's Law may relieve the hotel of liability, but it neither disposes of the victim's dissatisfaction nor does it protect the property's reputation. For example, in a large East Coast city a majority of hotels that had suffered from burglaries of guest rooms also had their post office boxes at the same station. Consequently, tagged hotel keys dropped in the mail by guests who had inadvertently failed to turn them in when leaving ended up at the same post office. In the course of an investigation by U.S. Postal Inspectors that was unrelated to the city's hotels, they nevertheless identified, arrested, and successfully prosecuted one or two postal employees who had been stealing keys and offering them for sale to hotel burglars. The asking price depended on the type of hotel and the clientele that it attracted. However, insofar as the victimized properties were concerned, the damage to their reputations had been done, along with an attendant, albeit relatively temporary, impact on sales.

The foregoing concerns aside, tagging adds to rather than prevents operating losses. As an example, some guests consider tagged keys acceptable souvenirs of their stay. Replacement costs time and materials. The same is true of guests who inadvertently walk off with keys and then discard them despite the fact that they can be dropped into a mailbox and returned at no expense. Even when tagged keys eventually return, the inn must go to the expense of replacing them in the meantime. If keys are returned, the hotel pays the postage; it also ends up with surplus keys, making controls and accountability more difficult. As a result, plain keys marked with only room numbers are both a more cost-effective and less risky solution to potentially embarrassing and expensive problems.

SALES, CREDIT, AND PUBLIC RELATIONS

Up to this point we have focused primarily on various aspects of loss prevention in relation to operations. For the most part our emphasis has been on efforts to secure assets and prevent losses where employees may be primarily involved, although their actions can also have an indirect affect on guests and ultimately on the hotel itself. However, it would be naive to fail to acknowledge that there can also be a risk of loss from the more direct inn-guest relationship with respect to sales to large groups, guest credit, and public relations.

Sales

Larger properties, mindful of the fact that being able to book large groups can contribute substantially to income and their promotional efforts, have sales departments in pursuit of such opportunities. Success means more than the sale of a number of rooms for a number of nights. It usually means the accompanying sale of function space, possibly lunches and at least one dinner in the form of a banquet, and increased sales in the inn's food and beverage outlets. A goodly number of these bookings may also involve space to be used by exhibitors who want to display their goods and examples of their services to the participants.

Obviously sales of this kind are desirable and much sought-after. At the same time they also can pose some risks to the hotels at which they are booked. By no means does this mean that the risks outweigh the importance and value of the business. It does mean that when sales of this magnitude are in the offing the sales and security departments need to communicate and cooperate with each other. If they do not, the projected profits may shrink, the sponsoring organization and its members may be dissatisfied, and the hotel's reputation may be in jeopardy.

From a security or loss-prevention point of view, the most significant threats to profits, the unhappiness of guests other than the function's participants, and to the inn's reputation can stem from one or more of three sources. One is the protection of exhibited materials, another is the uncontrolled misconduct of guests attending the function, and the third is the attraction of prostitutes to certain groups. While each of these will be discussed in greater detail, the most obvious point to be made here is the need for sales and security to work together before rather than after the sale is finalized.

When exhibition space is the issue, the factors that have to be considered are the receipt and shipment of exhibited materials and their protection while on display. Materials received in advance of the exhibitor's arrival should only be accepted and stored by the hotel's employees, in secure space set aside for that purpose, but not unpacked or otherwise handled by them. This restriction does not prevent the hotel's staff from helping set up exhibitions under an exhibitor's supervision, but it helps reduce the risk of a claim being filed against the inn should something be broken or missing. It also helps protect the property's reputation. To further protect the hotel's reputation and reduce the risk of claims for breakage or lost items, when the function has ended, hotel employees can help take down, pack, and arrange for the pickup of exhibited materials—but again, only under the direct supervision of the exhibitor.

The extent to which the exhibited items will need to be protected is something to be reviewed with the sponsoring group. If the inn's sales and security managers feel that the items may be at risk for any reason, they should voice their concerns to the sponsoring group, but the latter should make the decision on protection and by whom it is to be provided.

If the inn is to provide protection, the security director must take into account two critically important issues. One, what will be the impact on the department in terms of its ability to effectively discharge both its primary and secondary responsibilities? Two, how will these additional duties affect the department's ability to provide protection for both other guests and the property's assets while the function is taking place?

A realistic assessment of the sponsoring group's needs in relation to the security department's size and basic responsibilities may make it abundantly clear that for the inn to assume this obligation would be inadvisable. However, if the hotel can provide the called-for protection, it is highly unlikely that it can do so without asking at least some of its security officers to work overtime. In making the assessment of security needs, it is equally important that the security and sales managers take into account the nature and size of the group. Even if the security department is unable to provide exhibit protection, if a particular organization's booking may have an adverse impact on other guests and will require security officers to work extended hours, the cost should be charged against the group. Consequently, before sales personnel agree to provide protection, it is imperative that the security manager be informed. Only in this way can he or she project what the inn's cost of providing protection will be so that it can be included in the total contract price. If this is not done, it is conceivable that the function's sponsors will expect the hotel to absorb the cost, obviously reducing the property's profit margin.

Two different scenarios may also have to be considered when the matter of providing security arises under these circumstances; each has to be evaluated. The results may vary, depending on whether an inn regularly employs contract agency security officers or a proprietary security staff. In either case, once a need for additional protection has been established, the assessment referred to above must be made in order to determine the level of security required. Once this has been done, further refinement is needed before any commitment can or should be made to the sponsoring organization.

Whether to protect exhibits or ensure the comfort of other guests, there is less of a problem—and less of an impact on the hotel—when contract security officers are used regularly. During the function, there need not be any change in officers' assignments. Instead, based on the security manager's needs assessment, arrangements can be made for the agency to provide additional security officers. Knowing the hourly rate at which the agency charges the hotel for its personnel and the number of additional security officers and hours involved, the security manager can furnish the sales department with the sum to be included in the contract.

The problem may be more complex when security personnel are proprietary. If a large enough proprietary security department exists—one that can cover a sponsoring organization's needs and minimize guests' exposure to unruly function participants by working a reasonable amount of overtime—the security manager can calculate the additional costs to be charged against the function's agreement. However, the matter is not so easily disposed of when the security department itself, working a limited amount of overtime, can deal with guest-related concerns but is incapable of providing the degree of protection requested by the sponsoring organization.

Looking at guest-related issues initially, knowledgeable security managers generally have a good idea as to the times when the unruly behavior of some guests is most likely to disturb others. If these problems are to arise they usually will occur in the evening and may last well into the morning. Knowing this, as well as the room assignments of potentially unruly guests, allows them to reasonably project the number of security officers and amount of overtime to be worked so the cost can be added to the contract for the function.

Innkeepers who would argue that while it is appropriate to charge groups for the protection of exhibits, it is not good business to charge solely to cover guest-related issues, are being unrealistic. While it is true that the number of times when things may get out of hand are limited, there is ample evidence of persons attending some conventions or other functions being exceedingly disruptive. Not only have they disturbed other guests, they have also damaged hotel assets, including reputation, and there has been litigation when guests have felt that the security provided was wholly inadequate.

Two good examples can be found in incidents that took place during the 1990s. In one, out-of-town police officers, who had assembled in Washington, D.C., to dedicate a memorial, spent an evening at their hotel drinking too much, discharging fire extinguishers and in some cases their firearms in corridors, running up and down with few or no clothes on, and generally disturbing other guests. Finally the Washington, D.C., police had to be called to take them into custody.

The other incident involved a convention of active duty and reserve U.S. Navy and U.S. Marine Corps aviators in Las Vegas. There was excessive drinking, and a number of them, scantily clad, formed a gauntlet in a corridor, through which women, some of whom had no connection to the affair, were fondled or otherwise abused while trying to go to or from their rooms. Things got out of hand to the extent that the Navy and Marine Corps subse-

quently found it necessary to take disciplinary action against those participants who could be identified, as well as against superior officers who failed
to stop the proceedings. Insofar as the hotel was concerned, among its losses
was damage to some of its tangible assets and damage to its reputation, prolonged by the fact that some women guests sued the hotel, alleging that it
failed to provide an adequate level of security.

Sometimes, of course, a property's proprietary security department may
be able to provide adequate physical security for an exhibit yet not provide
the staff needed for other forms of protection requested by the exhibitors. As
we previously noted, just as security and sales managers who feel exhibit
space and its contents need to be secured should express themselves to an
exhibit's sponsors, so should they inform the latter when the hotel is unable
to do so with its own personnel.

In such a case, if exhibit sponsors ask what options are available, they
should be told that they can hire off-duty police officers (if allowed by the
local police department), they can use the services of contract agency security
officers, or while inadvisable, they can elect to proceed without any security
personnel. If they want a human presence, it would be entirely proper for the
security manager to provide general information about the fee structure for
both police and contract personnel, but it is unwise to show a preference for
one over the other or to otherwise attempt to influence the sponsor's decision.

The hourly rates charged for police officers, who have to be paid for a
minimum number of hours no matter how few they may work, almost invariably are considerably higher than contract agencies' charges. As a result,
sponsors often will choose to use agency personnel. If so, not surprisingly
they then may ask the security or sales manager to recommend an agency.
Should they do so, it is in the hotel's best interest to give the exhibit sponsors
the names of a few generally known agencies that might be contacted without recommending a specific agency. To do otherwise may expose the hotel
to the risk that the exhibit sponsors will consider it the recommended
agency's guarantor. Consequently, they might seek to hold both the inn and
the agency liable for any losses or other incidents that occur.

When exhibit sponsors ask for options and advice, to decline to show a
preference for either police or agency personnel, or to recommend a particular contract agency may relieve a property of responsibility if the sponsors become dissatisfied with the officers' performance. Another caveat must be
borne in mind by the security manager: Do not become involved with, or in
any way direct, the work of whatever outside security personnel the sponsors
choose. This detachment can help insulate the property from liability if
something for which outside personnel are responsible goes awry. Otherwise, the injured or wronged parties might well try to invoke the legal doc-
trine of principal and agent by alleging that whether police or contract

security officers, they were under the hotel's control and direction and therefore the inn is liable. It is worth noting that regardless of the outcome, the property must pay the legal fees and court costs involved with its defense.

Although the sales department is neither responsible for nor can it prevent prostitution, it is important that the security manager be kept informed of the anticipated nature and composition of large bookings since some functions may be more likely than others to attract prostitutes. Concern has lessened as an ever-increasing number of organizations now number both men and women among their membership, but to say the problem no longer exists is naive. Dealing with it can be a delicate matter.

The reasons for concern are justified and can vary, depending in part on the type of prostitute whose services are engaged. For instance, the high-priced, so-called "call girl" is far less likely to rob or assault a customer than is the "streetwalker." The latter charges far less, but her pimp may either expect her to rob a customer, or he will go to the room after she has left and commit the robbery. In the former situation the parties are discreet, and the risk to the hotel is minimal unless the customer commits an assault. In the latter, the activity tends to be blatant, and there is considerable risk to both the guest and the inn.

As a practical matter, trying to deal with the subject of prostitution may find one on the horns of a dilemma. To illustrate, geography can be a factor. Some countries are quite tolerant; as long as they are discreet, prostitutes can ply their trade even in the best of hotels. In others, of which the United States is a notable example, the puritan ethic will not tolerate prostitution. This is not to take a position on what is right or wrong; it merely faces reality.

Consequently, in places where prostitution is frowned upon, if an inn openly tolerates it, obviously its reputation can be adversely affected. On the other hand, if the prohibition is overzealously enforced, some guests may feel what they do in their rooms is their business, not the hotel's, and their privacy is being invaded. In its own way this, too, can have an impact on reputation. As a result, coping with prostitution challenges innkeepers and security managers alike.

Initially, it is of the utmost importance for the sales department to keep the security manager informed about large bookings; the manager can then evaluate the situation and plan on how to deal with a possible influx of prostitutes. Realistically, there is neither a single nor a simple solution to the problem. It is equally important for general managers to set a policy that they feel will be the least disruptive, risky, and embarrassing for the hotel.

With this in mind it would seem that a key element of such a policy would be based on the discretion of the parties involved—the guest and the prostitute. For instance, it is entirely possible that in terms of appearance and behavior a call girl having a drink in a lounge might be indistinguishable from a registered guest. Unless known to security for what she does, to approach her and ask her to leave could be more than a little embarrassing; it could be both awkward and problematic.

In contrast, a guest entering the hotel accompanied by someone whose appearance and behavior strongly suggest that she is a "street-walker" can be called aside and quietly asked if his companion is registered as a guest. If the answer is yes, he can be asked for her name and room number and requested politely to wait until her registration is confirmed. Under these circumstances, if the woman is a prostitute the guest most often will understand that she will not be allowed to accompany him to his room; at the same time he also will appreciate the fact that every effort has been made to minimize his embarrassment and discomfort.

The real challenge for general managers—and for their security managers in terms of policy implementation—is to be able to protect the property's reputation and its guests in ways that will not embarrass either the guests or the inn. Consideration must also be shown for guest privacy unless the issue of prostitution is so blatant as to jeopardize the inn's reputation and lead to the discomfort of other guests.

Credit

Thanks to modern technology, service industry losses, including those applicable to hotels, do not pose the same degree of risk that they used to. Nevertheless, the lodging industry's concerns are different from those of other service providers. For example, for retailers who do not extend credit and accept only cash, there is no problem. Those who allow customers to charge purchases face an element of risk, but they at least know the dollar amount involved should the customer fail to pay when billed.

In some respects the same is true for retail stores that accept third-party (bank or other) credit cards. Retailers pay a fee to participate in those plans, and in return they are ensured payment when they submit proper documentation. Again, the amount charged is known, and realistically, a major part of the risk involved is assumed by the credit card issuer. However, the modern technology used by so many retailers has greatly reduced the risk of loss. Unless a buyer succeeds in using a counterfeit credit card or one that has been stolen but not yet reported as such, both the store and the credit card company know the amount of the purchase at the time and point of sale, as well as whether or not it is within the range of the buyer's credit limit. If the purchase amount reaches or exceeds the credit limit, the credit card company will not authorize the purchase, and neither it nor the store suffers a loss.

The situation is different for innkeepers, even though many have access to and use the same technology, primarily because so much is unknown and

Presidente Inter-Continental–Cozumel

beyond the hotel's control. The only things certain are the price of the room and the fact that a guest's credit starts to run at time of registration. For example, despite what the guest says when registering, the actual length of stay may be for more or fewer nights than stated. Neither is there any way of knowing at the outset the extent to which the inn's other services—food and beverages in outlets or from room service, laundry, telephone, and even purchases made at newsstands or in the hotel's gift shops—may be added to the bill.

When credit card use first became a recognized and popular way of doing business, hotels that accepted them often asked registering guests how they intended to pay their bills. The method of payment would be noted on the folio, but little more was done even though credit card companies periodically sent plan participants hard copy lists of card numbers that had become invalid because they either had been reported stolen or the persons to whom they had been issued had exceeded their credit limits.

These voluminous lists made it impractical for a cashier to try to compare listed card numbers with those on credit cards presented by departing guests. This occasionally caused conflict between credit card companies and hotels. The former felt that they were being asked to accept a risk that could be avoided if hotels would check the lists and refuse to accept certain cards as payment; persons fraudulently obtaining credit could be detected.

In the late 1960s things began to change. It was suggested that both credit card companies and innkeepers would benefit if the latter initiated certain easily implemented and inexpensive preventive measures. The first was to continue to ask guests about their proposed method of payment when they registered. The second, if payment was to be by credit card, was to take an imprint of the card at that time. Last, night auditors would compare the imprinted charge forms with the card company lists. Appropriate action then could be taken if a guest proposed to use a card that either exceeded the person's credit limit or appeared to be stolen.

With the speed of technology preferred by credit card companies and their plan participants, the night auditor's role in minimizing losses of this kind has become obsolete. Now the attempted use of counterfeit, stolen, or "maxed-out" credit card can be detected quickly at checkout time. Of course, this fact does not justify a failure to try to at least minimize those losses that might occur, regardless of whether a credit card company or the inn will bear the brunt of the loss. At the same time the uncertainty issue remains, as does the inn's risk of loss in those cases, however rare, when a guest indicates that payment will be made by a personal or company check.

How might one minimize losses related to credit card use? Initially, distinguishing between hotels that depend primarily on business travelers (and perhaps tourists to a degree) and resort properties is helpful. Commercial hotels are less exposed than resorts to guests who incur sizeable bills, largely due to the length of stay and use of resort facilities. As a rule, business people and tourists tend to stay at a hotel for only a few nights, usually less than a week; at a resort, people stay for at least a week, possibly more. The question is, is it at all possible to reduce the risk insofar as significant sums may be involved? The answer is *yes.*

It is almost a matter of tradition for hotels to render bills weekly to guests staying for extended periods of time. However, there is no reason that invoices cannot be presented for payment either at the end of a week or when a certain amount has been reached; timing can be based on which event occurs first. This change recognizes that guests' spending habits differ.

To illustrate, let's say two couples stay at a resort for two weeks. Their room rates are the same. One couple prefers to be alone, using only the resort's food and beverage outlets and outdoor swimming pool. The second mixes freely, occasionally treats other guests to drinks, plays 18 holes of golf daily for which there are green and caddy fees, and charges souvenirs bought in the gift shop to the room. It is conceivable that the amount charged by the second couple will have reached the inn's set limit at the end of four days, yet the first couple's bill for the entire week will be half that amount. If the hotel's billing practice is made known when reservations are confirmed and again when guests register, problems that otherwise might be harmful to reputation can be avoided.

The rare occasions when a registering guest indicates an intention to pay by personal or company check can pose a problem. Persons known to the hotel, who have been guests before and established a credit record, would not seem to be cause for concern. However, if they are unknown, they should be directed to the credit manager. The latter, in the person's presence, should contact the bank on which the check is to be drawn to confirm the existence of an account in that person's or company's name, learn something about their banking and credit history, and ensure that the account contains sufficient funds to more than cover any bill incurred. If satisfied with the answers, the credit manager then can authorize the guest's registration with payment to be made by check.

Public Relations

Simply acknowledging the importance of public relations in relation to loss prevention is to oversimplify matters. The subject needs to be examined from the perspectives of three different relationships. The first deals with the security department and guests; the second with the public relations department and guests; and the third with the relationship between the security and public relations managers.

Although we shall be discussing the relationship of guests to loss prevention in detail in Chapter 4, the security and public relations aspect deserves some consideration at this point. Certainly guests will have contact with security personnel if an incident occurs, but they also may have contact at other times for any number of reasons. These contacts may range from a simple "Good morning" or "Good evening" to asking for directions to a store, a theatre, or a stadium where a sporting event is scheduled. The security officer's appearance, knowledge, and manner will contribute to or detract from the inn's public relations. If security personnel are easily identifiable, neatly and tastefully dressed, well groomed and well mannered, knowledgeable, and attentive to guests, whether responding to an incident or merely being of assistance, the hotel's public relations are enhanced. If they are not, rest assured that the opposite will be true.

Is there any justification for security's concern with the public relations department's relationship with guests? Yes, but only in a very limited way. It is important to remember that security's primary function is to protect the inn's assets and prevent losses to the greatest possible extent. One of the most valuable assets of any hotel is its reputation. As a result, to the extent that security managers can offer meaningful suggestions to public relations managers that will make a positive contribution to good guest relations, they should not hesitate to do so.

Without doubt a critically important aspect of good public relations involves cooperation and good communication between the security and public relations managers. Although there has been considerable improvement in this regard, some in the lodging industry still seem to feel that former law enforcement personnel make the best security managers. The rationalization that retired police officers can "get things done" because of their contacts or their investigative skills ignores the fact that their prior experiences also make them inclined to be somewhat secretive and not particularly adept at dealing with people in general.

The lack of people skills can certainly adversely affect the security-guest relationship; the tendency to be secretive can be more damaging to the hotel's overall public relations efforts. The underlying cause can be an attitude problem. As a rule, police personnel (and even some security managers who do not come from that background) are inclined to feel that they can ask all sorts of questions but that they are only obliged to provide answers to persons who are part of the criminal justice system. This bias could be contrary to an inn's best interests if a significant incident should occur.

If something happens that is considered newsworthy either because of its nature or the persons involved, the public relations manager, not the security manager, is the inn's proper spokesperson even if the incident is a security matter, such as a suspected crime or suicide. Once the news media are interested, the property's reputation becomes an issue, for better or worse, and the public relations manager is just as concerned with protecting that reputation as is the security manager. However, the former cannot do his or her job properly unless the security manager provides enough information to answer news media questions.

To illustrate this point, suppose there is a homicide or a suicide, and the police are called. They respond, along with television reporters who learned of the incident by monitoring police radio transmissions. The first member of the hotel's managerial staff to be properly informed and involved is the security manager. However, rather than providing the public relations manager with even minimal information, he or she focuses on trying to help the police. Queried by the news media, the public relations manager can only promise to try to answer their questions as soon as he or she has something to tell them.

To reporters this scenario most likely will imply that (1) the hotel is trying to cover up what happened to save itself embarrassment or worse, (2) the public relations manager is incompetent, or (3) a combination of the two. Now the reporters must indulge in speculation, at least up to a point. In truth there is no coverup, nor is the public relations manager incompetent. If there is any incompetence at all, it lies in the security manager's failure to communicate and cooperate with the public relations manager; the latter needs enough information to be able to satisfy the press inquiries and prevent speculation, as well as avoid unwanted and unnecessary publicity.

THE FRONT OFFICE

From a security/loss-prevention perspective, any discussion of front office operations has to consider several different activities. These include those of the bell staff, guest registration, guests' access to their rooms, and the telephone operators. Each of these functions, in its own way, can contribute to the protection of both the hotel's assets and its guests, and each will be looked at separately.

Bell Staff

In discussing the human resources department's role, we noted the importance of the preemployment screening of applicants, regardless of the job for which they were being considered, and of their being trained once hired, no matter their prior experience. In the long run it can be a costly mistake to view any position as trivial or to equate the level of that position with the intelligence of the person holding it. This is true whether the employee's direct contact with guests is very limited or frequent and ongoing.

With respect to the bell staff, it is not unusual for members to pick up and return guests' laundry and cleaning, often when the guest is absent. This gives them access to guests' belongings. Then, too, how they escort guests to their rooms, handle their luggage, point out the room's amenities and, if necessary, explain their use is important since in reality they will spend more total time than registration desk personnel with newly arrived guests. Using great care, so as not to frighten guests, they also should point out the locations of the stairways closest to the guest's room in case their use should become necessary. Equally important are their appearance, courtesy, and ability to answer questions about the hotel's services and perhaps even about the community. These multiple factors can affect the inn's reputation, a valuable asset in itself.

How prostitution can be a problem when certain types of large groups are involved was touched upon in our discussion of sales, but it is not necessarily limited to large meetings or seminars that are primarily or largely populated by unattached males. It can occur at other times and under normal operating conditions, but seldom without the bell staff being aware of it.

A common practice is for the bell desk, or at least some bell staff employees, to be near the main or primary entrance in order for them to be able to assist newly arriving guests. This also puts them in a position to help the security department by monitoring access, and certainly by reporting prostitutes' attempts to solicit customers in or near the lobby. However, for such monitoring to succeed there has to be more than good communication between bell staff and security personnel. The security manager must provide training in terms of what to look for and guidance with regard to how such suspected activity is to be dealt with. If this is not done and the bell staff is left to its own resources, there is the risk of embarrassment and possible litigation.

Conversely, the bell staff's unique ability to monitor access also may contribute to the problem in one of two ways. The first is a willingness to ignore the comings and goings of known prostitutes. The other is for them to actually arrange for prostitutes' visits when guests either hint, or say outright, that they would be interested in "having some company."

Another possibility not to be ignored is the bell captain who has his own list of prostitutes and is in fact their pimp. Regrettably, when this situation exists it is not unusual to find collusion between the bell captain and the security manager. As an example, at one first-class, big-city hotel the bell captain and security manager often boasted to other employees, including the general manager, about their joint efforts in keeping the property free of prostitutes, attributing success to their conscientiousness. This became a topic of conversation not only among their coworkers but also among other hotel security managers in the same city.

The hotel was part of a chain; and during a visit by the corporate security director, the security manager, wanting to impress him, bragged of his and the bell captain's success in dealing with the prostitution problem. This seemed to be the one achievement of which the security manager was proud. His speaking of it repeatedly aroused the security director's suspicion and prompted his initiating an investigation. It uncovered the fact that the bell captain and the security manager were operating their own prostitution ring within the hotel. They were indeed conscientious, but only in keeping out prostitutes who were not working for them. Among other things, this case proves that from a security/loss-prevention point of view, there is no such thing as an insignificant job in the lodging industry.

Guest Registration and Room Access

Good guest relations obviously are critically important to the success of any hotel, and they actually begin at the time of the guests' arrival at the inn's entrance. The way they are greeted and their bags are handled while being moved to the lobby are a starting point, but the first major step occurs when guests register. How they are dealt with at this time can be a factor in avoiding rather than contributing to later dissatisfaction and possibly other problems.

Whether traveling on business or for pleasure, the overwhelming majority of guests want their privacy respected. If this is not done, the result could be later problems for security to deal with. Announcing the name of any registering guest should be avoided, and while regular guests will be impressed and enjoy being recognized upon arrival, greeting them by name is inadvisable. The same is true with respect to their room numbers.

It is immaterial whether the inn has safe deposit boxes only at lobby level or they also are available in guests' rooms; it is when guests register that they should be asked if they want to use one. Since desk clerks have no way of knowing if guests have valuables with them, noting the offer of a safe deposit box and its refusal, where appropriate, is worth considering despite the limited liability set forth in that particular jurisdiction's Innkeeper's Law.

Whether properties have electronic access to rooms or still use keys, room numbers will be shown on the cards or keys, and they will also appear on the rooming slips handed to bell personnel escorting guests to their rooms. The use of electronic systems, with their coded cards, has made it unnecessary for guests to drop off and pick up keys when leaving or returning to their rooms.

However, where keys are still used, guests often will drop them off when leaving their rooms, and they will ask for them when they want to return. One of the major security issues for which the lodging industry has been criticized where keys are used is the ease with which they can be gotten from front desk personnel. Rarely will a person asking for the key to a certain room be questioned. This is illustrated by the case of a chain operation's corporate security director who, returning at night to the luxury property at which he was staying, asked for his key by room number. As the desk clerk retrieved the key from the rack, he checked the folio. The security director's initial reaction was that the clerk was security conscious and would ask for his name before handing over the key. Instead, the clerk gave him the key without question and wished him a good night by name. Despite the clerk's good intentions, laxity of this sort can contribute to guest room burglaries. A better practice, which guests appreciate, is to discreetly ask for the person's name and check it against the folio before handing over the key.

Occasionally front desk personnel are approached and asked for guests' room numbers. It makes no difference whether guests are celebrities or not; room numbers should not be disclosed. Instead, persons making such requests should merely be directed to the house telephones so they can call the guest.

Telephone Operators

Telephone operators fit into the scheme of things from a security point of view in two ways. One is how they should handle requests for guest information; the other is their role in case they get a bomb threat. Both are important, and hotel management should not treat either one lightly.

The security of guests is a constant concern, not only in terms of contact with front desk personnel but also with regard to the way in which incoming calls for them are handled by telephone switchboard operators. Whether those calls are placed from a house telephone or originate outside the hotel is immaterial. What is material are any instructions that guests may leave with operators regarding incoming calls.

Most guests do not object to calls being put through to their rooms or having messages left for them, but under no circumstances should operators give room numbers to callers. If callers ask for room numbers, their requests should be denied and the calls merely put through; if there is no answer, operators can offer to take a message, but nothing more. At the same time, on relatively rare occasions there may be guests who do not want any calls put through to their rooms; their requests must be honored.

A related but more delicate matter arises when instead of callers asking for room numbers, they ask if a certain person is registered. This leaves operators on the horns of a dilemma since they have no way of knowing the caller's purpose. For example, suppose a guest in the business of selling diamonds to jewelers regularly stays at the hotel on a fairly fixed schedule. A burglar specializing in hotel burglaries wants to steal the diamonds. However, before planning the burglary the burglar wants to confirm the salesperson's presence in town and at the hotel. The burglar calls, registration is acknowledged, and the diamonds are stolen. In litigating the matter, the guest convincingly argues that despite the Innkeeper's Law, if the hotel had not given the burglar the room number there would not have been a loss. Or it could be a call from an admirer to find out if a certain celebrity is registered and, learning that he or she is, comes to the hotel with friends to await an appearance by the celebrity in order to ask for autographs.

Consequently, if guests say they do not want any calls put through, it is fairly safe to assume that they would prefer that their presence not be made known. On the other hand, if guests do not state a preference and such inquiries are made, acknowledging registration is one thing, but providing more specific information is another. Again, answers to such questions should be limited to a simple *yes* or *no*.

Most bomb threats are made by telephone since identifying the caller is extremely difficult. Equally hard is answering a critical question: Is the call merely a threat, or is there actually a bomb? The only thing of which general managers can be certain is that these threats must be taken seriously. The safety of guests and employees is of primary concern, and the question of whether or not to evacuate must be answered. Although there may be telltale signs that can help distinguish between an empty threat and the actual presence of a bomb, they are only signs. They cannot be relied upon where lives are potentially at risk.

That a call is nothing more than a threat does not necessarily make it any less disruptive or traumatic. Operations come to a halt; if it appears that there is enough time before the threatened explosion, the hotel must be searched, evacuation must be considered, and if it takes place, hotel assets and guests' property are exposed. If there is a bomb, the knowledge that employees and guests may be injured or killed is not a deterrent to the bombers;

in fact, it is because of the extent of destruction to the inn and the number of casualties that may be involved that a hotel may be targeted.

From a general or senior manager's perspective, whatever decisions are made may subsequently be criticized. If the call turns out to be only a threat, but the property was evacuated, the criticism may be based on the downtime, loss of productivity, and what some perceive to have been an overreaction. If there is an explosion but no evacuation, and the general or senior manager on duty is among the survivors, he or she will be criticized for not having taken the call seriously.

As a result, general or senior managers on duty are in the unenviable position of having to make decisions, and in order for them to do so intelligently, they have to rely on the information that is given to them by the operator who took the call. Whether or not a bomb has actually been placed in the hotel, this information also becomes useful to the law enforcement agencies conducting the investigation and trying to identify the perpetrator.

Consequently, operators need two things. One, a bomb threat checklist; the other, training in how to handle calls of this sort. Both should be given to them by security. If the hotel is part of a chain, the checklist and general guidance should be provided by the corporate security director, with the local security manager involved with the training. If it is an independently owned property, providing both the list and training should be the responsibility of the security manager. How to deal with bomb threats will be discussed in greater detail in Chapter 5.

THE CONTROLLER

Other than a security director or manager, no department head has a greater role to play in preventing losses than a hotel's controller. As we have said repeatedly, among other things protecting assets requires that they be controlled and accounted for. These are functions with which controllers must be involved by virtue of their oversight responsibility for both cashiering activities and inventories, areas where shortages can occur.

When shortages occur in either cashiering operations or in the course of inventories, the question that most often arises is, are they due to honest mistakes or dishonest employees? An answer must be found, and until it is, no shortages should be ignored or simply written off. If the cause is an honest mistake, it must be discussed with the employee responsible to minimize the risk of a recurrence. However, if there either is no ready explanation or it appears that it may be a case of employee dishonesty, an investigation by the security manager with the controller's cooperation is warranted. To better understand the relationship between the controller and security/loss prevention, cashiering operations and inventories are best considered separately.

Cashiers

In the lodging industry there are usually three types of cashiers. General cashiers work in the controller's office, dealing with such matters as payroll, accounts receivable and payable, and preparation of "floats" or "banks" for front desk and outlet cashiers. Front desk cashiers deal primarily with departing guests paying their bills; they also make change for guests when necessary. Those working in food and beverage outlets also accept payment for bills and make change.

With the advent of credit cards, the use of cash to pay bills has been greatly reduced, but for some guests, especially in outlets, cash still may be the preferred method of payment. Regardless, to accommodate guests front desk and outlet cashiers must have some cash on hand with which to work. Consequently, it is important to recognize that all cash-handling activities may suffer losses, although the degree of vulnerability is not necessarily the same in every case.

In terms of vulnerability, general and front desk cashiers usually rank higher than outlet cashiers, with general cashiers being the most vulnerable. The variances are due to a number of considerations. Insofar as a possible robbery is concerned, general cashiers are the ones with access to the greatest amount of cash. Although they have less cash on hand, front desk cashiers also are possible robbers' targets because of their location in proximity to an exit. While outlet cashiers' stations are not immune to robbery, their locations, the volume of wait staff and guest traffic in the vicinity, and somewhat limited operating hours often help make them the least vulnerable to this type of loss.

Since one of the significant elements of robbery is the use or threatened use of force, to protect and minimize the risk of injury or death to employees or guests, or a hostage taking, it is imperative that all cashiers be instructed that in the event of a robbery they are to comply with whatever demands are made, not to resist. Instead, they should try to note as many details as possible about the robber's appearance, they way in which the robbery was staged, and the means of escape.

This compliance does not mean that inns have to be robbers' willing victims or that they are limited to hoping that employees and guests can provide detailed information to the police. There are measures that not only can help reduce the risk of loss, if not actually prevent it, but can also be helpful in the recovery of property and apprehension of the robbers.

The first method is to tightly control access to the space. As a practical matter, this control can be applied only to the controller's office. Card readers should be used at hotels with electronic or computerized access-control systems, and only members of the controller's staff should be allowed to enter.

In addition, in view of vulnerabilities other than robbery (yet to be discussed), their cards should be programmed based on the hours and days of the week when each individual employee legitimately needs access. At properties that still are on key-operated locking systems, access to the controller's office should be controlled by installing a combination lock with a key override. There also should be a clear understanding that whenever any member of the controller's staff is no longer employed by that department, regardless of the reason, the combination must be changed.

Similar isolation for front desk and outlet cashiers is impossible, but that should not preclude considering such physical security measures as alarms and either closed-circuit television or time-lapse cameras for all cashiering operations. Closed-circuit television, with videotape recording, can be used at properties with security departments where all such devices and alarm systems are monitored by security personnel. For inns that do not have a full-time security staff, time-lapse cameras that can be discreetly activated by cashiers can be equally useful.

While closed-circuit television or time-lapse cameras can monitor all cashiering functions and possible robberies, alarms may vary. Again, the question of whether or not the hotel has a full-time security organization has to be considered with respect to alarm monitoring. If it does, then obviously alarms should be monitored by security personnel and their activation should be referred to the police immediately. In the absence of a security staff, alarms, as distinguished from closed-circuit television, can be monitored at any station where at least one employee is always on duty.

For general cashiers, unlike front desk and outlet cashiers, alarms that can be discreetly activated by knee or foot pressure are effective. Using, or attempting to use, their hands for that purpose poses too great a risk for them and others working nearby. In any case, they always should have on hand a preset amount of paper currency, referred to as "bait money," for which the denominations and serial numbers have been recorded and safely stored, to give to a robber. This helps the police and prosecutors once an arrest has been made.

The situation is somewhat different for front desk and outlet cashiers who use registers. They, too, should be given "bait money," to be used in connection with register drawers that have a pressure-release alarm mechanism that is activated when paper currency kept on the pressure plate is lifted. In those drawers, the only currency used to apply pressure should be the bait money.

The amount of loss in case of a robbery can be further reduced by exercising good judgment and not giving front desk or outlet cashiers excessive sums for their "banks" or letting them keep large amounts of money on hand during working hours. As a practical matter, the primary role of cashiers is to receive, not dispense, money; they accept payment of bills and make change. Occupancy, forecasting, and experience with regard to the volume of guest traffic are factors usually taken into account when preparing the individual "banks" for these particular cashiers. Similar thought should be given to setting a limit on the amount of money that cashiers can keep on hand, and whenever preset limits have been reached, arrangements should be made to have the excess sums turned back to the general cashier.

Although the risk of robbery cannot be ignored, for the most part the risk of accepting counterfeit money is even greater. Although a videotape recording or film from a time-lapse camera can be helpful to investigators, a cashier's ability to detect a counterfeit bill and refuse its acceptance is preferable. Whether or not a hotel employs a security director or manager, the nearest office of the United States Secret Service should be contacted and asked to provide what training or help it can to cashiers to minimize the risk of their accepting counterfeit money in payment for a bill or in response to a request for change.

Insofar as cashiering losses are concerned, some will be due to honest mistakes. In fact, it is wise to be wary of a cashier who invariably checks out to the penny at the end of a shift. It is naive to ignore possible cashiering shortages caused by employee dishonesty when two steps can be taken to at least reduce the risk of such losses where cashiers work at registers. Cashiers should not be allowed to either change their register tapes or zero their registers. An inn's best interests are served when both of these tasks are performed by a member of the controller's staff.

Front desk cashiers also have a loss-prevention role to play at properties that still use a standard key-and-lock system by helping to recover keys from departing guests. We have already noted the expense involved when guests check out without leaving their keys. What matters is not the replacement cost of one or two keys; the cumulative effect over time must be considered. While an occasional guest may want to take a key as a souvenir of his or her visit, most guests have every intention of turning in their keys but, having put them in a pocket, forget that they have them. Consequently, unless a member of the bell staff has assisted the guest to the lobby and turns in the key, front desk cashiers should ask persons checking out for their keys. Obviously, cashiers must accept a guest's word that the key was left in the room or at the front desk.

From a cashiering perspective, with particular regard to the general cashier's job, the way in which the hotel's banking is done must be considered under the security/loss-prevention umbrella. This is true whether the general cashier or another controller's employee makes the deposits and withdrawals or the hotel employs armored car services.

In the latter case the risk of a successful or even an attempted robbery realistically cannot be ignored, and ample evidence supports the fact that in such instances the robbers and guards may become involved in an exchange of gunfire. This, in turn, can pose a threat to the safety and security of both guests and employees. Consequently, although the armored car service schedules stops at customer sites for its own convenience, the protection of guests and employees requires that the service at least be contacted in an effort to have it avoid stops at the hotel that set a pattern.

Avoiding patterns is far more critical if bank withdrawals and deposits are made by any hotel employee since that person's well-being is a factor. For banking purposes patterns can take several forms, depending on the bank's location. Times of day, days of the week, routes taken to and from, and even the container in which funds are transported, can reveal a pattern to someone who chooses a hotel as a robbery victim. Without minimizing the robbery potential inside a property, whether of a general, front desk, or outlet cashier, a robber sees less risk of apprehension and identification if the robbery can be committed on a public way.

This means avoiding all forms of pattern if banking is done by an employee, even if the bank itself is on the inn's premises or in an adjacent building. Since preparing deposits and the disposition of cash when withdrawals are made originate in the general cashier's office, routes between the hotel and bank should be varied from day to day regardless of where the bank is located. The time of day and, unless banking is done on a daily basis, days of the week should also vary. To use a brief or attaché case to transport deposits and withdrawals or using a woman's purse if banking is done by a female employee is far safer than using a typical bank bag. Not only is the latter easily recognized for what it is but it usually has the bank's name imprinted on the outside, thus advertising the bag's contents.

It is also helpful to not have the same person always do the banking if more than one person works in the general cashier's office. If not, consideration still should be given to the occasional use of another controller's employee for that purpose. Taking precautions to minimize the risk of robbery does not mean that robberies are automatically eliminated. Therefore to help protect employees—and ultimately help the police—all cashiers and employees making banks runs must be told that if a robbery is attempted they are to comply with the robber's demands rather than resist. Instead, their instruction should emphasize the need to remain calm and to try to carefully observe both the perpetrator's appearance and the way in which the offense is committed.

Inventories

Although properly a controller's function, inventories warrant separate consideration. Lodging industry inventories are not limited to fixed assets; they also cover such expendables as food and beverages. However, while other service industries, such as retailing, now can have access to current inventory data based on point-of-sale information (thanks to modern technology), hotel inventories do not lend themselves to this type of accountability or control. Earlier in this chapter we took note of asset accountability in relation to food and beverage operations, laundry, housekeeping, and engineering. From a hotel management perspective, taking inventories can serve a dual purpose: to reinforce the importance of accountability and help reduce losses and the risk of loss.

When unexplained shortages are uncovered by inventories, good accountability requires that an effort be made to determine the cause. Security has a role to play in this regard by conducting an investigation with three goals in mind:

1. To identify the conditions that allowed the losses to occur in the first place. Appropriate corrective action to prevent a recurrence cannot be taken unless this is done.
2. To identify those responsible for the loss.
3. To effect a recovery if possible.

From an investigative viewpoint, time can be a significant factor if reaching these objectives is to be successful, yet the way many inventories are taken hinders rather than helps the security/loss-prevention effort. While they may reflect an unexplained loss, the time between a current and previous inventory may be so great as to render a meaningful inquiry virtually impossible. Furthermore, not all inventories at any given hotel are taken at the same time; neither are all taken but once a year. Instead, the tendency is to schedule them at different times for different departments and functions. Consequently, if the loss-prevention program is to be effective, the intervals between various inventories must be scheduled in ways that are reasonable and realistic, at least in areas where unexplained shortages are most likely to occur. This does not necessarily have to mean that each and every one has to involve the controller, but it will require department heads' participation.

Properties that are part of a chain can expect to have their inventory schedules set by corporate policy. In other cases schedules can be established by general managers or by controllers with general manager approval. The question is, with what frequency and by whom should inventories be taken? Although there may not be a single answer that will satisfy the needs of all properties, the following program focuses on the goals of any inquiry prompted by unexplained losses.

Inventories taken, or at least supervised, by controllers:

1. All consumables at 30-day intervals.
2. Engineering equipment, tools, and related supplies every 30 days.

3. Housekeeping at 90-day intervals.
4. Food and beverages every 30 days.
5. Operating supplies semiannually.
6. Fixed assets such as furniture, room furnishings, office equipment, and so on, annually.

Taking inventories of fixed assets annually is adequate since their nature is such that their disappearance would soon be noticed. Nevertheless, accountability and control require not only that all fixed assets must be accounted for but also that they are to be found in the particular department or area for which acquired and to which assigned. This, in turn, means that upon receipt each one should have a numbered "asset tag" affixed, with a record kept of the number, the item on which it was placed, and the department or area to which it was assigned. Items serialized by manufacturers nonetheless should be tagged with those numbers added to the record set up for that particular item. The responsibility for protecting asset tags and recording the data should rest with the controller's office.

More frequent inventories should be taken by department heads or, where appropriate, by supervisors. However, since taking complete inventories would be impractical due to the time involved, using a random selection process based on those items most likely to be lost is acceptable. Here is a suggested schedule:

1. Engineering tools and related supplies, bimonthly.
2. Housekeeping department, at 30-day intervals, with floor setups checked on a weekly basis by supervisors.
3. Food and beverages, weekly.
4. Operating supplies, quarterly.

These inventories serve a dual purpose. They shorten the time frame insofar as the discovery of possible shortages is concerned, thus facilitating whatever inquiries may be deemed necessary. In addition, without being accusatory in any way, they serve as a deterrent to the possible misappropriation of assets by letting individual employees know that unexplained shortages will be detected within a reasonable time and that investigations will follow.

Consequently, taking inventories to account for and help control assets, regardless of category, is an important part of the security/loss-prevention program. It is also indicative of the need for security's integration into the inn's total operation instead of its continued relegation to the role of patrolling the property, inspecting parcels, and investigating allegations by guests that they are victims of crimes.

COMPUTER OPERATIONS

While the need to protect computer operations has existed since they became an integral part of business, security for information technology has become increasingly complex with the advent of distributed systems, personal computers, and various Internet connections. Where large computer rooms are still the norm, controlling access to the rooms and using passwords and gateways as primary sources of access control for data no longer are enough. As computer and modem use have grown, so have concerns about data protection, regardless of what might be a cause for loss. Firewalls and encryption are used with increasing frequency to help prevent unauthorized access to data and the losses that might result therefrom.

Regardless of the type of system used, the wide variety of data stored in a hotel's computer files needs protection. For example, the files may contain information on employees, payroll, advance bookings, guests, the inn's finances, sales promotion and marketing plans, and suppliers. However, from a loss-prevention perspective, the protection of both the equipment itself and the stored data has to be considered.

Chapter 2 discussed physical security in general terms. We now look at its application to computer operations at hotels that may have relatively large systems. With regard to equipment, central processing units (CPUs) tend to be placed in rooms with elevated floors, where the principal issues are control of access, which should be limited to programmers, and environmental factors that might cause a system to shut down.

To control access, electronic or computerized systems using card readers are best. They allow each programmer's card to be coded so as to limit access to only those days of the week and hours when that person is working. Due to the electric voltage flowing through the room, there often is a second door for emergency use even if the staff uses only one to enter. If there is, it either should be secured from the inside with an approved fire lock or access should be via a card reader. Without interfering with access control, but recognizing that emergencies can occur, highlighted, push-button-type power shutoffs should be inside the room, near both doors, so they can be activated by evacuating personnel to help reduce the level of equipment damage.

To further protect the equipment, smoke and rate-of-rise heat detectors may be needed, both above and below raised floors. Since the amount of equipment found in large computer rooms can generate a lot of heat, the need for smoke, and possibly heat, detectors is self-evident. Thought also should be given to installing water detectors under raised floors. The constant use of air conditioning for rooms of this kind may result in some water collecting under the raised floor, and a mix of water and electricity is a deadly combination.

Computer room fire-suppression equipment is another issue that must be addressed. Sprinkler systems generally are used to suppress fires, but the water–electricity combination understandably has raised questions about their use in computer rooms. Foam instead of water systems are an option, but cleanup can be difficult and time consuming, and equipment still may be damaged if either is used.

As a result, Halon, a system that can be programmed so it can be manually turned off if there is a false alarm, has been installed in many computer rooms. A gaseous system, it requires little or no cleanup if activated, with little or no damage to CPUs. Halon acts by literally "squeezing" oxygen, a component of all fires, out of the air, thus necessitating the immediate evacuation of employees unless there is a false alarm and the system is shut off during the timed interval before activation.

Regardless of whether a hotel has a computer room or uses a distributed system, data have to be protected. For this, most security directors or managers have recognizable limitations. As a practical matter, they can help in terms of providing physical security and suggesting equipment designed to minimize the risk of loss due to the theft of terminals, keyboards, and printers. However, the security department head with the technical know-how needed to protect operating systems is more the exception than the rule.

Conversely, absent specialization in computer or information technology security, most employees involved with a system's operation are unfamiliar with the physical and related security aspects. This tends to be the case with hotels where justifying having a staff member whose sole function is computer security might be difficult. Under these circumstances the best way to ensure operating system and data security is to have those responsible for security and information technology work closely together, with each contributing their expertise. This cooperation happens most readily and easily when security is fully integrated into all aspects of an inn's activities.

By no means are these the only important aspects of computer operations protection. Such issues as access to data, backup, and backup storage have to be considered. Fundamental to loss-prevention efforts in relation to computer operations is the need to limit access to data. For this two things are needed. One is to ensure that terminals are turned off completely when they are not being used for extended periods of time, including lunch breaks. Once a system has been turned on, with any display on the screen, nothing can prevent any reasonably knowledgeable person from accessing data. Logging on and off takes mere seconds, is easy, and involves no expense; however, supervisory employees must both set an example and ensure compliance.

Equally important, but possibly harder to implement, is the need for passwords in order to log on. At issue is how passwords are chosen and by whom. Some employers permit individuals to select their own, theorizing that this offers the best protection; others prefer to assign passwords.

Regardless of the method used, system integrity is enhanced when passwords, selected or assigned, do not lend themselves to easy identification with particular users; also, they should be changed periodically. Computer usage can be programmed for password changes at regular intervals. Certainly no problem exists if the information technology staff assigns passwords; they effect the changes and individuals are told their new passwords. On the other hand, if employees choose their own, they can be denied access if they fail to change their passwords at the prescribed time.

Despite the ability to force password changes, a major concern when they are chosen by individual users is the actual password selection. Too often the choice is based not on what will afford the best protection for a user's files but rather on something that is easy to remember—a nickname, date of birth or wedding anniversary, initials, hobbies, or the name of a spouse or a child. An easily remembered password also makes it easier for a person who is at all familiar with the user and who is interested in accessing that user's files to do just that. Consequently, the random selection and assignment of passwords at prescribed intervals provides a higher degree of protection than a system that allows individuals to choose even when changes can be mandated.

The need to protect information against loss may not automatically require the incorporation of firewalls, gateways, and perhaps even encryption into computer systems. The use of any or all of these safeguards to protect the system's integrity should be based on a threat assessment undertaken jointly by those responsible for computer operations and security. The assessment should take into account the nature and sensitivity of the data stored, the probability (as distinguished from the mere possibility) of unauthorized access or some other form of compromise, the impact that it would have on operations if successful, and the cost effectiveness of the measures to be adopted.

Regardless of the possible adoption of safeguards, remembering that losses related to computer operations are frequently caused by employees rather than outsiders is important. As a result, a computer operations loss-prevention effort can be enhanced by maintaining systems logs that reflect computer activity. These logs should be reviewed daily for any signs of questionable activity by whoever is responsible for the inn's information technology programs, and any indication of unauthorized access to or use of the system should be thoroughly investigated by that employee with regard to the technical aspects, with the security department head's help where it would be useful.

Properties that rely heavily on computers, whether on an in-house basis or on a contractual one with a company that performs services for them, inevitably find it necessary to back up at least some data without which operations generally could suffer if they are not actually brought to an abrupt halt. Thus backing up data is not done to preserve an inn's history; it is done to ensure the availability of important information so that operations can continue with only minimal interruption should data in use be lost for any reason.

Consequently, backing up data has to be done frequently, although the frequency cycle may well depend on precisely what and how much is to be backed up. Considering the reasons for backup, the need to make certain that the data are properly protected against loss becomes obvious.

To preserve and protect the usefulness of backed-up data against loss, they must be stored in a safe, secure environment regardless of whether computer operations are in house or handled on a contractual basis. From a loss-prevention perspective, both the environment and security are factors. With regard to the former, the space must be clean and have suitable temperature and humidity controls. Security requirements need to cover other situations that could result in a loss.

If not actually fireproof, the space should at least be constructed of fire-retardant materials. Furthermore, storing backup in close proximity to a computer room or any part of a facility in which a fire could occur is at best shortsighted and at worst, negligent. Access to the space in which it is stored has to be controlled; so does access to the actual backup. However, controls over access to space do not always equal controls over access to data, and those responsible for computer operations and security should visit any off-site storage facility and satisfy themselves with respect to the level of protection provided.

For instance, a security director became concerned upon visiting a company specializing in the storage of backup for a variety of customers, including some in competition with his employer. Environmental, fire safety, and access to the facility factors posed no problem; access to backup did. Records were kept on where all items in storage were placed, but the actual placement was on a random basis, theoretically to improve security. However, the storage firm admitted that random placement was accompanied by an element of risk. True, records would be checked whenever a customer wanted to withdraw backup, but random instead of segregated storage could conceivably result in that customer being given another firm's backup instead of its own.

SUMMARY

Effective security programs involve more than simply preventing crimes. Losses can also result from waste, mistakes, accidents, carelessness, and unethical behavior. Consequently, security must focus on dual but complemen–

tary goals. One is to prevent losses of any kind (including to reputation) to the greatest extent possible; the other is to acknowledge that some losses are inevitable and to hold their dollar value to the lowest possible amount. This means that security, as both a concept and a function, has to be integrated into all aspects of an inn's operations with the active participation of all department heads.

Since humans account for both most workplace losses and their prevention, the importance of the human resources role in the screening, selection, and training processes cannot be overemphasized. While a security director, where there is one, may possibly be of some assistance in screening and even some training, the primary responsibility for the staff's quality rests with human resources. However, once people are employed, trained, and assigned to their respective departments, they need to be properly supervised if losses are to be prevented.

That a goodly percentage of a hotel's tangible assets are "disposable" does not lessen the need for their protection against loss, beginning with their receipt. The less attention paid to how tangible assets are received, stored, and moved internally, the more vulnerable they are to loss, whether from theft, spoilage, waste, or breakage. The departments with the greatest need for, access to, and control over those assets, such as food and beverages, laundry, housekeeping, and engineering, must be held accountable for their use and disposition.

Other departments, however, should not be exempt from actively participating in the loss-prevention effort. When selling space for large functions, sales personnel need to think about what security may be necessary so that it can be discussed with the sponsors and suitable arrangements can be made. The unique nature of the lodging industry makes it susceptible to losses if an inn's credit policies are not clearly defined and followed.

One of a hotel's most valuable assets, albeit an intangible one, is its reputation. A damaged reputation can mean loss of business and income. While the security program is a key factor in trying to avoid occurrences that can damage reputation, the public relations staff works not only to preserve it but also to enhance it. Thus good, open communication between the security and public relations department heads is absolutely necessary if the PR head is to be able to answer media inquiries when there are significant security-related incidents.

The front office too has a role to play in loss prevention. More is involved than overseeing the bell staff and helping to prevent guests from being disturbed while in the lobby. How guests are treated upon arrival or when checking for messages, and how they are protected against unwanted visitors or telephone calls, are equally important. Failure to pay prompt attention to guests, treat them courteously, and respect their privacy is harmful to reputation and eventually to business.

Controllers are responsible for a variety of functions that can contribute to or help prevent losses. If inventories are not taken in timely fashion so they can be controlled, losses can occur, and finding out why they did can become increasingly difficult. The way in which banks are given to cashiers and closed out at shift's end, registers are zeroed and their tapes changed, keys (where still used) are recovered from departing guests by cashiers, and banking is done—all are inherent parts of an effective loss-prevention program.

The increasing use of computers for a wide variety of functions also adds to the user's vulnerability to loss unless suitable protective measures are in place. Whether losses are attributed to an operating disruption or unauthorized access to data, the results can be costly. The type of system used will dictate the extent to which physical security is a factor, but determining what kinds of data are stored in memory and how best to control access to those data, as well as ensuring the availability and safe storage of backup, are of the utmost importance.

Chapter 3 clearly explains how every phase of operations can have an impact on the profit picture by either contributing to or helping prevent losses. It also makes two crucial factors evident. First, security and loss prevention are synonymous; crime prevention is not security's only job. Second, optimal benefits can be achieved only when security is fully integrated into all operations rather than isolated from them.

REVIEW QUESTIONS

1. Explain why the preemployment screening of all applicants is particularly important in the lodging industry.

2. Why is the receipt, storage, and internal movement of assets of special importance to food operations?

3. What is meant by "FIFO," and why is its use important?

4. Give an example of how housekeeping can both suffer losses and help control them.

5. What is the preferred way to deal with the need for security personnel when a large function is being sold?

6. What makes the lodging industry more vulnerable than other service industries where the matter of credit is concerned?

7. Why are good communications and interpersonal relations imperative for the heads of the public relations and security departments?

8. Is it appropriate for front desk personnel or switchboard operators to give out guests' room numbers?

9. Unless an armored car service is used, what precautions should controllers take when going to or from a bank to make a deposit or pick up money?

10. Who is best qualified to decide on operating systems security when computers are used?

ENDNOTES

1. Gerald W. Lattin, *Modern Hotel and Motel Management*, 3rd ed. (San Francisco: W.H. Freeman and Company, 1977) p. x.

2. pp. A1, B5.

SECURITY SURVEY NUMBER 1

General

The ABC Hotel, located downtown at 333 West Myrtle Ave., Any Place, U.S.A. a city of over 350,000, is a 333-room property consisting of 148 rooms in its original building and 185 in a tower with a parking facility adjoining a portion of the latter. It has two main dining rooms plus two other outlets that offer more limited food service, one of which is primarily a lounge. There is a second lounge atop the tower. An eighth-floor convention center offers a wide range of function rooms and banquet facilities. On the tower's top floor there is a combination indoor swimming pool and health club.

Physical Security

Access, Design, and Layout

These aspects of physical security are so interrelated as to warrant their being considered together. The primary means of street-level access for both guests and the general public are doors fronting on Main, Columbus, and Howard Streets. Persons who use the parking facility have direct access from floors 2 through 5A of the ramp to the tower's elevator bays on those floors; thus, they have virtually unrestricted access to both the tower and original building without their first having to proceed to street level. There also is an employees' entrance, as well as doors on either side of the primary freight elevator used for shipping and receiving.

Although there have not been any major security problems, the hotel is vulnerable, and the potential for a wide range of activities contrary to its best interests, as well as those of its guests and employees, is undeniable. This vulnerability is due to easy perimeter access, now uncontrolled but for the presumed controls in force at the employees' entrance and the shipping/receiving doors. The former reportedly is locked from 10 P.M. to 6 A.M.; the latter are secured at day's end. However, when they are open, there are few if any controls over ingress and egress. Furthermore, there are no controls with respect to the doors fronting Main, Columbus, and Howard Streets or to access via the parking ramps at levels 2 through 5A.

Persons using the Columbus and Howard Street doors at least are subject to at least some observation by front-desk personnel, but those entering via the ramp or Main Street doors do so wholly unseen. Once people enter through the Main Street doors, they can go directly to the tower elevators without detection; thus they have free access not only to the tower floors but also to the original building by using 6 as a transfer floor. The same is true of those entering the tower by way of the parking ramp.

This virtually uncontrolled ingress and egress makes it easy to steal both hotel and guest property, which admittedly has already occurred; it also increases the risk of guests being assaulted. This may result in damage to reputation, with an attendant decrease in occupancy and loss of income.

Some corrective steps can be taken with only nominal expense and minimal inconvenience. Other measures may involve more substantial expense, but it can be amortized over time and, whatever the cost, prove more economical than trying to cope with some of the hazards by adding more security personnel.

Initially, two possibilities exist with regard to the employees' entrance. One, an electric lock could be installed on the inner set of doors with a timekeeper (or a security officer) to exercise control over ingress and egress and also check outgoing bags or parcels to ensure that no contraband is being taken from the hotel. Two, electronic locks and card readers could control both ingress and egress. They could be programmed to record times in and out in lieu of a timekeeper or security officer; but without either posted at the door, nothing would prevent the unauthorized removal of hotel or guest property.

Key-operated fire locks could be used on the shipping/receiving doors. The doors should be closed and locked except when shipping/receiving activity is occurring. A sign on the outside of the doors should instruct drivers to see the timekeeper (or security officer), who then would call for a storekeeper to unlock the door and accept deliveries. The key for this lock should be kept on the storeroom key ring and controlled by having the ring signed out and in at the front desk. Security should have a key for emergency use only. This procedure would effectively restrict the use of these doors without inhibiting or otherwise interfering with legitimate hotel operations.

Based on the property's experience in terms of guest foot traffic, thought should be given to securing all but one of the street-level doors during predetermined nighttime hours. The unsecured door should be the one most easily observed by front-desk personnel. Fire department–approved fire locks, such as those mentioned above, would permit these doors to be locked without in any way interfering with their emergency use as exits from the hotel. This arrangement would allow front-desk employees to more closely monitor and control street-level access during hours when foot traffic is minimal but risks are somewhat higher.

These restrictions should not result in guest inconvenience. Convenience is relative; only those used to unrestricted access would even notice, and they would have no effect on persons using the parking ramp. Furthermore, with locking scheduled for a time when experience shows that most guests who have gone out for the evening have returned, it is unlikely that this procedure would create any significant problems with guest relations.

Not yet addressed is the matter of access control via the parking ramp elevator lobbies. Corrective action would require the single largest expense for physical security and an expenditure of effort. However, in the long run the following solution would be far less costly than hiring four or five additional security officers to do nothing but monitor closed-circuit television.

1. Install one wide-angle lens, CCTV, fixed-position camera in a tamperproof housing in each elevator bay offering direct ramp-to-tower access. They should be installed on the wall above the elevators and focused primarily on the fire tower emergency exit door opposite since the stairwell would be the most likely used escape route to the ramp. Properly installed, wide-angle cameras should provide reasonable coverage of the doors leading to and from the ramp area and elevator bays.

2. The monitors should be the smallest but most easily seen size, mounted in one or two banks and located in the parking attendant's office to be monitored by him or her.

3. The system should be supplemented by installing a magnetic-type door alarm that would activate an audiovisual signal in the office to attract the attendant's attention and focus it on the particular door, camera, and floor level involved.

4. Upon seeing a suspicious-looking departure from the tower via the fire stairwell or elevators, the attendant would communicate via two-way radio directly with security officers, so that an attempt could be made to detain a suspect leaving on foot or to get a motor vehicle's description and registration.

Labor and material costs aside, the attendant's office might need some alterations. The only viable alternative would involve installing the monitors in the security office, and that would require hiring four or five additional security officers to monitor the system around the clock, an expense that cannot be justified in addition to the initial labor and material costs when an option exists.

Access, design, and layout concerns are present with regard to the tower's top floor, which has the Star Room, a high-volume lounge that features name entertainment, an indoor swimming pool, and a health club. There is a rear exit from the Star Room, and the elevator bay, lavatories, and fire tower stairs are admitted sources of concern since occasional "walkouts" have become a problem. Guests in this category have avoided paying bills ranging from as little as $8 to as much as $125.

Merely installing an approved fire lock on the Star Room's rear door does not seem to be an acceptable solution. The "walkouts" or "skips" often use the fire tower stairwell rather than wait for the elevator and risk being confronted by the Star Room manager. Under these conditions a quicker response by the manager is needed in questionable situations. This can be achieved with minimal expense by doing the following: Install two lights, each with its own distinctive color and tone signal, next to the light now used to alert the manager to incoming telephone calls; one should be activated by the opening of any rear door and the other by the opening of the fire tower door.

While curbing lounge losses is important, the swimming pool area has a far greater potential for loss and/or adverse publicity. This is true, despite locks on the three doors leading to it, due to the following: The pool cleaner often fails to lock the doors when he leaves the area; the Star Room manager has a key since entertainers use the health club space as a combination dressing room and lounge; and guests are welcome to use the pool even though no full-time pool attendant or lifeguard is on duty.

At times, both guests and trespassers, the latter including teenage children, have been found in the pool in the absence of a pool attendant or any other member of the staff. In the event of a lawsuit arising out of an accident that resulted in either injury or drowning, a jury might not be swayed by a defense argument that the injured party assumed the risk and that the ABC Hotel is not liable.

The ABC Hotel should immediately ask counsel for an opinion to determine whether the presence of a lifeguard or pool attendant is mandated by law whenever the swimming pool is open. Regardless, it is in ABC's best interest to have a properly trained lifeguard or attendant on duty whenever the pool is open for guests' use to ensure their safety and keep unauthorized persons out of the area.

The pool cleaner's admitted failure to always lock the door, as well as the health club's use by entertainers, as previously noted, could result in injury to or the drowning of an intoxicated Star Room patron or an entertainer. Consequently, the following additional steps are needed to reduce the risk of such happenings.

1. Pool cleaning should be done only when the attendant or lifeguard is physically present and on duty.
2. The latter then should be responsible for ensuring that all doors to the pool are closed and locked when the pool is closed and prior to his or her departure.
3. If the practice of allowing Star Room entertainers to use the health club is to continue, that space should be suitably isolated from the pool, and the Star Room manager then should be issued a key that provides access to only the health club space.

A number of supply and housekeeping closets were found to be unlocked. Aside from the risk of their contents being stolen, tolerating this practice is unwise. Should there be a bomb threat, when time would be critical, each would have to be searched. These closets—and all others—should be closed and locked except when authorized personnel are physically present and working in or within direct sight of them.

The Dutch door immediately inside the housekeeping department can control access to the department's inventory only when it is used properly. To do this requires keeping the lower half closed and locked at all times other than when bulk transfers are being made; all other transactions should be handled "over the counter," a practice not currently followed. The same is true relative to the main storeroom's Dutch door, its use, and corrective action needed to improve the loss-prevention effort.

A half door, or gate, is directly behind the front desk, and a full door leads from the lobby proper to the back office and front office manager's space; however, as they now exist nothing prevents unauthorized persons from entering the general area. An electric lock that can be opened by front-desk employees by merely pushing a button would enhance protection without imposing any hardship on authorized personnel.

Some storerooms, such as the liquor storeroom, are equipped with multiple locks to protect their contents, yet the door hinges are exposed and in no way secured. All storeroom doors should be inspected, and exposed hinges should have one or more of their pins frozen or pegged to prevent their easy removal and the unauthorized, and even undetected, access to their contents.

The reservations and payroll offices have doors, but anyone can walk in, thus needlessly exposing both employees working there and the records and other assets found therein to some risk. The existing doors should be replaced with Dutch doors, the lower halves always closed and locked during business hours and all business done "over the counter." This would improve protection for the staff and assets.

The personnel (and employment) office is on the original building's second floor, a location that gives trespassers both a ready-made excuse if found wandering around the floor and a chance to roam around the entire hotel with the aim of stealing from either guests or the hotel. Employees admit that more than once they have seen one or more persons, alone or in groups, wandering around the second floor who, when questioned, said they were looking for the employment office, yet when given directions merely left the floor. An effort should be made to move this function to a location adjacent to the employees' entrance, where access is controlled.

Storage Facilities

Suitable, secure storage facilities must be provided for such things as a range of records, check stock, and inventory stored in various outlets as well as the back of the house. That some of the latter are expendables does not reduce the need for protection.

Although suitable locks have been provided for back-of-the-house storerooms and refrigerated boxes or coolers, it has been determined that those locks frequently are not in place and properly secured after hours when there is neither any activity in the area nor any need for them to be accessible. In the interest of preventing losses, department heads and supervisory personnel must be made to understand that they will be held accountable for losses incurred due to a failure to ensure that their respective storage facilities are properly secured when access is not needed.

The Do Re Mi Lounge's liquor is not secured once the lounge closes since the entire outlet is locked. However, both security and bell staff personnel reportedly have or can get keys to the lounge. If this is true, bar stock is at risk of being stolen by employees with access.

The cabinets in which Do Re Mi liquor is kept should be locked when the lounge closes. The keys should be controlled the same way as the lounge's door keys. If possible, all bar stock on the rail should be placed in the cabinets, but if there is not enough room, locking the cabinets, improving key controls, and prohibiting after-hours access by security and bell staff will help reduce the risk of loss.

Most records, both active and inactive, are kept on site in metal file cabinets with plunger locks. For security purposes the locks are inadequate. In addition, employees who fail to properly protect the keys increase the risk. Since space itself is a valuable commodity, all active and inactive records should be separated and reviewed. Unless there are legal requirements for retention, inactive records should be destroyed. Those that must be kept should, if legally acceptable, be put on microfilm or microfiche and stored in smaller cabinets that can be locked and that are specifically designed for that purpose.

Cabinets in which are stored all active personnel, payroll, and accounting records, and copies of purchase orders or contracts kept in the purchasing department, should be protected by using security bars that are secured after hours with changeable-combination padlocks. When necessary the combinations can be easily changed with a special key provided by the manufacturer.

Backup for all computerized data should be stored off site, possibly in a nearby bank safe-deposit box, volume permitting. If this is not possible, a secured, bonded, limited-access, fire-retardant facility should be used.

Check stock, insurance policies, and other legal or essential documents are now kept in the controller's office in either a locked cabinet or a locked closet, the key to which was once lost. The nature of these items would justify their being kept in either a safe or safe-type filing cabinet, the combination to which is given to only those employees with an absolute need to know it. An alternative would be to keep them in a safe-deposit box to which access is similarly restricted.

While the safe-deposit boxes for guest and hotel use are satisfactory, the safe into which cashiers put their deposits is incapable of holding all deposits, especially those made over busy weekends. At least one weekend loss is known to have occurred because the depository was so full that envelopes were sticking out of the opening.

Although buying a larger safe would solve the problem, it would be a needless expense. Instead, since the bank with which the hotel regularly does business is just across the street, a deposit should be made as late as possible on Friday. If there is still not enough room in the safe for weekend deposits, an additional deposit could be made late Saturday morning since the bank's Saturday hours are 9 A.M. to noon.

Despite the fact that the safe-deposit boxes themselves are satisfactory, their present location exposes guests to full public view when they put valuables into them or take them out. This exposure increases the level of risk to both the guest and the hotel, yet any meaningful corrective action at this time would involve considerable expense. If in the future the front-desk area is remodeled, it should provide privacy for guests using safe-deposit boxes. However, until that time the suggestion that an electric lock be installed to help control access to the front desk should be implemented.

Housekeeping still uses some keys to access storage facilities. When not in use the keys are hung on pegs in a wooden cabinet with double doors, secured after hours with a screwed-on hasp and key-operated padlock. This cabinet should be replaced with a one-door, steel cabinet expressly designed for key storage. Keys to this cabinet should be issued to only the executive housekeeper and his or her designee.

Locks and Locking Devices

Security for storerooms and other back-of-the-house storage facilities would be improved if all exposed door hinges had their pins either pegged or otherwise frozen as previously noted. In addition, where hasps and padlocks are used, hasps on metal doors should be spot-welded rather than screwed on. Those on wooden doors should be held in place with half-headed screws to make their removal more difficult, noticeable, and time consuming.

Although electronic locks have been installed on guest room doors, their use was not extended to high-ticket stores such as liquor and wine storerooms. Under the circumstances a suitable alternative would be the use of time-recording locks for both doors. They would not interfere with authorized access, but they would provide better controls and much better after-hours accountability than the existing locks.

All key-operated padlocks, other than those already cited, should be replaced with those having changeable combinations. Being able to change combinations as needed offers better protection and is less expensive than buying new key-operated ones.

Guest Rooms

Electronic door locks, plus dead bolts to provide additional protection for guests while in their rooms, are satisfactory. Without peepholes, however, guests must open their doors to identify callers and are thereby needlessly subjected to risks. True, guests cannot be compelled to use peepholes even when available, and many do not, but having them can reduce claims that the hotel was negligent if a guest is assaulted or robbed. Therefore, peepholes should be installed. In doing so allowance should be made for guests with disabilities who may not be able to use those inserted at the standard elevation.

Two other matters related to guest room protection deserve mention. One has to do with hangers. When they are not adaptable for home use, the hotel benefits since the risk of their loss is minimal. The other matter concerns early makeup signs or tags for guest use. Hung outside doors, they usually indicate that guests are out of their rooms, thus offering opportunities for burglaries. Security can be improved by dispensing with these signs and using tent cards, or something comparable, asking guests to call a particular housekeeping extension if they want their rooms made up early.

Lighting

Lighting in all parts of the hotel and the parking facility is acceptable with but one exception—the eighth floor, where, in the absence of any functions, most lights are turned off leaving a significant part of floor in darkness. The urge to conserve energy needs to be weighed against risks that include, but are not limited to, assaults against guests or employees and the theft of valuable art that enhances the appearance and attractiveness of the function rooms. Light may not prevent a range of security problems, but it is an effective deterrent. Minimum lighting standards should be set and maintained for the eighth floor rather than keeping it in almost total darkness.

Alarms

In addition to the recommended access controls to the swimming pool and health club, thought should also be given to installing a magnetic contact alarm on the doors leading directly into the pool space that, when activated, would generate an audiovisual signal at the switchboard. A security officer then could be directed to investigate the cause without delay.

The hotel relies on a standby emergency generator in case of a power failure. However, none of its refrigerated units in which perishables are stored are equipped with temperature alarms. Consequently, a sudden or prolonged drop in temperature might go unnoticed, resulting in a good deal of spoilage, loss of inventory, and loss of income. Temperature alarms for these units should be considered.

In the absence of holdup alarms, front-desk cashiers are vulnerable. To make matters worse, the switchboard is located in the same part of the lobby, so that in case of a robbery any reaction would have to be deferred until after the robber's departure.

A last-bill, pressure-type alarm should be installed in the register drawer; it would be activated when the cashier complies with a robber's demand, but it would not alert the robber. Although other alarms can be routed to the switchboard, its location means that this one should go to a central station for a quick response. In addition, installing a time-lapse camera behind and above the cashier's position, tied into the alarm's activation, would provide investigators with photographs of the robber and robbery.

At present the executive office receptionist is not in a position to have direct contact with anyone, other than by telephone, should she feel threatened by someone in the area. An under-the-desk alarm that can be discreetly activated should be installed. An audiovisual signal, easily distinguished from the one used for pool protection, should be located at the switchboard and a security officer dispatched to the executive office if the alarm is activated.

Emergency Equipment

Firefighting equipment is available and easily identified in terms of location; however, water extinguishers predominate. This could be a problem since some fires, such as electrical or grease fires, cannot be contained or suppressed with water.

Despite the fact that the fire department must be called immediately in case of any fire, there should be an in-house response pending its arrival. In addition to staff, a well-meaning guest might try to fight a small fire. In an emergency of this sort it is doubtful that whoever reaches for an extinguisher will read its label or try to determine a fire's source to ensure that the right kind of extinguisher is being used. This can be more than dangerous; it can be disastrous. Therefore, the property's in-house firefighting capability would be improved if all extinguishers were the dry-chemical, all-purpose type.

Administration and Operations

Personnel Practices and Procedures

Most problems are caused—and can be prevented—by people. Employee access to both the hotel's assets and guest property adds to the importance of the preemployment screening process.

The employment application used is both detailed and in conformity with federal and state laws. However, human resources personnel are not always careful in reviewing each one. Things that require explanation, such as unexplained gaps in time, frequent job changes, accepting a job with lower wages and/or a more difficult commute, failure to say why the applicant left a job, omission of a supervisor's name, tend to be overlooked or ignored. Human resources personnel seldom bother to contact personal references, and in many cases the limited information provided by former employers is accepted without asking if the applicant would be eligible for reemployment. These deficiencies can prove costly and embarrassing; the required corrective action is self-evident.

While department heads rightfully accept or reject applicants sent to them, they sometimes make hiring decisions without informing human resources. This needs to be corrected. Department heads should not only send every applicant back to human resources, but they should also let human resources inform the applicant of their decision. If the decision is favorable, all forms should be completed, starting dates agreed upon, and a written confirmation should be sent to payroll. This can help reduce the risk of payroll padding.

Aside from being given a copy of the employees' handbook, there is no orientation for new hires. Merely asking new employees to certify the receipt of the handbook, pledge to abide by the rules, and having their signatures witnessed is inadequate. They must be made to understand their roles in protecting the hotel's assets, protecting guests and their property, and in preventing losses.

All new hires should undergo a general orientation session conducted by human resources; the security/loss-prevention aspect should be handled by the security director. Thereafter, each should meet with his or her department head, be given a department-specific orientation, and told about policies not necessarily in the handbook, such as no free-pouring or free drinks by bartenders, no opening guest room doors for persons who claim to have misplaced their cards, and so on. After these departmental sessions have been completed, the department head should make a notation in each new employee's file, giving the date and confirming that orientation has been given and by whom. In the interest of keeping the staff abreast of new or changed policies or other matters of concern to the hotel, department heads should also meet with their staffs from time to time.

All employees are issued photo identification badges. Although they must be shown to the timekeeper upon reporting for work and are useful for check cashing on payday, employees are not required to wear them. Instead, all employees wear name tags whether their jobs are uniformed or not. Conceivably some guests may be in their rooms when the latter are being serviced by housekeeping or when engineering gains access to make a repair. If so, guests should have something more to rely on than seeing housekeeping or engineering uniforms. Concern for guests' protection suggests that housekeeping and engineering personnel be required to wear their photo identification badges while at work.

While all employees wear name tags, which can be useful for identification purposes, their effectiveness is reduced not only because they are all the same, but also because there is no distinction in the uniforms worn by certain groups of employees. Room service, outlet, and banquet waiters, as well as bartenders, all wear the same uniform, and even the hotel's management staff, seeing any one of them on a guest floor, might simply assume the person is authorized to be there when in fact they might not be. The name tags should be kept, but they should be color-coded by department or function. This would help reduce losses, whether of assets or time, by making it easy to detect employees in a part of the hotel where they do not belong.

From time to time employees bring parcels to work or take some home. Arrangements should be made for incoming parcels to be checked with the timekeeper when employees report for work. In addition, other than parcels in this category, employees should not be allowed to remove anything from the hotel without having a prenumbered, dated, parcel pass signed by the appropriate department head(s) with a full signature, not initials, describing whatever is being taken.

If an employee is allowed to borrow any hotel property, the pass also should indicate when it is to be returned. Passes should be completed in triplicate, with one copy kept by the authorizing department head, one copy by the timekeeper, and the third by the employee to be returned with any hotel property that is being taken on loan. Regarding the latter, timekeepers should have a tickler file for their copies, to be reviewed on a daily basis as a way to ensure that borrowed assets are returned.

Better control over access to, and accountability for, personnel records is needed in the interest of employee privacy. Presently there is no accountability when files are removed for any reason. A charge-out system indicating who has what files, when they were removed, and for how long they are to be kept is a reasonable safeguard, provided that the human resources manager regularly reviews the charge-outs to ensure that only authorized persons with an absolute need have access to personnel information.

Controller

In addition to the controller's function, this section covers cashiering practices, cash handling, and guest credit. A suggested solution for the excess accumulation of cash over weekends was discussed under the Physical Security heading.

All mail, other than that addressed to registered guests, is delivered to the controller's office in plastic laundry bags and open boxes. Although it consists largely of checks and invoices, mail addressed to other departments is included and then is sorted for further delivery. This system is time consuming. To the extent that it delays the opening of mail containing checks and their processing and deposit, interest income is lost.

All mail should be delivered initially to the front desk and sorted there. Only mail addressed to the controller, or not specifically addressed to other departments, should be delivered here. Envelopes should be opened upon receipt; if they contain checks, the latter should be removed, stamped with the date, time, and "For Deposit Only," posted to the proper accounts, and deposited. Invoices should continue to be matched against purchase orders and other supporting documentation before they are paid.

There is no inventory of office machines, with or without serial numbers. Neither is there an inventory of the artwork mentioned earlier, although the general manager has the information in the form of a list. Photographs and/or detailed descriptions of the artwork are not available. Color photographs should be taken and detailed descriptions of the hotel's artwork should be prepared; both should be retained in the controller's office safe.

Insofar as the office machines are concerned, the controller should maintain an accurate and current inventory of each item, listing the following: of what the item consists (e.g., computer keyboard, typewriter, calculator, etc.), brand name, date of purchase, and the department to which it was assigned. Serial numbers, where available, should also be recorded. Serialized asset tags with the hotel's name affixed to each item, with or without a manufacturer's serial number, also would help prevent loss. The controller should inventory all such machines semiannually, using as a basis the previous inventory. In addition to making certain that all are accounted for, their location should also be confirmed.

Night auditors should continue to change cash register tapes and zero registers. However, retaining large sums of money until cashiers' shifts end can contribute to possible losses, regardless of the reason, and adds to the cashiers' vulnerability. Since their main function is to take money in rather than pay it out, there is no real reason for continuing this practice.

Cashiers cannot be expected to take the time to count cash and reconcile accounts whenever they have substantial accumulations of cash. However, excess cash could be placed in a sealed envelope with the cashier's name on the outside and taken to the controller's office for counting and reconciliation at the end of that person's shift.

Each front-desk cashier is given $1,000 when going on duty. Only some of the cash goes into the register drawer; the balance is kept in a box underneath. Since the distance between the front desk and safe-deposit boxes is negligible, cashiers would not be inconvenienced if cash not in the register was kept in a safe-deposit box.

One cashier frequently keeps her purse directly below her register. Without impugning her honesty or integrity, this practice by any cashier should be discontinued.

Guest credit covers more than room charges; it also can include charges in outlets and shops. The latter is a potential source of loss. Signatures and room numbers on checks, by themselves, are insufficient proof that a person is a registered guest. In some outlets and shops, the staff asks for a look at the cardkeys of those signing their bills; in others this is not done. Asking for cardkeys should be standard practice in all outlets and shops when guests charge purchases.

Inventories

Office machine and artwork inventories have already been discussed. Food and beverage inventories are supposedly taken on a 28-day cycle; there is no uniformity with respect to other departments. Existing controls are weak and exact data are lacking. Not knowing what really is on hand can cause some department heads to requisition replacements. If time is a factor, the pressure on purchasing to replace what may only seem to be missing can prevent getting the best price and is a needless expense.

For some storerooms and other rooms containing assets, key-operated locks are still used for protection. Although keys and locks are maintained by engineering, there is no current engineering key and lock inventory. The available records are more than five years old. A complete key and lock inventory should be taken and repeated on a daily basis.

General housekeeping inventories are taken every 90 days; floor linen closets are checked daily. However, the controller does not actively participate in these or any other departmental inventories. Frequently those responsible for assets and taking inventory feel hurried and admit to being careless. Apparent shortages or overages may be ignored, while an attempt to reconcile the numbers may be excessively time consuming.

Placing all departments on a perpetual inventory basis would improve controls and accountability. If done, however, department heads should nevertheless reconcile their inventories on a random but regular basis. Furthermore, annual or semiannual inventories should be taken and reconciliations made by the controller.

Food and Beverages

There are five outlets. Two are full-service restaurants; two are primarily beverage outlets but offer limited food service; and one serves only drinks. Registered guests can also use room service, and both food and beverages are available for a wide range of functions.

The food and beverage director, steward, and executive chef occasionally spot-check garbage. If outlet managers were to participate, inspections could be made more often, preferably on a regular basis. In the interest of preventing losses, they should look for signs of waste, excessive breakage that might indicate careless handling of glass or other ware, or a loss of flatware due to negligence on the part of employees who clean trays or scrape dishes.

Other measures, not now in place, could also help reduce food costs. Locks on freezers and coolers, whose contents can be consumed on the premises or used in any home, are not always secured. This is particularly noticeable when kitchens are not in service and the only persons present are porters doing cleanup. In addition, items that need refrigeration were seen sitting on worktables after hours instead of having been properly stored. Managerial and supervisory oversight of these areas need to be improved.

Despite the fact that food and beverage inventories are supposed to be taken on a 28-day cycle, as noted under the Inventories heading, this schedule is not strictly followed. The food and beverage director says food production inventories are taken monthly; the executive chef says annually. It also appears that instead of a complete inventory, a monthly inventory is limited to two freezers. The only available liquor inventory is more than 120 days old. Not only is a better overall system called for, but the controller's regular and active participation is needed in these inventories.

Outlet liquor is supposed to be coded, but the policy is not always enforced. The lack of coolers and storage space for banquet floor liquor, especially acute when large functions are scheduled, is also a problem and has resulted in some thefts. To alleviate the coding problem, delivery schedules should be arranged to allow ample time for coding upon receipt. Replenishing bar stock on a bottle-for-bottle exchange basis should continue, but in addition, outlet managers should regularly check bar stock to make certain that bartenders' personal stock is not being substituted.

Other food- and beverage-related matters also suggest a need for closer staff supervision. To illustrate:

1. A young couple carrying two paper bags, each with a Chinese restaurant's name and logo, walked into one outlet without waiting to be seated, picked up knives and forks from a table, and left without being questioned by the hostess, wait staff, or cashier.

2. The cashier in another outlet left the register, located near the door, unattended for well over two minutes without telling anyone.

3. Although smoking is allowed in the lounge, a bartender smoking while on duty made a poor impression. In addition, shortly after a party of five reordered and paid for their drinks, they left, glasses in hand, without so much as a word from the bartender.

4. A room service order of ice cream was received in liquid form due to insufficient ice in the serving container.

Purchasing, Receiving, Storekeeping, and Requisitions

Without questioning the integrity of the person now in the job, assigning these multiple functions to one person is not in the hotel's best interests. Any savings in terms of salaries could be more than offset by losses if the job-holder were less than honest. The possibilities for a conflict of interest—soliciting or accepting kickbacks from suppliers, or accepting deliveries and sending copies of delivery tickets to accounts payable without actually confirming quantities or quality—cannot be ignored.

Corrective action can be taken in several ways:

1. Although most purchases are based on department heads' requisitions, the general manager should set limits above which purchases would require his or her approval or that of the executive assistant manager.

2. Purchase orders should be reviewed randomly but regularly to see if certain suppliers seem to get most of the business. If so, other reputable vendors should be contacted by either the general or executive assistant manager and asked if there is any particular reason for their exclusion. This can help uncover possible or actual kickbacks.

3. One copy of all purchase orders should be sent to accounts payable and another to the cost controller, pending receipt of the goods or services. The cost controller, when accepting deliveries, should actually verify the weights or quantities received to ensure that they conform to the purchase order. Any possible discrepancies should be noted on a copy of the delivery ticket, and it, plus a copy of the purchase order, should then go to accounts payable so that vendors can be paid; no payments should be made without proper documentation. To avoid backed-up deliveries, par-

ticularly of perishables where spoilage is a factor, the purchasing manager and suppliers should agree on delivery schedules.

4. Immediately following verification, the receiving dock should be cleared, and all delivered goods should be moved into their designated storerooms or coolers or to the departments for which they are intended, as is appropriate.

5. The greatest loss potential lies in the receipt of foodstuffs and beverages subject to short weights or counts, substandard quality, spoilage, or breakage. The risk of such losses can be reduced if the food and beverage director, executive or sous chef, and outlet managers make periodic, unannounced, uncoordinated visits to receiving to personally weigh or count and check the quality of select items and ensure that the measures in the preceding paragraph are being implemented.

6. All stored goods should be issued only upon the receipt of a written requisition signed by a department head or his or her designee. For the kitchen, in addition to the executive and sous chefs, the former may also authorize certain specific personnel, such as the pastry chef or the salad chef, to sign requisitions to fill their respective needs. To minimize the risk of spoiled foodstuffs or the obsolescence of other items, all requisitions should be filled on a first-in-first-out basis.

7. Inventories on a 28-day cycle should continue, but with the controller's participation.

Two other procedural matters need attention. Storekeepers should be required to use their assigned lockers and not allowed to keep clothing or other personal items in storerooms. The Dutch door at the main storeroom's entrance should be closed and secured at all times other than when bulk shipments are being moved in or taken out; all other transactions should be handled "over the counter."

Sales

The sales department should continue its practice of informing security when certain types of functions or "persons of consequence" will be using the hotel's facilities and more than routine protection may be needed. However, some functions have special needs; then, sales personnel often tell them that they must provide their own security but that sales will make the necessary arrangements.

Advising a group that it has to provide its own security is quite proper, but the hotel is better served if it does not become involved with making the arrangements. The current practice might be construed as making the hotel a guarantor of the outside service, and should a problem arise or a loss occur, the function's sponsors might blame, or even seek redress from, the hotel.

When the sales and security managers agree that a function will require additional protection beyond what is normally provided, they should so advise the function's sponsors, tell them that they need to make their own arrangements, and either suggest the "yellow pages," or give them a list of companies that can be contacted. However, the sponsors should also be asked to have the person responsible for their protection contact the security manager so that all security activities can be coordinated for the function's duration.

Engineering

Several deficiencies that can result in losses exist. The chief engineer, in his job for five years, has never gone beyond "thinking" about taking an inventory. Thus there is no inventory of assets for which this department is responsible, and without one there can be no inventory control system. The controller should arrange for a complete physical inventory of all engineering assets, and a perpetual inventory system should then be set up.

Work orders are available, but they are not used. Most work is done in response to calls from either the rooms division or housekeeping. Nor are engineering personnel required to turn in parts that have been replaced so they can be accounted for and either repaired, salvaged, or sold as scrap or junk. Not using work orders or exchanging parts offers unlimited opportunities for losses.

Work orders, in triplicate, should be required before any routine work is done. In an emergency the work can proceed with the chief engineer's verbal approval, but a work order should then be completed as soon as the emergency has passed. The chief engineer should keep one copy; one should be used by the mechanic as a parts requisition that is submitted together with all items that were replaced; and the third copy, with the time and date of completion, should be turned in to the chief engineer when the work is done. All copies should be kept for a year and used to reconcile requisitions, inventories, work orders and to ensure that all work orders have been completed.

Key and Combination Controls

Combinations, whether for padlocks or safes, should be made known only to employees with an absolute need to know. Neither status nor seniority should have a bearing on this policy. Whenever an employee to whom a combination is known no longer needs the information, regardless of the reason, or whenever there is even the slightest suspicion that a combination has been compromised, the combination should be changed without delay.

Some keys still are used by employees, but no records exist of to whom they were issued or why. Keys should be issued by engineering only on the basis of written requests in duplicate, signed by the person's department head and giving the reason for the issue. The employee receiving the key should also sign the form. One copy of the completed form should be sent to human resources to ensure that keys are turned in when employees are terminated; the other should be kept on file by engineering until the keys are returned to it.

Keys should be issued only if they are essential to job performance. Occasionally keys may be needed for temporary use, in which case they should be signed in and out to reflect the dates and times of issue and the names of both issuers and recipients.

Housekeeping

The current inventory system and the practice of issuing all supplies on an exchange basis should be continued but with one modification. The executive housekeeper, inspectors, and maids check linen closets daily, but only to make certain each has adequate supplies. This determination is based on what is seen, not on count. Thought should be given to having either the executive housekeeper, inspectors, or both, take a floor count once a week to supplement the inventory controls in place.

Occasionally the executive housekeeper and a houseman check outgoing trash, frequently recovering assets, flatware included that would otherwise be lost. Based on the results as reported, these inspections should be done daily rather than occasionally, with department heads taking turns in overseeing the work.

Housekeeping reports the loss of uniforms, particularly by waiters and bar porters, despite the policy of requiring a uniform deposit. Between 80 and 100 are replaced annually because they were not turned in by persons leaving the hotel's employ. A contributing factor may be that some employees launder and clean their own uniforms; also, uniform exchanges take place on Monday mornings, yet employees are paid or terminated on Fridays.

The hotel should do all cleaning and laundering of uniforms. Allowing uniforms to be removed from the premises opens the door to losses; conceivably, terminated employees could return in uniform for any number of reasons that could prove costly. Another safeguard would be to have all uniforms turned in before paychecks are distributed on Friday; clean ones would be issued at the beginning of the employee's next working day.

A controlled loss program might be a useful training vehicle for the housekeeping department. If the executive housekeeper periodically removed one or two items from a guest room, such as linens, pillows, blankets, wall hangings, or terry-cloth bathrobes, it would test how much attention housekeepers and inspectors pay to detail. This can be especially helpful since one of the executive housekeeper's concerns is the fact that English is not the first language of many housekeepers. If the plan is implemented, the staff should be given to understand that the program is being used as a constructive educational tool, not for the purpose of chastising or embarrassing anyone.

Front Office

Telephone operators do not give callers guest room numbers. This practice should be continued.

There is no formal reporting by the bell staff of light or seemingly empty luggage brought in by arriving guests. Since some guests will take hotel assets as souvenirs or for other reasons, the executive housekeeper should be informed so that particular attention can be paid to the contents of the rooms occupied by guests with suspiciously light suitcases.

Security Department

Organization and Supervision

The security staff numbers six, the manager included. The timekeepers and garage ramp attendants also report to the manager. According to the duty roster, one security officer has no regularly scheduled hours, three members of the staff (including the manager) work a 40-hour week, and two work a 32-hour week. The intention is to have one officer on duty per shift during a normal work week, with some overlap when required for major functions.

Working a regular shift in addition to managerial duties, the manager lacks the flexibility needed to effectively supervise the staff. Under current conditions the department is faced with two choices: (1) security personnel, timekeepers, and ramp attendants, whose shifts differ from the manager's, either need not be concerned about possible off-hours vis-its by the manager to ensure that they are on duty and performing their jobs properly, or (2) have the manager work far in excess of 40 hours a week, which would be unproductive.

From the duty roster it appears that only one of the full-time, 40-hour-a-week offi-cers has two successive days off, but on returning to work he works a double shift. Fur-thermore, last year security officers worked a total of 902.5 overtime hours, for which they were paid time and a half. These hours equal almost half of those of a full-time em-ployee. The wages amount to about 68 percent of the annual base rate for one full-time se-curity officer.

The entire security staff is male. This can be a disadvantage in dealing with security matters that concern women. Considering the number of women guests and employees, the organization would benefit if its composition was more representative.

Based on the normal activity level and the hotel's security history, a staff of six, plus the manager, timekeepers and ramp attendants, would improve protection and the de-partment's morale. All should be scheduled to work a 40-hour week, arranged so that days off can be successive, and under normal conditions all personnel would have a mini-mum of 16 hours off between tours of duty. This would put a second officer on duty dur-ing those hours on Thursday, Friday, and Saturday when the greatest need for additional coverage exists, and it would give the manager more flexibility for supervision. It would also create an opening for which a qualified woman should be considered. Aside from the foregoing, and in the interest of departmental efficiency, a part-time person should be hired to do typing, clerical work, and filing. It might be possible for security to share such a person with another department.

Security officers do not rotate shifts; this should be changed. Shift rotation, on a quarterly basis, has advantages: It helps boost morale by recognizing that officers have private lives; it equalizes income by way of shift differential; and it means that over time each member of the staff becomes familiar with the hotel and its activities at all hours of the day and all days of the week. The latter advantage can be most important in case of an emergency.

Selecting and Training Personnel

Selection and training are critically important. Not only may some encounters with guests and other employees occur under rather trying circumstances, but the behavior of security officers can also have legal implications.

One current member of the staff is an off-duty police officer, hired because of his experience and in the hope of a rapid response should police assistance be needed. Police experience and security experience, however, are not the same. Furthermore, it is unfortu-nately true that the authoritarian approach to which police officers are accustomed in dealing with people can backfire in the private sector in general and in the lodging indus-try in particular. Those inclined to equate courtesy with weakness can cause a host of both guest and labor relations problems.

Neither police nor prior security experience should be seen as an asset or a liability in choosing security personnel. Of greater importance are appearance, manner, and good communications skills, both oral and written. A high school education or its equivalent should be required. College graduates interested in security careers and willing to start as security officers should not be arbitrarily turned down. In view of the number of guests and employees for whom English is not a first language, having security personnel who can communicate in the most frequently used foreign languages would be helpful. The selection process should also take into account an applicant's physical ability and emotional stability with respect to their probable response to an emergency, no matter how infrequently one may arise.

Newly hired security officers now get four hours of training; there is nothing in the way of in-service or refresher training. Training consists mainly of learning the hotel's layout in order to make rounds, how to fill out tour reports, and how to monitor and reset (where applicable) the existing security systems. Considering the potential for incidents and how the conduct of officers in dealing with them can lead to complaints and even litigation, the need for an expanded training program for all security personnel exists.

In addition to matters already covered, additional instruction is needed in such subjects as guest and employee relations, officers' authority, report writing in general, the fundamentals of investigation and how to interview incident victims and witnesses, the identification of incident scenes and preservation of evidence, safety, the hotel's security-related policies and procedures, how to conduct a search, and the right to arrest or detain people.

Training should be given to all new hires regardless of their previous experience. At least twice a year, in-service training should cover either operating or hotel policy changes and new developments in the field of lodging industry protection. To be effective all training should be done by persons qualified to discuss specific topics.

Given the ready availability of both a physician and the city's emergency medical service, training in first aid does not seem to be necessary. However, training in cardiopulmonary resuscitation and possibly in the use of a portable defibrillator should be considered.

Responsibilities and Authority

Although the responsibilities can be as broadly or narrowly defined as the general manager wants them to be, certain fundamental duties must be performed. The security staff is responsible for protecting and conserving the hotel's assets, including its reputation. It also must provide for the security and safety of all persons (guests and employees) lawfully on the premises and for the protection of their personal property.

An unavoidable responsibility is to patrol the hotel. In doing so tours must be made so as not to establish clearly identifiable patterns. It is also important for patrol personnel to look for any possible sources of loss, such as defects that might result in persons being injured, and not to focus primarily on completing rounds within a preestablished time frame.

To expect the staff to discharge its responsibilities without authority is illogical. Therefore, the general manager must make it clear to all employees that security's role is to be respected, and cooperation is to be forthcoming. With respect to authority, the security staff's is derived from that of the general manager under the legal doctrines of agency and master and servant.

Although it is not problematic insofar as routine duties and responsibilities are concerned, the question of authority can be costly, particularly if issues of search and seizure or arrest and detention are involved. Since the general manager's authority in these areas is no different from that of any private person, the same is true of that given to the officers. At the least, an abuse can generate bad publicity and embarrassment; at the worst, it can mean a lawsuit and a sizeable plaintiff's judgment. Consequently, training related to any aspects of the law should be given only by counsel.

Records and Communications

The records system is of little value as constituted in that it really cannot be used effectively as a working tool; it reflects past activity, but only in a historical sense. To use it for planning purposes or in an investigation would be an exercise in futility.

A records system needs to be developed that will help the manager learn from what has happened in order to plan for what may happen. It need not be complicated or expensive, but it should allow for quick and easy retrieval and should enable the manager to detect trends or patterns in relation to incidents. For example, if certain types of incidents seem to occur with great frequency, at certain times, or in certain parts of the premises, attention can be focused on those problems in an effort to solve them. The system can also be used easily to keep the general manager informed about the overall loss-prevention picture.

Security officers have direct two-way radio communication, but all messaging is done "in the clear" and can be overheard by anyone. A simple code, preferably a numerical one, could be helpful for several reasons. While all transmissions should be brief, they nevertheless would be further shortened. This is useful in emergencies when time is of the essence. A number code would lessen the risk of confusion in transmissions. An additional benefit would be that in an emergency, even if guests or other employees should overhear a transmission, code use would lessen the risk of their being concerned or panicked by overhearing a "clear" one.

Uniforms and Equipment

Security personnel are not uniformed. The hotel would be better served if they were uniformed for easy identification by both guests and employees, but a police or military type of uniform would be inconsistent with the hotel's image. Instead, color-coordinated uniforms consisting of blazers, slacks (with skirts as an option for women), shirts, and ties, with the hotel's logo and the word "Security" on the left breast pocket of the blazer, are recommended. Personnel should also be issued name tags to be worn in plain view for the benefit of guests and employees. In addition to being a deterrent, they also become easily identifiable.

No security personnel are armed, and some may carry handcuffs, but all carry police-type badges and "Public Safety Identification Cards." The carrying of badges and the carrying, wearing, or use of handcuffs or weapons of any kind should be discontinued. Security officers to whom any of the foregoing are issued rely too often on these symbols of authority and ignore the need for tact and discretion in problem solving. If officers encounter problems that, in their considered opinions, cannot be tactfully and peacefully resolved, police assistance should be requested.

There also is the risk of their exceeding what legal authority they actually have. To display a badge could conceivably lead to charges of impersonating a police officer. To use or try to use handcuffs involves physical contact, which could result in a lawsuit for false arrest and false imprisonment, and it could prove even more costly if the person taken into custody is injured.

Insofar as equipment is concerned, patrol personnel rely on two-tone signal papers. Paged security officers then must find a telephone before they can take action of any kind. This can mean a loss of valuable time, especially if there is an emergency while they are otherwise engaged and do not answer the page immediately. Moreover, if there are developments about which they should know as they proceed to the scene, they have no direct communication, and the same is true if, upon arrival, they need additional help and must spend time searching for a telephone. The pagers should be replaced with direct two-way radio communication.

No flashlights, notebooks, or pens are issued to the staff. Flashlights should be given to patrol personnel whose tours may require them to enter parts of the property that are dimly lit. Notebooks and pens should be provided by the hotel instead of relying on officers to furnish their own.

Police Liaison

Good relations with the police are important, but they should not be abused by either security or police personnel. Although some security personnel like to think of themselves as members of the "police fraternity," as evidenced by the police-type badges and "Public Safety Identification Cards," the fact remains that they are not. Under normal circumstances their first duty is to their employer, not the police department.

Asking for police assistance, when needed, or cooperating with police when asked to do so is perfectly proper and can be mutually beneficial, but only if all requests are handled in strict accordance with existing laws and court decisions. For example, security personnel should not ask for information to which by law the private sector is not entitled; neither should they automatically release information about guests or employees to the police that, for privacy reasons, should be released only upon receipt of a court order. Police liaison matters must be handled carefully and discreetly, and the parameters of the cooperation between security and the police should be defined by the hotel's attorneys before any action is taken.

Emergency Procedures

The principal emergencies to which the hotel is most likely to be exposed, other than those that may be weather related, are fires and bomb threats. Although weather forecasting in many cases allows ample time for preparation, the same cannot be said of fires and bomb threats, both of which are unexpected events that require a prompt response. Nevertheless, emergency procedures that are flexible, except for notification and decision making, rather than rigid, provide for the best response. Since the hotel has procedures, this section deals only with aspects where some improvement may be possible.

Surprisingly, emergency staffing under the current procedures needs to be reevaluated. Despite operations around the clock, throughout the year, the existing staffing plan seems to be based on the premise that most emergencies arise between 8 A.M. and 6 P.M., Monday through Friday. Consequently, the hours when the greatest number of people are most likely to be on the premises appear to be inadequately staffed. This does not mean that more security and other employees are needed; it does mean that those on duty at any time are given emergency assignments that will ensure an immediate and efficient response by the staff.

Fire Procedures

Employees are cautioned not to use water or soda acid fire extinguishers on oil or electric fires. This imposes a burden on any employees involved with firefighting pending the fire department's arrival if they are unfamiliar with the equipment and do not have time to determine extinguisher types. It is suggested that all extinguishers be the multipurpose type and that the fire department be invited to provide proper training in their use.

Security officers are designated as members of the "fire crew." This presupposes that more than one will be on duty whenever a fire breaks out, and it also implies that they will help fight the fire. They should not be involved with the firefighting effort, but one should be at the entrance to lead the responding firefighters to the scene. That aside, their focus should be to help evacuate guests and employees and to protect guests' property and the hotel's assets.

The chief engineer, or the senior engineer on duty, should be in charge of the firefighting effort until the fire department arrives and then should act as liaison with the fire officer in charge. This is important since the engineering staff is most familiar with the location of the hotel's controls, valves, firefighting apparatus, ventilation systems, and so on.

Should evacuation be called for, there is no way to identify guests who have disabilities and may need help in the process. A way should be found to discreetly tag their registration cards and to note pertinent data with respect to the nature of the infirmity and help that might be needed, so that security, and responding fire and police personnel, can provide assistance without delay.

Bomb Threats

Virtually all bomb threats are made by telephone. The recipient, most often a switchboard operator, should try to get as much information as possible with regard to both the threat and person making it. Each should have a copy of the existing "Threatening Phone Call Information Log" under clear glass or plastic where it can be easily seen if a threat is received. In addition, the information for which they should be alert needs to be expanded to include data about the caller's state of sobriety or agitation, use of ethnic, regional, or trade idioms, and familiarity with the property, its employees, or guests.

That most bomb threats tend to be brief, hurried, and false does not guarantee that a call fitting this profile is a hoax and can be ignored. Consequently, it is imperative that immediately following receipt of a threat all available information should be given to the general or senior manager on duty. Only he or she should be authorized to decide if the police and fire departments are to be called and whether or not to evacuate the hotel.

Unless the general or senior manager on duty feels an explosion is imminent, based on the available data, the property should be thoroughly searched. Since employees are most familiar with the hotel and most likely to notice anything unusual, they must be involved in the search with or without help from police or fire personnel. Each department should search its own area; the bell staff, housekeeping, and employees who can be spared by other departments should cover public spaces; special attention should be paid to stairwells. Electrical closets, mechanical control rooms, linen closets, slop sinks, and such must be searched unless they are always closed and locked in the absence of authorized personnel. All deliveries should be refused until the emergency has passed, and all access to the hotel must be tightly controlled.

Anything unusual noted during the search should not be touched or even approached; the general or senior manager on duty must be informed immediately. If the police and fire departments have not yet been called, they now should be. At the same time, security should seal off and keep clear the immediate area in which the object was found, and a minimum of two floors above and one below should be evacuated pending the object's examination and disposal by competent authority.

If evacuation is ordered, employees responsible for protecting any tangible assets should endeavor to secure them before leaving their stations. Their immediate supervisors should try to verify that this has been done before they themselves leave.

Chapter 4

Guests and Loss Prevention

This subject is not one to be looked at from a single perspective only. Just as those engaged in retailing—another service industry—know that their very survival, aside from profits, depends on having customers, innkeepers understand that guests are the lodging industry's lifeblood. If occupancy drops, profits drop; if it remains low for an extended period of time, even staying in business may become difficult if not actually impossible. Another similarity is that retailers suffer losses attributable to both employees and shoplifters, and hotels suffer losses caused by employees and guests.

However, there is also a significant distinction between the two industries. Retail customers are on the premises for brief periods of time and carry very limited amounts of personal property if any. Their exposure to risk tends to be more a matter of safety than of theft, and while their protection should not be ignored, the concern is less than that required for the security of hotel and motel guests. With respect to the latter, they see a hotel or a motel as a "home away from home" no matter how short or long their stay. Thus they invariably have at least some personal, and possibly even business, assets with them. Consequently, the need to protect them and that property is of the utmost importance.

An additional concern is the fact that we now live in an extremely litigious society that can contribute to a further erosion of profits. Some guests encouraged in part by those lawyers whose television advertisements seem to ensure a client's victory, may file a suit for damages at the slightest provocation. Despite insurance coverage, if a plaintiff wins such a suit, a hotel's profits can be adversely affected at least to an amount equal to a policy's deductible clause. Even if damages are not awarded, poor publicity stemming from the mere filing of a lawsuit, let alone from a trial, can have a negative impact on reputation along with an attendant, albeit indirect, effect on profits. The fear of losses due to guest grievances is further compounded by some so-called consultants who regard all guests as possible victims and litigants.

No one questions the importance of protecting guests and their property and of taking reasonable precautions toward that end. However, hoteliers also need to understand that lawsuits, the occasional "skip," and the credit risks discussed in Chapter 3 are not the only ways in which guests can contribute to losses. They can do so by damaging or taking an inn's tangible assets, a matter to be considered in greater detail later in this chapter.

For the sake of clarity we shall discuss guests and loss prevention from three different points of view: First, we shall look at protecting persons (and their property) who are traveling alone or with their families; next, we shall consider the protection of persons and property when conventions or large groups are in attendance; and finally, we shall examine the need to protect the inn's assets from guests.

GUEST PROTECTION

Protecting Persons

In Chapter 2 we discussed the evolution of physical security and how modern technology has contributed, and continues to contribute, to guest protection. However, over the years other changes have occurred, mainly with respect to the traveling public. Whether traveling for business or pleasure, women have become an ever-growing part of that public. Some properties, aware of this phenomenon, have already taken steps to provide additional protection for women guests; but those that have not need to address the issue. Although we look at other aspects of guest security in chapters to follow, our concern at this point is the protection of individuals and their property.

The process begins with the arrival and registration of guests. At properties with door attendants, guests expect help with removing their luggage from taxis, their own automobiles, or an inn's airport shuttle. At this junction baggage is vulnerable to theft unless guests stay with their luggage until it is transferred to the lobby—carried inside by a member of the bell staff—or kept under the watchful eye of the door attendant.

The risk of theft decreases when guests carry their own bags inside or accompany the bell staff carrying them. The risk increases at motels that have neither door attendants nor a bell staff, and when guests traveling by automobile elect to drop off luggage and register before parking their cars. Where there are door attendants or a bell staff, if is best to ensure that bags are moved as quickly as possible from outside to the vicinity of the front desk; then they should be watched over by the bell staff until they accompany guests to their rooms. The responsibility for protecting their luggage obviously must rest with the guests themselves at properties that employ neither door attendants nor bell personnel.

The registration process itself has a role to play in preventing losses and protecting guests, and staff training as it relates to the overall security effort is essential. In this respect it is important to remember that a property's overall approach to security, not merely when guests register, must be one that provides an acceptable level of protection in ways that will not frighten guests. How to deal with the subject of security with guests is one of the first things that front-desk personnel must be taught. Failure to keep this in mind can conceivably lead to a reduction in occupancy, a point worth illustrating, although the following was a situation that would have involved front-desk employees only indirectly.

A major, politically active conglomerate had a wholly owned hotel/motel subsidiary. A number of the hotels were owned, while others were managed under contract with the owners; the motels operated under franchise agreements. The conglomerate and the subsidiary each had a corporate security director; the subsidiary's had a dotted reporting line to the former. Within the space of a very few months, to embarrass the parent corporation, an opposition organization exploded small bombs in lobby-level men's rooms at two hotels; in both cases the inns were called in advance. There were neither injuries nor deaths as a result of either bombing and the repairs cost each hotel less than $2,000.

Immediately following the second incident, the parent corporation's security director demanded that the subsidiary's security director order all properties using the hotel division's name to buy and install x-ray machines and to inspect all incoming guest luggage, brief or attaché cases, and shopping bags. The expense factors, limitations, and impracticality of his directive, if it were implemented, were pointed out. Among other things, guests would want to know why their luggage was being x-rayed. Once told, concern for their personnel safety could easily prompt them to go to any one of a number of nearby hotels or motels. Nevertheless, he was adamant. The subsidiary's security director, supported by the hotel/motel division's president, refused to go along with this idea. The parent corporation's security director had failed to consider the total impact of implementation to the subsidiary, its reputation, revenue, and relations with franchisees.

Other issues are also involved where front-desk personnel are concerned. For instance, when addressing guests they should speak their names as quietly as possible, and there is no reason to mention their room numbers. Aside from the fact that room numbers are on the rooming slips given to members of the bell staff who escort guests to their rooms, they are also on the keys or coded cards needed for access. Front-desk personnel also contribute to loss prevention when they ask how guests will pay their bills and when they tell guests about any time limits relative to the submission of bills, as discussed in Chapter 3.

Guests should be asked if they want to use a safe-deposit box, which may be located behind the front desk or in the guest's room. If the guest declines, a note should be made on the folio for the hotel's protection. Women traveling alone should be asked if they have a preference as to room location. They also should be told if there are security or other employees available to escort them to their rooms or to parking where it exists, once they have settled in, and how to avail themselves of that service. In addition, based on the inn's knowledge and experience, all guests should be told if there are any particular hazards in any parts of the city that they might be tempted to visit. While this, too, can be a delicate subject, in the long run it can be in the hotel's best interest to at least alert guests to such possible risks.

In many respects protecting guests (and their property) once they are in their rooms can be difficult, mainly because so much depends on the guests themselves. Even when the entire staff, and especially security personnel if employed, are on the lookout for people who just do not seem to belong, either because they are wandering the corridors or using stairwells instead of elevators, no hotel realistically can guarantee that only authorized persons are on the premises.

As a practical matter, trying to prevent all possible acts of trespass would be impossible, and the cost of hiring security personnel would be prohibitive. Even with an acceptable preemployment screening process, the risk of an employee-instigated incident cannot be ignored. The widespread use of closed-circuit television or security officers on the floors might make guests feel fearful or that their privacy was being invaded. As a result, while innkeepers must take reasonable measures to protect guests, guests also have a good deal of responsibility for their own protection while in their rooms.

To help illustrate this point, let's say there is a knock at the door and a voice says, "Room service," or "Engineering." Although the guest has neither ordered room service nor called about any maintenance problems, he or she opens the door without even looking through the peephole. A stranger enters, robs or assaults the guest, and leaves. Or suppose a male guest telephones a so-called "massage" service and gives his room number. A woman who could easily pass for a guest, judging by her appearance and behavior, arrives and goes directly to the room. After completing her business, she steals the man's wallet before leaving the room.

In the first example, tent cards in guest rooms can be helpful. They should convey a message to guests about what they should or should not do when there is an unexpected knock at the door. For instance, guests should not freely or willingly give their room numbers to strangers no matter where they meet them. If they have not ordered room service, say so to the person on the other side of the door without opening it. If the person claims to be from engineering, call the front desk for confirmation. Even if the answer is in the affirmative, look through the peephole for a uniform and photo identification badge before opening the door. In the second case, since the entire incident resulted from the guest's behavior, practically speaking there was nothing that the hotel could have said or done to prevent his loss.

If tent cards are to be effective for security purposes, they must be tastefully worded, eye-catching, and strategically placed so that they will stand out, attract guests' attention and cause them to be read. This is especially true at properties where so many tent cards may be displayed, advertising various outlets and other features in which it is hoped guests will take an interest, that one focusing on protection may easily be overlooked or ignored.

Protecting Property

Innkeepers find themselves on the horns of a dilemma when guests allege that something of value has been stolen or damaged. In reality, a hotel can do only so much to protect guests' property. Again, speaking practically, in most cases the primary responsibility for protecting personal property rests with the guests themselves. Then, too, there is the question of legitimacy with respect to the complaint; did the guest actually suffer a loss, or is the allegation made for other reasons? Certainly it is in an inn's best interests to take affirmative action if a complaint appears to be legitimate; however, to automatically assume legitimacy without making a thorough investigation can be costly. The guest whose claim is valid, although understandably upset by the loss, nevertheless should understand the inn's position vis-à-vis an inquiry as a condition precedent to any form of compensation.

Thus the subject of protecting guests' property has to be considered from two different perspectives. One, what can and should hotels do? The other, what role do guests themselves have to play in this regard?

As we have already said, regardless of whether all safe-deposit boxes are accessible only via the front desk or also are installed in individual rooms, asking guests if they want to avail themselves of a box when they register, and noting their acceptance or rejection on the folio, is helpful. Some guests will not only elect to take advantage of safe storage facilities, but they will also appreciate being reminded of their existence.

Some guests, however, at inns where the only safe-deposit boxes are at lobby level may decline the offer since they consider going to and from the lobby to get things out or put them back an inconvenience. As an example, guests with valuable jewelry might want to change certain pieces when they change their clothes. But the fact that they are assuming the risk will not necessarily prevent them from seeking compensation if the jewelry is stolen.

A greater problem arises when an item of value, such as a fur coat, simply will not fit into any type of safe-deposit box. One option is to have a suitably safe storage facility, with access thereto both limited to specific employees and electronically controlled, where such garments can be kept; guests can be given tickets or tags similar to those used by checkrooms. For hotels with security departments, a storeroom could be within the space allocated for the security office; if not, it might be near the safe-deposit box room on the lobby level.

Most guests who complain about losses will allege that something was taken from their rooms during their absence. This raises two possible issues: one, access to the rooms; two, unless there are signs of a forced entry, the suspicion of employee involvement. If locks to rooms have spring bolts, the risk of unauthorized entry by way of a credit card, plastic, or flexible tool to slip the bolt can be reduced by installing pick-plates. Made of metal to cover the bolt housing on the door's exterior, they need not be aesthetically offensive. With respect to employee involvement, the risk can be reduced if all applicants are properly screened, as set forth under the human resources heading in Chapter 3.

Other claims may be based on the alleged loss of or damage to items of clothing sent for laundering or dry-cleaning. To minimize the risk of such complaints, all items, upon being received at the laundry, need to be examined for valuables that may have inadvertently been left by guests, things that could cause damage, or preexisting damage to garments, as discussed in Chapter 3 in connection with the laundry. This should be done whether the work is to be done in house or is sent out.

As implied by the word "motel," a contraction of the words *motor* and *hotel*, guests staying at these properties most often arrive by car and want to park. While fewer hotel guests may need parking, some properties nevertheless have their own garages or will arrange for parking at facilities with which they have contracts. Notwithstanding the fact that the required standard of care is based on reasonableness, trying to explain what is reasonable to someone who is distraught because a motor vehicle has been damaged or stolen does not lend itself to good guest relations, and a damaged or stolen car may result in litigation.

If parking is made available on the premises, the previously discussed provision of escorts for women guests at their request should be extended to all guests, especially those who may be fearful during hours of darkness. However, in reality this solves only that part of the problem that deals with guests going to rather than from their cars. In the latter instance they cannot ask for escorts from their automobiles to the inn unless they carry portable telephones. This does not mean that nothing can be done for their safety.

An effective, but by no means absolute, deterrent is good lighting for all parking facilities. Adding occasional patrols by security or other assigned personnel, or the use of monitored, closed-circuit television cameras, reduces the risk to guests and of damage to or theft of motor vehicles. In this regard, television can be used to better advantage in open parking areas such as those found at motels. In garages more likely to be associated with hotels, concrete columns support upper levels and limit the monitoring of any section. Under these conditions, strategically placed microphones can be installed, set at levels to detect the sound of breaking glass or a person's outcry—as a significant contribution to the protection of guests and their vehicles. Installing telephones in parking lots or garages and connecting them directly to the front desk or a security office may give both guests and inn management a false sense of security since the instruments can be—and often are—stolen or vandalized.

As we have already noted on more than one occasion, just as guests have a major role to play in protecting themselves, the primary responsibility for protecting their property also rests with them. Periodically, one reads about guests who, having failed to use a safe-deposit box, report the loss of substantial sums of money or jewelry from their rooms. Unfortunately, when such incidents do occur, the news media tend to focus on the victim's celebrity and loss; they make little or no mention of the fact that the guest did not take advantage of the offer of a safe-deposit box.

It is unreasonable to expect innkeepers to protect guests against losses due to their own laxity, yet the risk of adverse publicity and damage to reputation, which can lead to other kinds of losses if ignored, means that complaints of this sort must be acted upon in two ways. One, the media must be made to understand (in a way that will not alienate the victim), that the loss occurred because the latter chose not to use a safe-deposit box. Two, the incident must be reported to the police and a thorough investigation must be made.

Since, as a rule, front-desk personnel cannot know whether or not newly arriving guests are carrying with them large amounts of money or valuable jewelry, it is important, as we have said, to offer the use of a safe-deposit box at registration and to note acceptance or refusal on the folio. Furthermore, the eye-catching, strategically placed tent cards in rooms telling guests how they can help protect themselves should urge the use of safe-deposit boxes for the protection of any valuables they may be carrying with them.

PLANNING FOR CONVENTIONS AND LARGE GROUPS

In the discussion of sales in Chapter 3 we mentioned some of the loss-prevention issues that can arise when conventions or large groups are booked. Large bookings are desirable because they generate substantial revenues for properties. Some hotels get more business of this kind than do others. Inasmuch as every business wants to be profitable, many inns understandably will actively solicit conventions and large groups. However, in doing so, from a security and loss-prevention perspective, a hotel may find itself on the horns of a dilemma. It wants to accommodate the conventioneers or persons in the large group without ignoring the comfort and needs of its other guests.

The problems posed by conventions or large groups will vary, depending largely on the particular organization or group that has booked space. For example, many organizations or groups will need nothing more in the way of security consideration than certain measures we took note of earlier in the text. For the most part they will be well behaved and pose no problems. However, other functions will involve organizations or groups whose behavior may do more than disturb other guests; it may result in damage to a hotel's assets. Two noteworthy examples have been cited, one in Washington D.C.

In both cases the host hotels, and most assuredly their other guests, were victimized by such aberrant behavior. However, hotels do not necessarily have to forego income generated by booking conventions or other large groups. It simply means that more attention has to be paid to detail both in selling space and assigning rooms for such bookings.

There is no reason that sales personnel should not make an effort to learn something about the history of groups whose business they are seeking. How have they behaved before? What has been the impact on other guests and guest services? Have they caused damage to hotel property? Have any special security measures been necessary? They also should be candid with groups that they are trying to book by asking questions about the nature of the event; have the sponsors encountered any particular problems in the past?

In reality, the answers to these questions should lead to a cost-benefit analysis: Will the benefits of booking this group outweigh what its presence may cost in other respects? If all the answers are favorable, there is no cause for concern. If any are not, however, can the issues be dealt with satisfactorily through the use of security personnel? Prior experience with a certain group by either the hotel attempting the sale or by others will dictate the answer. If it is in the negative, the inn's management may elect to pass on the booking. If it is in the affirmative, the cost of providing adequate security, whether by working the existing staff overtime or bringing in contract agency personnel to help, should be included in the total cost of the agreement signed by the sponsoring organization.

PROTECTING HOTEL ASSETS FROM GUESTS

To deny that some guests, however few, either steal from or damage hotel property would be naive. We have already taken note of ways in which the theft of keys, where still used, can be minimized. The theft of certain disposables, such as shoe-shine cloths, small sewing kits, bars of soap, and small bottles of shampoo, as souvenirs not only is to be expected but is also a legitimate part of overhead. However, significant damage to or the theft of other and more expensive items by guests can prove costly and have an impact on profits. Therefore, losses stemming from guest misconduct need to be addressed.

The realization that losses of this kind can and do occur is best illustrated by the fact that virtually all hotels and motels have taken steps to minimize the theft of television sets by bolting them to tables or incorporating them into cabinets or larger pieces of furniture. A property that had silver bed lamps on night tables found it necessary to have them bolted down to prevent their theft. Other hotels, victimized by the theft of such things as terry cloth bathrobes and towels, have taken to putting signs or tent cards in rooms informing guests that these items may be purchased. These measures are worth considering by inns that have not already adopted them.

Helpful as the foregoing measures are, they are not the only things that can be done. A first step in developing an effective approach to the problem requires lodging industry management to understand and accept the concept of security/loss prevention as an integral part of overall operations. In other words, managers should not try to solve the problems by either relying solely on security or ignoring it altogether. Instead, they need to recognize the fact that losses attributable to aberrant guest behavior resulting in property damage or theft are often best dealt with by housekeeping and, to a lesser degree, the bell and room service staffs. Then, too, to acknowledge the impossibility of totally preventing such losses is to be realistic; to decry any effort to at least try to minimize them is a sign of poor management.

The roles that can be played by housekeeping, the bell staff, and room service personnel in reducing the risk of loss with respect to room service setups was discussed in Chapter 3. Beyond that, the bell staff represents a logi-

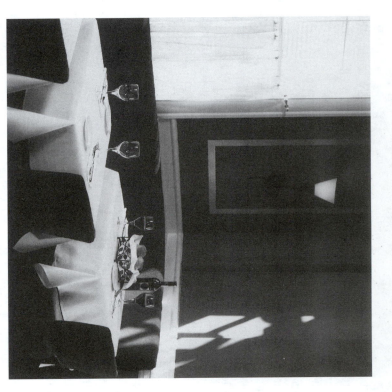

Anago, The Lenox Hotel—Boston

cal starting point in looking at ways to deal with other guest-related losses. For example, when helping newly registered guests to their rooms, they should be alert for bags that seem to be empty or unusually light. In this instance the front desk should be told as soon as possible, and the information should be relayed to the executive housekeeper. True, light or empty bags may signify nothing more than that the guest intends to shop while in town, but the possibility that they may be intended for the planned appropriation of hotel assets prior to departure should not be ignored.

Upon entering guest rooms the bell staff normally will take time to show guests where the room's various amenities are and how to use them. This also gives them an opportunity to quickly examine the room and ensure that all its furnishings are both in place and in good condition. Without being too obvious, a similar inspection should be made whenever they either collect or return laundry or dry-cleaning.

That housekeepers service their assigned rooms does not necessarily guarantee that all furnishings are accounted for and undamaged. Certainly they will notice if items with which they normally have contact are missing, such as bed linens and hand and bath towels. But what about terry cloth bathrobes hung in closets, drapes, or perhaps even hair dryers or coffee makers? Housekeepers should understand that servicing rooms includes making certain that all assets, of whatever kind, normally in those rooms are actually there and that they are not damaged. Discrepancies should be reported without delay to their supervisors, and both the executive housekeeper and front desk should be alerted. All supervisory room inspections should be made to ensure not only that rooms have been properly serviced but also that no assets are missing or in need of repair.

Making these multiple examinations of a room's contents can serve several purposes. Not only do they help maintain a high quality of service, but their frequency also helps to isolate the time frame within which thefts of or damage to assets may have occurred. This, in turn, makes it easier to identify the guest who was registered and, when appropriate, to ask for compensation for the loss that the hotel otherwise would have to absorb.

SUMMARY

Recognizing that without guests inns cannot survive, it behooves hotels and motels to provide a reasonable amount of protection to those guests and their personal property. However, there is not, and cannot be, a single industry-wide standard with regard to what is "reasonable." In reality, when guest are injured or suffer losses, the question of reasonableness too often is determined in a courtroom and by the totality of the circumstances.

The expression "Totality of The Circumstances" would include, among other things, a property's location, incident history, use of physical security, and both the presence and training of security personnel. It could even consider whether the victimized guest was cautioned about possible risks. Despite the absence of specific standards, but bearing in mind what constitutes "the totality of circumstances," it is not unreasonable to expect innkeepers to provide protection for their guests.

Perhaps of equal or greater concern is the realization that hotels and motels cannot be the absolute guarantors of their guests' security. On the contrary, they are limited in what they can do to protect them and their property because so many of the injuries and losses are attributable to guests' carelessness or negligence. The challenge for the industry is to educate guests with respect to their own roles in loss prevention.

Under normal conditions, using certain physical security measures, carefully screening applicants, properly training employees, and noting the offer of and refusal by a guest to take advantage of an inn's loss-prevention facilities may not eliminate claims. However, they can be mitigating factors insofar as their settlement is concerned.

Rarely will a property book so large a convention or other large group as to achieve 100 percent occupancy. That means two things: Depending on the group, the risk of damage to or loss of assets is ever present, and other guests still have to be accommodated. Consequently, before trying to sell such bookings, a cost-benefit analysis is worth considering.

It would be foolish to ignore the potential for the loss of or damage to an inn's assets or to assume that it is limited to major bookings. Other guests can contribute to the problem in their own ways. They can leave without paying their bills, deliberately or negligently damage assets, or steal assets of some value that will have to be replaced. To effectively confront these issues by preventing, or at least minimizing, the scope and magnitude of such losses requires innkeepers to integrate the security/loss-prevention model into all aspects of operations and involve a property's entire staff.

REVIEW QUESTIONS

1. What distinguishes the lodging industry from retailing with respect to its exposure to the public?

2. Why is insurance coverage by itself inadequate from a loss-prevention perspective when guests file claims?

3. At what point in time should innkeepers become concerned with the protection of their guests and their property?

4. Who is or should be responsible for protecting guests' bags when there is neither a bell staff not a door attendant?

5. What do hoteliers need to remember in creating programs for guest protection?

6. With what employees should the guest-protection effort begin?

7. How can front-desk personnel assist with loss prevention for both guests and their employers?

8. In reality, who has or should have the primary responsibility for the protection of guests and their property? Why?

9. In what ways can guests be educated for their own benefit to help prevent losses?

10. Are losses attributable to guests confined to only conventions or large groups?

General

The CD Motor Lodge is an 86-room property located at the junction of two main high-ways, one an interstate, in Small Town U.S.A., a community of about 75,000. Guest rooms are in three two-story buildings; the lobby and front office, coffee shop, restaurant, and two lounges are in a fourth. It has two main function rooms, one in building three and a larger one in the building housing the front office. Guests park on two sides of the property. A high occupancy rate is maintained year-round.

Physical Security

Design and Layout/Access/Technology

The four buildings are connected by enclosed walkways, resulting in a U-shaped configu-ration around an open-air swimming pool and patio. Each guest room building has two floors; the fourth building is a modified split-level with a basement, in which are the back-of-the-house facilities, a sauna for guest use, and George's, a combination lounge and discotheque. The lobby, front desk, and general manager's office are on the second level; and the third, which also has the enclosed walkway and principal function room, consists of a coffee shop, the kitchen, the dining room, and a service bar. The Stonewall Lounge is on a fourth level.

That this property historically has had virtually no losses due to inadequate security does not mean that the potential for such problems can be ignored. The major concerns are (a) the ease with which people can enter and leave buildings due to the number of un-secured access doors, (b) the total absence of any safe-deposit boxes for guest and staff use, (c) no protection for the front-desk cashier in case of an attempted robbery, and (d) staff complacency that assumes guaranteed immunity from security problems since none have occurred to date.

In light of the property's history, it appears that implementing some of the sugges-tions that follow can be deferred until a greater need actually exists. However, the imple-mentation of others should be considered now.

Access control is virtually nonexistent. What does exist consists of the following: The knob on the outside of the single receiving door has been removed, and the door is closed and locked except when actually in use; the Stonewall Lounge's emergency door is secured with a fire lock; some doors to outlets and the pool, when secured, are locked with chains and key-operated padlocks or keyed locks. All exterior doors to guest room buildings have panic hardware, always in the unlocked position.

Moving the receiving door's hinges from outside to the inside, or at least pinning them to make their removal harder, would improve protection. So would replacing all ex-isting key-operated padlocks with changeable-combination padlocks with shrouded shackles. Change keys for the latter should be kept in the general manager's safe and combinations given only to those whose need to know is absolute. Exposed screw heads on hasps where padlocks are used should be replaced with half-headed screws.

If, as reported, there have been no real problems with the theft of hotel property from guest rooms, skips, room burglaries, or assaults on guests, the use of panic hardware on exterior doors can be continued, but the practice should be closely monitored. However, the first sign of any change should warrant considering the installation of alarmed fire locks that, upon any unauthorized opening, would send an audiovisual signal to the front desk.

The few guest requests for safe-deposit boxes are handled by giving guests standard safe-deposit box envelopes, a receipt for their property, and putting their valuables in the general manager's safe. Reportedly, he alone has the combination.

The lack of proper safe-deposit boxes can pose problems. Despite using envelopes and receipts, what impact does storing guests' valuables have on the inn's liability should something happen to them? If only the general manager has the safe combination, guests who have stored valuables can be inconvenienced in her absence. On the other hand, even if only one other employee is given the combination, the risk of loss increases. These points apply equally to the way in which hotel keys and outlet receipts now are safe-guarded.

Safe-deposit boxes in great numbers are not needed. However, installing possibly six in the vicinity of the key rack, for guest and hotel use, is worth considering.

There are fire and sprinkler alarms, but no holdup alarms. The front-desk cashier's location in relation to the main entrance, parking area, and two main highways for escape means that the threat of an armed robbery should not be ignored. Nevertheless, the likelihood that one will happen is regarded as improbable simply because there has not been one. This rationalization is naive inasmuch as a competing property, directly across one of the highways, has been victimized on several occasions.

Although the nature of this hotel, its guests, and the hours and activities of its lounges make locking the lobby doors impractical, the following three things can be done to improve security and help the police if a robbery occurs:

1. Install a pressure-released type of holdup alarm, linked directly to police headquarters, in the cash register drawer. If this connection cannot be made, tie the alarm into a reputable central station alarm office.

2. Make certain that a packet of bills, whose serial numbers are recorded and kept in a safe place, is always on top of the pressure switch and is to be used only in case of a robbery.

3. Install a time-lapse camera directly behind the cashier's position, tied into and activated simultaneously with the alarm. This type of camera would prevent wasting film, eliminate confusion, and provide the police with a robber's photograph.

Insofar as technology is concerned, while none of the food refrigeration units have temperature alarms, their installation should be considered. This would reduce the risk of spoilage and waste in case of a problem in any cooler that caused an unexpected, and possibly prolonged, drop in any unit's temperature.

Lighting; Locks and Locking Devices

Interior and exterior lighting, parking lots included, is satisfactory. No changes are necessary.

Some comments have already been made with respect to locks. The Best lock system permits easy core rotation whenever any possible compromise is suspected. However, the current practice of key controls and core rotation must be continued in order to ensure the maintenance of the lock system's integrity.

Guest Rooms

Doors have spring bolts and chains; they do not have peepholes. Room keys are tagged. Replacement keys are made and lock cores rotated regularly by a licensed, bonded, local lock-smith. "Do Not Disturb" and early makeup signs are available for guest use.

The latter should be modified to eliminate the early makeup portion. Such requests usually mean guests are not in their rooms and can encourage unauthorized entries. This, in turn, can result in thefts, even though reportedly none have so far occurred.

Garment hangers fit into a slotted metal bracket that is attached to a pole; they are not the kind normally found in homes. Thus this is a saving to the inn.

Guest protection would be improved if peepholes were installed in all doors. A further enhancement would be to angle the slides into which chains are inserted and remove excess links so that chains are at maximum tightness when in place as doors are opened.

In the interest of both economics and security, key tags should be removed and room numbers stamped on keys without further identification. Absent any assurance that guests who take keys will return them by mail, replacements are made by the local lock-smith; this is an expense. If keys are returned, the hotel absorbs the cost of postage, another expense, and it also results in a surplus that makes accountability more difficult and adds to the risk of security breaches. The general manager expressed the opinion that the owner is considering a major renovation. If so, conversion to an electronic or computerized system is suggested.

Storage Facilities

Except for the lack of temperature alarms in refrigerated units, as previously noted, physical security appears to be satisfactory. However, the liquor storeroom's controls would benefit from changing the existing lock to a time-recording one.

Parking Facilities

While lighting is adequate, and in the absence of any reported thefts, vandalism, or assaults, changes are not suggested at this time, restripping the almost invisible lines would make parking easier for guests. Nevertheless, the facilities should be closely watched, and if problems do arise, thought should be given to installing two closed-circuit television cameras in all-weather housings, with pan and tilt, with monitoring done at the front desk.

Administration and Operations

Personnel Practices

A standard application form is used, but there is no uniformity in preemployment screening; neither are viable applicants given physical examinations. The human resources manager relies on department heads to do their own screening and hiring.

Some department heads hire on the basis of employees' recommendations of friends without further inquiry. Others limit themselves to contacting the previous employer and asking "personal police contacts" if applicants have criminal records, the names of personal references are not even requested. Personnel files are inadequately maintained, and there is no employee identification system.

The only orientation for new employees, given by their respective department heads, focuses solely on the department's work. The property's overall policies are not discussed, nor is there any mention of security.

The application form used is inadequate and needs to be revised; preemployment screening needs to be improved. Applications should ask more detailed questions about prior employment, including dates, salary or wages paid, supervisors' names, and reasons for leaving the job. The names, addresses, and telephone numbers of three personal references should be requested.

Preemployment screening should include a careful review of the application. An explanation should be sought from the applicant with respect to any unaccounted-for periods of time and frequent job changes, especially if the latter indicate taking positions for less pay and/or more difficulty in commuting to work.

All previous employers should be asked to verify the information provided by the applicant. In addition, even if unwilling to say anything more, they should be asked if they would be willing to rehire the applicant. Personal references should be contacted. On occasion they may say things about the applicant that to them are positive, yet the information may raise questions about suitability in the prospective employer's mind. Inasmuch as the use of "personal police contacts" for criminal history information violates the state's laws on the subject, this practice should be discontinued immediately.

Physical examinations for viable applicants, or at least for new hires, warrants consideration. The possibility cannot be ignored that an applicant for a food service job might have a communicable disease or that applicants for the bell staff of storekeepers jobs might have preexisting conditions that could be aggravated by the nature of their work. However, it must be clearly understood that if such examinations are agreed to, they must not be used to circumvent the provisions of the Americans with Disabilities Act.

All new employees should undergo orientation, notwithstanding the fact that some may have lodging industry experience. The latter is no assurance that learned habits are acceptable in their new jobs. With this in mind, orientation should first deal with the inn's overall policies, procedures, and work rules. Next, the security/loss-prevention program should be discussed, including what it consists of, its importance to the property and consequently to the staff, and the need for employee participation and cooperation. Individual department heads should then discuss their respective operations and what they expect of their staffs.

Despite the relatively small number of employees, people are on duty around the clock, as in any hotel. To expect every member of the staff to recognize all the other employees is unrealistic, uniforms notwithstanding. Furthermore, from the standpoint of guest protection, housekeeping and engineering uniforms are not unique. Arrangements should be made to issue photo identification badges to all employees and to have them worn by housekeeping and engineering personnel while on duty.

Guest Credit/Cashiering/Banking Practices

Guest checks in outlets do not have space for guests' names, room numbers, and signatures. On occasion this has confused guests and cashiers alike and resulted in incorrect postings. The checks need to be changed in this respect.

During the survey only one outlet cashier called the front desk in an attempt to confirm registration for a signed check. Admittedly, at times an outlet customer has given a room number and signed with an illegible signature. This potentially costly problem can be minimized if persons who sign checks and give room numbers are politely asked by the wait staff to show their keys.

Otherwise, cashiering practices appeared to be satisfactory in ringing up charges and presenting bills promptly and in closing register drawers between transactions. The night auditor should continue to zero all registers and change their tapes.

The general manager does all banking, varying the time of day but not the route taken. She also uses a standard bank carrying bag when making all deposits and withdrawals. Every effort should be made to vary the route taken, not merely the time. Her safety also would be improved if something less obvious than the bank carrying bag was used when going to and from the bank.

Inventories/Receiving and Stores

Food, beverage, and housekeeping inventories are taken monthly. The general manager takes the liquor inventory; the executive chef and the housekeeper take the food and housekeeping inventories respectively. The chef also does all food receiving and storekeeping. Requisitions for the withdrawal of supplies are not used.

Practically speaking, in view of the property's size and staff there is little room for change in these procedures. Nevertheless, it would be helpful if the general manager took food and housekeeping inventories at random intervals and, on a regular but random basis, verified both the quality and quantity of supplies being delivered.

In addition, and despite the property's size and informality, it would also be prudent to adopt some form of written requisition for all department heads to use in withdrawing supplies. They would provide the controller with a basis for reconciling sales, purchases, and inventories, something that does not now exist.

Garbage and Trash Disposal

The executive chef or members of his staff check garbage daily and frequently recover flatware or other items that were disposed of carelessly. This practice can pay for itself and should be continued.

Neither the executive housekeeper nor anyone from her staff regularly checks trash disposal. However, she admits that on those occasions when an inspection has been made, certain assets, such as washcloths or nearly full furniture polish or soap containers, have been recovered. This suggests that daily trash inspections would be justified.

Food and Beverages

For the most part, current practices seem to be acceptable. Liquor sold in both lounges is measured; this should be continued. However, liquor bottles are not coded even though there are two lounges and a service bar. For improved inventory control and to reduce the risk of bartenders occasionally selling from their own "private stock," a code system should be adopted.

Both lounges, the coffee shop, and the dining room seem to be well maintained insofar as housekeeping is concerned, and service is good except for the fact that the presentation of checks for coffee shop counter service is very slow. Since patrons who choose to sit at the counter tend to be in more of a hurry than others, their checks should be presented promptly.

Housekeeping

The executive housekeeper's small office also serves as the department's operating storeroom, and as a result supplies for daily use are kept to a minimum. While this is good, it does not justify allowing housekeepers to enter the office and help themselves to supplies instead of their being issued by the executive housekeeper. This practice should be changed, and hereafter all housekeeping supplies should be issued on an exchange basis.

Linen closets are frequently left unlocked, with doors open, although no housekeepers are to be seen on the floor. This encourages guests to "borrow," if not steal, especially when the swimming pool is open. This can have an impact on laundry as well as linen replacement costs. Consequently, linen closets should be closed and locked unless a housekeeper is actually present.

Guest rooms are not provided with plastic bags into which wet bathing suits can be placed. This, too, can lead to the loss of bath towels when guests who take a last-minute swim need something into which to put a wet bathing suit. Putting plastic bags with the inn's name imprinted thereon in guest rooms, especially when the pool is available to guests, should be considered. The cost of doing so would be considerably less than that of replacing bath towels.

Engineering

During this survey the engineer was seen in various parts of the hotel, including the lobby and food service areas, in his undershirt. This does little for the property's image and calls for corrective action by the general manager.

He also habitually leaves the maintenance shop for extended periods without closing and locking the door. Aside from possible security problems, this could have an impact on certain operating and safety considerations. The shop door should be closed and locked whenever he is absent.

Security Department

That a department as such is unnecessary does not mean security is unimportant. The general manager should designate one employee for each shift, especially when she personally is not at the hotel, who will be responsible for making whatever decisions are necessary for the security and safety of the inn, its guests, and employees.

There are no security records; consequently, no data base is available for either planning purposes or a possible defense in the event of litigation arising from a security-related incident. All such incidents, including fires and bomb threats, should be reported to the general manager in writing and reviewed periodically for possibly emerging patterns that would suggest a need for additional loss-prevention measures.

Emergency Procedures

Fire extinguishers are not multipurpose, nor are any employees trained in their use. This can pose problems. The hotel would be better served by (a) replacing the existing extinguishers with multipurpose units and (b) asking the local fire department to train a representative number of employees in their proper use.

In addition, two extinguishers, near rooms 311 and 335, were missing. They should be replaced immediately. None of the extinguishers in buildings two and three had dated tags to show when they were last inspected. This, too, needs to be corrected.

There are no written emergency procedures. They need to be written down and copies given to all employees. The following are among the items to be included:

1. All fires, regardless of size or location, should be reported immediately to the fire department and then to the general manager or, in her absence, to her designee. Pending the fire department's arrival, when the senior fire officer present will make all decisions related to the fire, the general manager or her designee must make an initial evacuation decision based on the fire's size, location, volume of smoke, and risk of spread. Meanwhile, appropriate action should be initiated to contain the fire and prevent its spread.

2. All bomb threats must be reported to the general manager without delay. She will decide if the police and/or fire departments should be called and whether or not to evacuate the property. The decision should be based on an assessment of the information given to her by the threat's recipient, most likely a telephone operator. Thus it is essential that the latter get as much information as possible about the exact time, place, and reason for the bombing; type of explosive used; the caller's sex, possible age, accent or speech impediments, voice pitch; use of idiomatic or regional expressions; familiarity with the property or any of its employees or guests; background noises; possible use of a pay telephone and any indication as to whether the call is local or long distance. The call's length can be a factor—a brief call most often being a hoax. However, under no circumstances should the length of the call be the sole basis for an evacuation decision.

3. Regardless of evacuation, unless an actual explosion seems to be imminent the entire property should be searched by employees since they are most familiar with the inn and best able to detect anything unusual. Each department should search its own area, with housekeeping also handling guest floors. Departments with staff present in excess of those needed for their own area searches—such as dining room and kitchen—should make the surplus available to help search stairwells, locker rooms, public and parking areas.

4. If suspicious-looking objects are found, they should not be touched, the area should be secured, and the general manager notified. If she has not already called the police, she will do so now, evacuate the affected area, and move the evacuees far enough away from the secured area to minimize the risk of injury from flying debris or glass if an explosion occurs.

5. Attention must be paid to evacuating guests with physical disabilities, especially those on the second floor of any building. Folios of disabled guests should be red-tagged when they register and their names, room numbers, and nature of disability noted so that the information can be made available to the police and fire departments and special attention can be given to their evacuation.

6. If evacuation is ordered, regardless of the reason, and time permitting, personnel responsible for the property's assets should make every effort to properly secure them before leaving the premises.

SECURITY SURVEY NUMBER 3

General

The Excel Motor Hotel is a property with 205 rooms on fifteen floors and a basement at 711 Memory Lane, Academe, U.S.A., a city of about 135,000 within a metropolitan area of over 1.5 million people. The hotel comprises a specialty restaurant, two lounges, an outdoor swimming pool on the fifth floor, function rooms, and a limited number of parking spaces on its Memory Lane side plus tiered parking on its east side. Close to two major academic institutions and several industrial firms, it enjoys a respectable occupancy rate throughout the year with seasonal increases, particularly from mid-May through mid-September.

Physical Security

Design and Layout/Access/Technology

The tiered parking area is the primary parking facility. Bordered by Francis St. to the east, Prince St. to the north, and an adjacent shopping center to the south, these three sides are protected, either in whole or in part, by a cyclone fence topped with barbed wire strands that angle inward on the east and south sides. Cars enter and leave via a ramp, reportedly controlled by an attendant 24 hours a day, seven days a week, assisted by a chain and/or bar, depending on the hour.

In theory, foot traffic to this parking space is limited to the ramp or two doors on the hotel's east side, one of which is locked from 5 P.M. to 6 A.M. daily. In practice, trespassers, car thieves and vandals included, admittedly have entered by either climbing or cutting the fence, particularly on the south side, lower parking level.

People can enter and leave the building on two levels by way of multiple doors with little real control. A basement door leading to the main parking area is secured with a fire lock from about 5 P.M. to 6 A.M. All other arrivals and departures are at the lobby level on the first floor. The main doors—two sets of double doors with a space between them—are never secured; neither is the door behind the general manager's office leading to the parking area.

A perimeter door next to and behind the bell captain's desk, as well as the receiving and compactor doors, are locked daily from about 5 P.M. to 6 A.M. An emergency door with a fire lock admittedly is left open on occasion, but it is checked and, if unlocked, it is secured at 5 P.M. The door near the bell captain's desk, when secured, is protected with a fire lock; the compactor and receiving doors are locked with padlocks. There are also three basically unprotected doors leading to the walkway on the Memory Lane side, one from the Publican Lounge and two from the currently unused Barque Lounge.

The telephone equipment and electrical rooms, engineering, housekeeping, food, beverage, and general storerooms, a locker room, and a time clock for employees other than those employed in the Red Rose Grille, are in the basement. Thought is being given to installing a laundry near the liquor storeroom. The basement is accessed via fire stairs, two passenger elevators, and a service elevator that does not go above the third floor.

The door to engineering has a dead lock; the shop is relatively small, and access is controlled by the engineer when he is present. However, he occasionally absents himself for several minutes without closing and locking the door. With the inn on a key-lock system and the key masters, blanks, and key-making machine in the shop, this practice is an unacceptable risk and should be discontinued.

A door near engineering, which leads to other back-of-the-house facilities, is secured with a keyed padlock at 5 P.M. daily, but screwheads for the hardware are exposed. They should be replaced with half-headed screws to make their removal more difficult.

Housekeeping's access controls are satisfactory with an alarmed door that also is on a timer. However, supplies are at risk because they are close to the department's employees' lounge and partially concealed from anyone's view. Locked metal storage or supply cabinets would help reduce the risk of loss of housekeeping supplies.

A Dutch door controls access to the food storeroom. This door, and those to dry and liquor stores, have dead locks and are alarmed as protection against possible burglaries. The liquor storeroom door is also secured with a keyed padlock. None of these storerooms have temperature alarms, although the refrigerated units do.

Temperature alarms should be installed in the food and liquor storerooms, with a time-recording lock for the liquor storeroom. The latter would improve security without interfering with operations by identifying those who enter and indicating how long they stay. This would be most helpful from an accountability standpoint when there is an after-hours need for access.

Thought is being given to installing a laundry. If this is done, access should be controlled via a Dutch door.

On the first floor is the front desk (reception, cashier, and telephone switchboard), behind which are two offices. One is the general manager's. It can be entered through a door off a short corridor that leads to an always unlocked door to the main parking area. The other, designated for reservations but also used for counting money, like the general manager's, has a large window facing the same parking area. The window is lightly coated, reportedly to prevent observation of the money-counting process. The door from the corridor to the two offices is supposedly locked after 10 P.M.

In addition, the first floor has function rooms, the sales office, the Publican Lounge, and public toilets. The Barque Lounge space now is used to handle function overflow, and space formerly used as a coffee shop serves as a temporary storeroom.

The Red Rose Grille and Lounge, main kitchen, and four guest rooms are on the second floor; eleven guest rooms, main ballroom, a banquet kitchen, and function liquor storeroom are on the third. Floors four and five have guest rooms, but the former also has a housekeeper's closet for night storage and emergency supplies, with a linen chute inside the closet. The swimming pool is on five. Guest rooms are on all the remaining floors. The building has three fire towers, only two of which extend to all floors; the third goes only to the base of the pool.

Alarms

In addition to the alarmed spaces already cited, the pump and boiler room doors also have contact alarms. There are also smoke alarms and fire alarm pull boxes throughout the hotel. When activated, all the inn's alarms are received at the front desk. All these installations show an awareness of and concern for security and safety.

Nevertheless, there is no holdup alarm for the front-desk cashier's use in case of a robbery. This needs to be corrected. The installation of a pressure-type alarm in the cash drawer is suggested. It would be activated only when "bait money" (a small packet of bills whose serial numbers have been prerecorded and kept by the controller) is given to a robber. If the police department agrees, the alarm should go directly to headquarters, considering the latter's proximity to the hotel.

Parking

Due to problems of vandalism and theft of automobiles parked in the main area, parking attendants are now employed on an around-the-clock basis. This represents an annual cost of over $65,000 for a staff that may help prevent thefts, but whose impact on vandalism and trespass may be negligible. Several viable but less costly alternatives should be explored.

If possible, one such measure would be to reverse the barbed wire atop the fence so that it would angle away from, rather than into, the area. Whether this can be done within the confines of the hotel's property line will have to be examined. Regardless of this, a zoned alarm system for the fence, including the section adjacent to the shopping center, is worth considering. Monitored at the switchboard, it would indicate the access point, thus initiating a prompt response by either employees or the police.

Extending the fence line at the top of the main parking area ramp, as needed on the Memory Lane side, would be helpful if accompanied by the installation of a heavy duty metal arm at the ramp entrance/exit. To enter, guests would take a ticket from a dispenser; this would elevate the arm. Tickets would be redeemed for a specially designed slug, issued by the front-desk cashier, that, when deposited, would raise the arm and allow cars to exit.

A closed-circuit television camera with a 45-degree pan and tilt and a high-density spotlight focusing on the ramp entrance/exit would be an additional deterrent. It should be mounted in an all-weather, theft-proof housing on a corner of the building facing the ramp. The monitor should be portable to allow its use at either the switchboard or some point behind the front desk.

The foregoing combined measures represent an expense. However, it would be a one-time cost that could be amortized overtime. Their adoption would improve main parking protection, help combat the existing theft, vandalism, and trespass problems, and properly used, save the money now being spent for full-time attendants.

Another matter is space utilization. A combination of weather, traffic, and carelessness result in wasted space. Not important when occupancy is down, it can be crucial when it is up. Markings not clearly visible should be repainted, and signs should be posted at regular intervals asking drivers to park within the lines.

During the survey, two automobiles, whose ownership could not be determined, were parked near Memory Lane on the receiving door side despite the fact that other spaces were available, and there did not seem to be a reason for their being where they were. The risks stemming from this are self-evident, especially if they are employees' cars. A "No Parking at Any Time" sign should be posted along the entire length of this side of the building, and the policy should be enforced.

Access Controls

The inn was robbed twice within the past year. Its location relative to city streets that are available as escape routes increases the need for improved access control; therefore, securing both innermost sets of lobby doors from about midnight to 6 A.M. warrants consideration. One set can be secured with panic hardware to deny ingress but not egress; the other, with an electric lock with an emergency fail/safe. The latter would be controlled at the front desk, with the aid of a fixed-position, closed-circuit television camera in a theft-proof housing and speaker microphone, mounted in the vestibule.

Trespassing neighborhood children admittedly have entered via the main lobby doors and gotten to guest floors. Turning the bell captain's desk 90 degrees to the right would help reduce, if not eliminate, the problem by making it much easier to see people before they reach the lobby. An added benefit would be the bell staff's ability to react more quickly in helping newly arrived guests carrying luggage.

It is unrealistic to consider securing the lobby doors while ignoring the risk posed by leaving the parking lot door near the general manager's office always unlocked. This practice is largely for the staff's convenience. This door should be secured with a fire lock from at least 6 P.M. to 6 A.M. daily.

Although the emergency exit near receiving, equipped with a fire lock, is locked at 5 P.M., it is admittedly left open on occasion. Considering how close the door is to both the back of the house and the Memory Lane parking spaces, this door should be secured at all times. If there is a valid reason for opening it, other than an emergency, the door should be unlocked by a member of management who is present for the duration of the opening and who relocks the door thereafter.

To improve perimeter protection and reduce the risk of larcenies of hotel assets, the three doors leading to the walkway parallel to Memory Lane should either be alarmed or have fire locks. If alarmed, monitoring should be audiovisual at the front desk. At present anyone with access to the Barque Grille or Publican Lounge can easily take assets, such as furniture, for transfer to a car parked in one of the Memory Lane spaces.

Miscellaneous

Parenthetically speaking, room television sets are neither anchored to table tops nor are they alarmed. Three were stolen, albeit by employees, within the past year. The cost of alarms and anchors should be explored, and the least expensive deterrent should be installed.

Internally, in view of the location of the safe, the safe-deposit boxes, and the use of the reservations office for counting money, keeping the corridor door to the front office locked at all times deserves consideration. An electric lock, with its release mechanism at the switchboard, is recommended. Thus only those with a real need would be allowed to enter; others would be kept out.

The glass window in the reservations office should be replaced with Lexan (or its equivalent) and completely recoated to prevent outside observation of money counting. The door to the room should be closed and locked from inside whenever counting takes place.

The Publican's entrance is directly opposite the front desk, but its door to the Memory Lane walkway is neither alarmed nor otherwise secured. This can be risky, especially at night when front-desk employees may be busy or distracted. The idea of installing a tape-switch alarm or something similar, set to activate only when the lounge is closed, should be explored.

Locks and Locking Devices

Back of the House

While the entire hotel is on the key-lock system, some keyed padlocks are also used to supplement back-of-the-house security. All keyed door locks have changeable cores. Only as long as keys are tightly controlled and accounted for, and cores are changed at the slightest suggestion that security has been compromised, can the system be retained. Shortcomings in either or both routines will invalidate the system's integrity and require installation of more secure locks or locking devices.

Combination padlocks (with shrouded shackles where appropriate), with the change key kept by the general manager, would offer better protection than the padlocks now used. Lost keys require new locks, but being able to easily and quickly change combinations would make this unnecessary. As a result, the inn would enjoy better protection and benefit from the savings realized by not having to buy new padlocks.

Several doors on which padlocks are used have hasps, but the screwheads holding them in place are easily accessible, and the value of the locks is markedly decreased. Hasps on metal doors and/or door frames should be spot-welded; half-headed screws should be used for those attached to wood.

Guest Rooms

Spring locks and chains are used on the doors; tags are not attached to keys. Doors do not have peepholes. "Do Not Disturb" and early makeup signs are on inside doorknobs. While keys frequently have to be replaced due to losses, their not having tags is both a security and an economic advantage, and the practice should be continued.

Peepholes are inexpensive and easily installed. This should be done in the interest of better guest protection.

Spring locks do not provide optimum protection, but until such time as a decision is made to replace them with an electronic system, a program of regularly scheduled core rotation should be instituted. Cores also should be changed whenever keys are reported missing.

Chain locks should be realigned and angled so chains on opened doors are taut. All excess links should be removed so there is only enough play in the chains to allow them to be inserted in slides when doors are fully closed.

Use of the early makeup sign should be eliminated in favor of tent cards advising guests who want early makeup to call housekeeping. Displaying early makeup signs tells burglars that rooms are sold and that the guests most likely are out.

Personnel Practices and Procedures

The inn uses a standard application form, and despite its having a human resources manager, department heads do their own screening and hiring. Consequently, there is no uniformity in preemployment screening. It ranges from rather perfunctory to relatively thorough. As an example, one department head calls only one former employer, asks no questions about eligibility for reemployment, and contacts only one personal reference. Another asks the eligibility question but contacts no personal references.

The current application needs to be revised and preemployment screening improved. More detailed questions about previous jobs are needed, including dates of employment, beginning and ending salary wages, supervisors' names, and reasons for leaving. So are the names, addresses, and telephone numbers of at least three personal references.

Before sending applicants to department heads for interviews, human resources should carefully review all applications and determine an applicant's whereabouts for all blank periods of time. Furthermore, frequent job changes should be explained, especially if they tend to indicate taking positions for less pay and/or more difficulty in getting to and from work. Only viable candidates should be sent to department heads for additional interviews.

Department heads interested in hiring someone should contact all previous employers and verify the data provided by the applicant. Among the questions asked should be one regarding the individual's eligibility for reemployment. Personal references also should be contacted. They occasionally say things that they view as positive, yet their comments may raise legitimate questions about suitability in a prospective employer's mind.

An orientation checklist is used for new employees. The general manager tries to orient all new employees, and individual department heads are asked to provide additional orientation with respect to their department's work. In addition, the executive hostess gives her staff a tour of the entire property. Unfortunately, the roles to be played by employees in loss prevention is not part of the program.

Orientation for new employees should continue but be expanded to include a discussion of what security is and how employee involvement can contribute to loss prevention. No one should be excused because of prior lodging industry experience. Practices acceptable to other employers may not be acceptable in their new jobs. Additional benefits can be realized if department heads periodically discuss security with all their personnel at staff meetings.

A good illustration of the need for orientation and training occurred in a busy Red Rose Grille one morning during this survey. At 8:14 A.M. an emergency exit alarm, accidentally activated and sounding in the kitchen, was heard in the dining room until it was deactivated about seven minutes later. However, upon first hearing the alarm a bus boy walked from the dining area toward the kitchen loudly chanting, "Fire, fire, fire!" Despite guests being upset while the sound continued for a long time, the staff ignored the situation. Not one member of the staff made any effort to calm and reassure guests or to tell them what to do if there actually was a fire.

Employees are not issued any form of hotel identification other than their uniforms. To assume that all employees know each other is unrealistic, and with respect to guest protection, housekeeping and engineering uniforms are not really unique. All members of the staff should be issued photo identification badges, in addition to the name plates now worn, and the former should be worn by all housekeeping and engineering personnel while on duty.

Parcel passes are not required of employees carrying things from the inn. However, the executive hostess checks packages being taken by her staff, and both the food and beverage and general managers periodically inspect lockers. Nevertheless, a number of employees are really untouched by either procedure. As an additional deterrent, department heads should regularly but randomly inspect all parcels being taken from the property by employees. For optimum effect the inspection points should vary. If this suggestion is implemented, it is imperative that there not be any form of discrimination in terms of the inspections and that all members of the staff be treated the same.

Key and Combination Controls

The only combination is the one on the safe outside the general manager's office. The general manager and the controller have the combination. However, to the best of the general manager's knowledge the combination has never been changed, although there have been changes among those with access to the safe. The combination should be changed without delay, and at any future time when a person who knows the combination no longer needs it.

Back-of-the-house and housekeepers' keys seem to be adequately protected after hours, but hanging housekeeping keys and engineering masters on open boards is unwise. Security would be much improved if these keys were kept in small, metal, key cabinets hung on walls in their respective departments and kept locked except when access is needed. The cabinet keys should be controlled by those who need access.

There is no meaningful inventory of keys to guest rooms or areas at the back of the house. On occasion the front office manager inventories keys, but for all practical purposes the results are meaningless.

An inventory should now be taken of all keys. Thereafter, room keys should be inventoried daily and those for the back of the house at least weekly. Cashiers and the bell staff should ask departing guests for their keys. In addition, a small but clearly marked locked box for keys, secured to a big and heavy object at or near the front desk, could be useful for guests who have paid their bills. This would be an improvement over having them leave them atop the front desk counter where they can be picked up by virtually anyone.

The foregoing concerns and the rate at which room keys reportedly have to be reproduced are worrisome. Notwithstanding the ease with which lock cores can be rotated, the high volume of lost or misplaced keys prevents truly effective rotation. Therefore, the earlier recommendation for consideration of a new, electronic lock system is reaffirmed.

Guest Credit/Cashiering Practices

In general there does not seem to by any reason for changes. The night auditor should continue to zero registers and change their tapes.

For the most part cashiers have their own banks, but this is not true of lounges when more than one bartender is working. However, weighed against the risk, the cost of changing this particular practice cannot be justified at this time. As a result, management must exercise constant vigilance to ensure accountability for all cashiers' banks.

Food and beverage outlet guests frequently sign their checks and enter a room number, but no attempt is made to verify the fact that the person is registered. Thus nothing prevents someone who is not registered from signing and entering a room number; losses have admittedly occurred. Continuing this practice can mean additional losses. Guests who charge should be asked to show their room keys, and their numbers should be checked against check entries.

Banking is done by either the general or front-office manager using a green bank bag with the bank's name clearly imprinted thereon. That the bank is more than a mile away adds to the risk involved with this practice despite their effort to avoid a pattern by using different automobiles. There would be less risk if, in addition to not using the same car, they varied the times of day and routes taken to and from the bank. Of equal or greater importance, they need to use something less conspicuous than the green bank bag when going to or from the bank—possibly a brief or attaché case.

Inventories, Receiving, and Stores

Food and beverage and housekeeping inventories are taken monthly. In addition, the food and beverage manager occasionally takes a weekly inventory while the executive housekeeper takes frequent floor counts.

Despite the basic acceptability of these practices, their main drawback is that those accountable for these assets are also involved with the inventories. This situation can be unfair to them and the hotel in case of discrepancies. A regular inventory schedule should be established for each department, with the controller actively participating in a prescribed number of rounds during the calendar year.

Receiving and storekeeping are handled by the steward. The latter checks all deliveries for quality and quantity; so does the food and beverage manager on a random but regular basis. All stores, and particularly foodstuffs, are issued on a rotating first in, first out basis. None are issued without written, dated, and signed requisitions, and distribution to departments is acknowledged with a receipt from the appropriate department head. The only exception to the requisition procedure involves foodstuffs delivered to the kitchen in response to a requisition from the executive chef. There does not seem to be any reason for change in theses practices.

Garbage and Trash Disposal

As the general manager secures certain perimeter doors at 5 P.M., he also spot-checks trash collected near the compactor door. The steward inspects trash and garbage every morning before he disposes of it. These checks should continue.

In addition, although the steward's garbage inspections have been useful in recovering carelessly discarded silverware and, on occasion, the attempted theft of foodstuffs, he is untrained in detecting other disposals that, while unrelated to theft, may have a bearing on food costs. As a result, the hotel might benefit from regular but random observation of the steward's inspections by both the general and food and beverage managers.

Food and Beverages

In the steward's absence the executive chef receives all food deliveries. In doing so he satisfies himself with respect to the quality and quantity. The executive chef prepares all requisitions for stores, and unless he is too busy with preparation, he checks what is sent to the kitchen. Preparation is based on a combination of forecasts and standard Red Rose Grille recipes. There is no reason for change.

The food and beverage manager and the steward are the only ones with access to liquor stores. All bottles are coded, and liquor is issued only on a bottle-for-bottle exchange basis. Each of the hotel's bars has its own bar stock, which is checked by the food and beverage manager three or four times a week. Changes in these procedures are unnecessary at this time.

Liquor for all drinks was measured, but in the Red Rose Grille's lounge the bartender, in serving guests at the bar, did not always serve a first drink on a fresh cocktail napkin. This suggests indifference, false economy, and sloppy housekeeping that reflects adversely on the hotel's image and can affect sales. This needs to be remedied by proper instruction to all bartenders.

A server in the Red Rose Grille did not ask if a guest wanted a cocktail before dinner, wine or beer with dinner, dessert, coffee or tea, or an after-dinner drink. Some diners may not want any of the foregoing, but others who might not take the initiative nevertheless might order in response to a suggestion. Consequently, failing to ask diners if they want these "extras" represents a potential loss of sales. Again, servers need to be instructed with regard to this matter.

Housekeeping

Aside from previously made recommendations, no other changes seem warranted at this time.

Bell Staff

The bell captain always cautions guests arriving in automobiles to not "leave anything valuable, visible." This often prompts guests to ask if there is a problem protecting guests' cars, to which he answers "occasionally."

This answer could have an impact on the inn's liability if an incident occurs since it implies knowledge without regard for suitable preventive measures other than a verbal warning to guests. The bell captain and staff should be instructed to simply point out that it is merely a suggestion for the guests' benefit and that the hotel has taken steps to try to prevent anything from happening. This is a factual statement, and further improvements were recommended in an earlier section of this report.

Sales

Recognizing that certain functions may necessitate protection of guests' property, the sales staff advises sponsors to make their own arrangements. This may relieve the hotel of liability, but it ignores the possible need to protect the hotel's assets and guest who are not involved with the function.

All functions should be evaluated on their own merits, and placing the responsibility for security on the sponsors of those that may need special attention is a sound approach. By the same token, since the hotel does not have its own security department, if a given function may attract persons whose presence could create problems for other guests or who pose a threat to public spaces of the inn itself, the sales department and general manager must decide whether or not special arrangements will be needed for the hotel's protection; and then they must act accordingly.

Security Department

The property neither has nor needs a full-scale security department. It does need one employee per shift, except when the general manager is present, to whom the responsibility for security and safety is assigned. This person should be able to make decisions when called upon to do so.

At present a night bellman has the task of making watch-clock rounds, varying the patrol times. To ensure complete tours a paper disc is inserted in the watch clock to record a stop at each station; blank discs are kept in the bell captain's desk.

All blank clock discs should be secured and in the custody of either the night auditor or night desk clerk with a single disc issued to the night bellman prior to the start of each tour. The person issuing the disc should date and initial it before giving it to the night bellman.

Even without a security department, records of security-related incidents, fires and bomb threats included should be kept. They should be working tools for the general manager's and owner's benefit, not merely history, and reviewed from time to time to see if there is enough activity to justify employing a minimal but full-time security staff.

Emergency Procedures

The only written emergency procedures relate to shutting off and resetting the internal fire alarm system. While too-precise emergency procedures can be self-defeating, written guidance nevertheless should be provided for the staff to minimize the risk of confusion and improper response. This is particularly true in case of fires or bomb threats.

All fires, no matter their size or location, should be reported immediately to the fire department even though trained employees may try to contain or control small ones pending the department's arrival. Once the fire department has been notified, the general manager, or in his absence, his designee, should be informed. Until the fire department arrives, the general manager must make the initial evacuation decision based on the fire's size and location, the volume and density of the smoke, and the risk of spread. Once the fire department has arrived, however, the senior fire officer present makes all decisions, including those related to evacuation if this has not already happened.

Bomb threats, usually made by telephone, should be reported immediately to the general manager. Depending on the information given to him by the person who took the call, he will decide not only if police and/or fire department help should be requested but also whether or not to evacuate the property. While his decision will be influenced, at least in part, by the length of the call (brief calls most often are a hoax), this should not be the only criterion on which to base a decision on whether to evacuate.

Toward this end, telephone operators, who are the most likely recipients of a bomb threat, should have displayed under glass or clear plastic the kinds of information to record and to try to elicit from the caller. Among them are the date and exact time of the threat; reason for the bombing and type of explosive device being used; anything that will help localize a search; the caller's sex, possible age range, accent or speech impediment, voice pitch, and use of regional or idiomatic expressions; familiarity with the hotel, its employees, or any of its current guests; background noises; possible use of a pay telephone; and any indication as to whether the call is local or long distance.

Unless the general manager feels the threat is real and explosion is imminent, and regardless of whether evacuation has been ordered, an effort should be made to search the hotel and parking areas. The search should be conducted by employees who are in the best position to detect anything unusual. Each department should search its own area, with housekeeping also covering guest room floors. Departments with more staff than they need to thoroughly search their own space—such as kitchen and dining room employees—should make the surplus available to help cover stairwells, locker rooms, parking areas, and other parts of the property to which the public has access.

Any area in which a suspicious-looking object is seen should be secured, the general manager should be informed, and he then should call the police if he has not already done so. If evacuation has not yet been ordered, it should be, with evacuees moved far enough away from the hotel to minimize the risk of their being injured or killed by flying debris or glass if an explosion occurs. However, if evacuation is ordered, to the extent that it is possible employees responsible for the inn's assets should try to secure them before leaving their stations.

Emergency plans also need to consider the possibility of having to evacuate guests with disabilities, including hearing problems, who might need help. This is especially important in a high-rise property such as this one.

Folios of guests in this category should be discreetly identified when they register. Their names, room numbers, and nature of the disability (if known) should be noted and given to the bell staff and to responding police and fire personnel to facilitate the evacuation of these guests by providing what help may be needed.

Procedures aside, fire extinguisher locations are clearly marked. However, the extinguishers themselves contain water and are not adaptable to all kinds of fires. Nor have any employees been trained in their use.

Fires can occur at any time, and time is of the essence in fighting them. Consequently, time cannot be wasted to read instructions on how to use an extinguisher or to determine its suitability for fighting a particular kind of fire. In many ways using the wrong kind can be dangerous. Therefore, thought should be given to replacing the water extinguishers with the multipurpose type and to having certain employees on each shift trained by the fire department in their proper use.

In today's world of commerce and industry, the term "risk management" tends to be associated with buying insurance to cover certain types of losses. In fact, it is not unusual for large organizations to have risk managers and risk management departments. However, before discussing the various matters to be covered in this chapter, understanding the different perspectives of the insurers and the insured may be helpful. What follows should not be construed as lessening the need for and value of insurance. Rather it is intended to alert the uninitiated to some of the realities to be faced.

For instance, entities that buy insurance do so to protect themselves against perceived risks, but in the parlance of insurance companies it is the insured entity itself that is the "risk." To insurers or carriers, the risks to which organizations feel they may be exposed, such as burglary, theft, fire, property damage, personal injuries, and so on, are "hazards."

In addition, when insurance companies recommend—or on occasion, require—that certain things be done, the insured may indeed benefit, but in reality the carrier may benefit more than the insured. True, the former may be less exposed to certain hazards, but the insurance company's goal in wanting changes made is more attuned to reducing its own exposure to claims on which it may have to make payments.

If carriers feel that an excessive number of claims have been filed against an insured risk, they may refuse to renew the policy or even cancel it altogether. Should either of these events occur, the entity tries to find a new carrier, and if it succeeds, it will undoubtedly pay more for its coverage than it had been paying. If unsuccessful it becomes self-insured, meaning that it has to absorb the entire cost of losses due to claims. However, as long as the policy remains in effect, the insured pays premiums for the coverage, and the insurer continues to collect them.

Insofar as the cost of coverage is concerned, the cost of total protection against claims would be prohibitive. Thus policyholders agree to accept deductible clauses that will vary in range and reduce the cost, but in doing so they also realize that even when a carrier pays on a claim, the amount of the deductible is an out-of-pocket loss for the insured. To illustrate, if a guest is injured and wins a judgment for $50,000, and an inn's deductible is $25,000, the carrier pays only half the total, and the hotel pays the balance.

RISK MANAGEMENT AND LOSS PREVENTION

Regardless of whether or not a hotel has a security department as such, it is important to understand the difference between risk management and security. Even though insurance companies make recommendations to policyholders that are intended to reduce the latters' exposure to certain hazards covered by the policy—as much for the carrier's benefit as for that of the insured—insurance does not prevent losses. It can only reduce their cost to the hotel.

By way of contrast, we have repeatedly pointed out that the objective of effective, fully integrated security/loss-prevention programs is twofold: (1) to prevent as many losses as possible and (2) to reduce to the greatest extent the dollar cost of those that are inevitable. Contrary to what many people believe, security's efforts to prevent losses are not confined to crimes; they are equally concerned with other possible sources of loss, as noted earlier in the text.

An examination of these differences should make it clear that, ideally, the risk management and security/loss-prevention functions complement rather than compete with each other. Regrettably, this is not always the case even at the level of large corporations that employ both corporate risk management and security directors.

Where both risk and security managers are employed, whether at corporate or property level, each may see the other as a threat; there is relatively little communication between them with a view to doing what is in their employer's best interest. In the final analysis, the latter suffers. At inns where security departments do not exist, those responsible for risk management are inclined to think that their insurance policies will prevent losses and provide all the protection they need.

Consequently, regardless of whether or not there are risk and security directors at corporate headquarters or managers at individual property level, the responsibility for making certain that these different but complementary activities are fully understood and properly coordinated largely rests with general managers. The reason is that the greatest exposure to hazards and claims exists at the local level. They need to appreciate what each of these different but complementary activities involves and to ensure that neither one is ignored. To accomplish this they also have to make certain that the members of their staffs to whom they have assigned responsibility for risk management and security/loss prevention, even if there are no departments as such, communicate with one another and work well together.

Failure to work together can be costly in several ways, one of which is a willingness to bow to pressure that insurance companies may try to exert to have changes made. Not all of their recommendations may be cost effective or meaningful in terms of reducing either the various hazards to which the insured may be subjected or the number of claims filed. Nevertheless, some insurance companies are less concerned with what it will cost policyholders to do as they want than they are with protecting themselves.

Before agreeing to satisfy an insurer's requests, those responsible for an inn's risk management and security/loss prevention need to do three things. First, evaluate the basis for the carrier's concern; does it really pose a threat to the hotel's best interest? Second, if it does, analyze the costs and benefits to be derived from following the carrier's recommendations. Third, determine whether or not an equally satisfactory but less expensive solution is possible.

Working well together with respect to managing risks and the loss-prevention effort serves another purpose as well. For instance, when risk managers are aware of their insured's concerns and discuss them with the person responsible for loss prevention, the analyses outlined above can be done and steps taken to protect the hotel's best interest. Conversely, when the person with security responsibility feels that there has been a significant reduction in a hazard, its impact on the coverage carried should be discussed with the risk manager.

To this point the need for all innkeepers to make certain that their properties have an acceptable level of both physical and operational security/loss prevention has been made clear. Equally important is the need for them to have sufficient but not excessive insurance. However, where the matter of sufficiency is concerned, one aspect of insurance is often overlooked at properties employing security officers: coverage for security operations.

Interaction with other people, whether they are guests or employees, is an inherent part of security work. While most employees interact with each other, and many do so with guests, the likelihood of their being charged with alleged involvement with an assault, false arrest and false imprisonment, libel or slander, or invasion of privacy is rare. Not so with respect to security officers. No matter how carefully selected, trained, and supervised they may be—matters discussed in detail in Chapter 7—confrontations cannot always be avoided. When one does occur, the possibility that a claim may be filed against the hotel cannot be ignored. Despite this, neither risk nor security managers may think of such possible incidents as "hazards"; or if they do, they may not consider them hazardous enough to justify having them covered by insurance. Again, good communication is essential if this kind of costly mistake is to be avoided.

PLANNING AND PREPARING FOR EMERGENCIES AND DISASTERS

Neither insurance coverage, risk management, nor loss-prevention programs can prevent or avoid emergencies or disasters since they are sudden, unexpected events that require an immediate response. While both emergencies and disasters result in the disruption of normal activities, disasters are always accompanied by injuries to persons or property, or even by death. That neither may happen with any frequency or regularity is no excuse for failing to be prepared for their occurrence. Since at the very least they are disruptive, some loss is inevitable, but the cost of that loss can be minimized if an effective security/loss-prevention program is in place.

Planning entails knowing what is to be done in case of an emergency or disaster and communicating this information to all employees; preparing involves actively taking steps in anticipation of the event's arrival. However, to make meaningful plans and realistic preparations, one first has to have some idea of what might happen.

Emergencies or disasters can be the products of persons or acts of nature; therefore, anything is possible. However, since the cost of planning and preparing for all possibilities would be prohibitive, one needs to weigh probabilities against possibilities. In doing so, geography has to be considered with respect to certain acts of nature. It is within this framework that priorities then have to be set.

In doing this analysis, reality tells us that events attributable to persons will be harder to deal with since human behavior can be completely unpredictable. To illustrate, a person may act deliberately, such as calling in a bomb threat, or an accident or someone's carelessness may cause an injury or property damage. In contrast, thanks to modern science and technology, coping with acts of nature can be easier. Today many events, among them hurricanes, blizzards, ice storms, and even tornadoes—at least to some extent—can be forecast.

Consequently, for planning purposes the first step is to identify those situations that are most likely to occur, particularly acts of nature. For instance, earthquakes can conceivably occur anywhere in the United States, but they are more likely to occur in California than in New York. There is a greater likelihood of hurricanes in New England than in the Midwest, and vice versa with respect to tornadoes.

After the probable risks or hazards have been identified, whether due to human or natural acts, the next step in the planning process is to decide on how to react to such events. Keep in mind the fact that the response will not necessarily be the same in all cases. However, among the many things to be considered are the question of evacuation (whether complete or partial), search procedures in case of a bomb threat, what to do if there is a fire or power failure, how to protect exposed glass in a hurricane, or what to do to keep walkways passable in an ice storm. In other words, plans for any given emergency or disaster consist of what will have to be done in response to that event.

To be meaningful, however, plans must also be set forth by whom they will be put into effect; that is, what roles are to be played by each department and its personnel? Illogical though it may seem, plans for what to do in case of emergencies or disasters may be quite adequate, yet staffing may be woefully inadequate for implementing those plans. Unfortunately, the timing of such events is not limited to the hours between 9 A.M. and 5 P.M., Monday through Friday, a fact that some hotels and motels may fail to take into account despite the lodging industry's around-the-clock operations.

Preparations, like plans, should be based on events that are most likely to occur. In some cases preparing may be limited to occasional drills or exercises such as searching for bombs, holding fire drills, or actually using extinguishers to put out small, supervised fires. Choosing certain employees and training them in the use of fire extinguishers is in itself a form of preparation.

Other types of preparation may involve ensuring that materials needed to help cope with an event are, or would be, available. For instance, properties with a lot of glass exposure in regions likely to have hurricanes would do well to arrange for suppliers to hold for them heavy plastic sheeting or plywood with which to cover windows that might be blown out. Properties in places likely to suffer from ice storms should make certain that sand-and-salt mixtures are close at hand. Taking such steps does not necessarily mean buying, paying for, and keeping these supplies in inventory; it does mean making arrangements in advance to ensure their availability. Otherwise, a last-minute effort to obtain them may prove to be of no avail.

A hotel located in the Southwest, part of a small chain of luxury properties, is a case in point. With properties in different parts of the United States, the chain's corporate policy required all hotels to monitor local weather conditions in order to be prepared to deal with forecasts of unusually bad weather. A local forecast predicted a severe ice storm two days before it actually struck. Despite this, the management staff, and the security manager in particular, either failed to keep abreast of weather forecasts or chose to ignore the prediction. Only after the ice storm struck was a search initiated for a sand-and-salt mixture to be used on the sidewalk, especially in front of the main entrance. By then it was too late; all suppliers were sold out. Both a guest and his adult daughter, while leaving the hotel, fell and were injured, the parent very seriously. As expected, a lawsuit was filed; the case was settled out of court.

To this point we have looked at risk management in relation to loss prevention. We also have discussed the need to plan and prepare for different kinds of emergencies and disasters at some length, but largely in general terms. Now it is time to be more specific with respect to some of the things with which innkeepers are more likely to be confronted—some caused by people, some by nature, and some by both.

EVACUATION AND ACCOUNTABILITY

Two aspects of planning and preparing for emergencies and disasters might be described as generic since they would have application in both cases. They are (1) being ready to evacuate if it becomes necessary to do so and (2) trying to ensure that evacuation is complete.

Any number of emergencies, accompanied by disasters or not, may call for evacuation. Included would be such things as bomb threats, fires, or certain acts of nature. Therefore, an obvious first question is, how should evacuation orders be transmitted? Historically, audible alarms were the accepted standard, but as increasing numbers of persons with impaired hearing or vision began to travel, innkeepers were obliged to think about ways in which all guests could be alerted to the need to evacuate. Audible alarms may not be heard by hearing-impaired guests, and flashing or blinking lights may not be seen by those with impaired sight. Therefore, the most logical way to signal the need to evacuate is to use a combination of audible alarms, flashing or blinking lights, and messages transmitted through television sets. With respect to the latter, hotels that cater to foreign guests would be well advised to have the messages displayed in languages representative of most foreign visitors' countries. In choosing any system, the main concern is to facilitate the prompt and safe evacuation of everyone on the premises.

Next is the evacuation itself, something that should be taken into consideration at the time guests register. A note should be made of every guest with a disability who would need help in an evacuation, and every effort should be made to assign those guests to rooms on floors where they can be removed from the hotel with minimal effort. The notations should include the nature of the disability, type of help that would be necessary, including any special equipment, and room assignment. These notes would serve to facilitate a rapid and easy response by staff members (or emergency rescue personnel) and help to ensure those guests' evacuation.

Evacuation information is frequently posted on the inside of room doors with or near a copy of the Innkeeper's Law. Relying solely on this posting is unrealistic since many guests do not take the time to look at either. Therefore, when guests are shown to their rooms, it is worthwhile to have the bell staff point out the exits nearest to the room. Thought might even be given to posting, at regular intervals in hallways, copies of both primary and secondary evacuation routes for each floor. Highlighting secondary as well as primary routes is most important since there is no assurance that in a real emergency the primary route will be clear. If the posted routes are large enough, attractively framed and placed under glass, they can be of benefit to both guests and employees without in any way being aesthetically offensive.

Regardless of whether or not management elects to post evacuation routes in guest floor hallways, they should be posted in the back of the house. Since employees' assignments may result in their being scattered throughout the property, their evacuation instructions should be to leave by way of the nearest available exit rather than a specific one.

When an evacuation is ordered, accounting for people is of prime importance, especially in structures open to the public such as retail stores, office buildings, and hotels. Since hotel guests are free to come and go as they please, accounting for their whereabouts is impossible. The only possible exception might apply to those guests to whom help would have to be provided.

With respect to employees, however, everyone who reported for work for his or her shift should be accounted for as quickly as possible so that emergency personnel, upon arrival, can attempt to rescue those unaccounted for. To expedite the accountability process and ensure that all employees have been safely evacuated, each department should be assigned a predesignated assembly point to which departmental personnel should report upon leaving the hotel. Allowing a reasonable amount of time, based on a property's size and configuration, but as soon as possible after evacuation has been ordered, using a two-way, hand-held radio or cellular telephone, each department head should report his or her department's status to the general, resident, or senior manager on duty. Missing employees and their last known whereabouts should then be reported immediately to the public safety agency that has responded to the alarm, regardless of the reason for the evacuation.

A question that can arise with regard to an evacuation is, must it be total, or can it be partial? There is no single or simple answer. Rather, it is a judgment call on the part of the general or senior manager then on duty based on the nature of the event and the most current information at his or her disposal.

For example, suppose a small fire has broken out in an area where it can be easily contained, the fire department has been called and is enroute, and the fire is being dealt with by either a sprinkler system or employees with fire extinguishers. Does this situation warrant evacuating and traumatizing everyone in a twenty-story, two-hundred-room property? In the case of a bomb threat, does the available information suggest that a possible detonation is imminent, or is there possibly time for a search of the premises?

After an evacuation, everyone affected is usually eager to reenter. The question is, is it safe to do so? Once again, the decision really has to be based on the type of event that prompted the evacuation.

Suppose there was a bomb threat, the hotel has been searched, and nothing was found. There is no reason that guests and employees cannot reenter the building. But in the case of fire, explosion, tornado, earthquake, or hurricane, the event's severity and its possible effect on structural integrity must first be assessed. For instance, the fire department having put out a major fire does not by itself necessarily guarantee that the building is structurally safe. Consequently, to prevent additional or future losses, if there is any question about possible structural damage, reentry should be deferred until qualified engineers have determined that the building is structurally sound and that it is safe to reenter.

BOMB THREATS

Bomb threats are almost invariably made by telephone, and the callers may or may not also cause actual bombings. Their motives will vary. To some a threat is just a prank to frighten people and disrupt activities. For those who actually send or place explosives, the motivation may be anger, revenge, or extortion; or the intention may be to make a political statement or to strike back against perceived socioeconomic injustice.

Uncertainty is the principal problem in deciding what to do. Is the call only a threat, or is there really a bomb on site? Is immediate evacuation necessary, or is there time to search for a bomb before deciding? To react to a mere threat by evacuating is disruptive and traumatic; it also can be costly. Having failed to evacuate if an explosion does occur is even more traumatic and costly; it can be downright disastrous. Regardless, a decision must be made, and the responsibility for making it rests with the general or senior manager on duty when the call is received.

Difficult as deciding may be, it cannot be done intelligently without first having access to all available information, and that can come only from whoever received the call. As a rule, unless a caller knows someone's extension, the vast majority of bomb-related calls are handled by switchboard operators.

Therefore, in order to provide helpful information to the person who must decide whether there is time to search or whether to evacuate, a bomb-threat checklist should be at each operator's station, preferably under glass or clear plastic. The checklist reminds them what kind of information to seek from the caller, as well as what to listen for. If a caller merely says that a bomb will go off in ten minutes and then hangs up, obviously there is little an operator can do. However, if an operator can get any information about the caller, and possibly about the place from which the call is being made, and relay it to the general or senior manager on duty, the quicker a decision can be made.

Single-sentence calls and quick hang-ups tend to be more in the threat category; longer calls tend to be more serious. Nevertheless, the length of a call alone should never be the sole or even the primary determinant in terms of what to do or not do. The ability to get information about the time of the explosion, the kind of device being used, and where it has been placed would be ideal, but it is highly unlikely that any answers will be forthcoming.

Meaningful information, however, can be gleaned by listening carefully to the caller. Is the caller male or female, seemingly a youth or an adult? Is his or her speech clear and easily understood, or is it muffled or slurred, suggesting that the person may be under the influence of either alcohol or drugs? Does the caller have an accent? If so, what kind? Does he or she use expressions or colloquialisms that are associated with a particular region or ethnic group? Of special importance is whether there is anything in the message indicating that the caller is familiar with either the property itself, an employee, or a guest. If there is, it may offer a motive.

Then, too, there is the matter of background noises. Is it completely quiet, indicating that the call is made from a very private or secluded place? Or is there music that might be coming from a jukebox, and thus possibly from a bar? What about noises made by such things as automobiles, buses, streetcars, subways, or aircraft? And what about other "street noises" such as sirens or the whistle of a police officer directing traffic?

Answers to all the foregoing serve a dual purpose. Certainly the ability to carefully but quickly evaluate those related to the caller will play a major role in management's deciding what to do. Answers to questions about both the caller and background noises can be helpful to the authorities in trying to identify, and hopefully apprehend, the person who placed the call.

Regardless of any evacuation decision, it is possible that the nature of the call itself is such that it appears there is time for a search. However, management should not wait for a bomb threat before deciding how a property is to be searched. Plans must be made in advance if a search is to be conducted in the shortest possible time and the most efficient and effective way. Since hotels and motels operate around the clock and bomb threats can be made at

Guestroom, the Lenox Hotel–Boston

any time of day or night, all employees have to be involved in the search, and they have to know what they are to do. This means making assignments in anticipation of such an eventuality and holding periodic drills to ensure that all members of the staff know what is expected of them.

In this respect it is important to remember that using employees to search is not a sign of callousness or disregard for their safety; logic dictates their involvement. It must be presumed that they are the ones best qualified to detect anything out of the ordinary in those parts of the inn in which they work or to which they have access. This truism is evident from the fact that even when police and fire departments are called and respond to bomb threats and prepare to search, they will ask to be accompanied by one or more employees for that very reason. When to seek their help is another part of management's decision-making process, although they will usually be called upon receipt of a threat.

For illustrative purposes, housekeepers, including the housestaff, would check all facilities to which they have access or in which they work, such as function rooms and linen closets. The kitchen staff, including storekeepers, would search all kitchen areas and storerooms; food and beverage outlets would be handled by the wait staff and bar employees. Engineering and laundry personnel would search their areas, while members of the bell staff and security department would handle so-called public spaces.

Chances are that if the police and fire departments are called, the property will be evacuated when they arrive if not before. However, if evacuation has not taken place and something out of the ordinary is found during a search, the precise location of the suspect item must be isolated and secured against intrusion by unauthorized persons; evacuation should then be ordered without delay. If evacuation has occurred, regardless of by whose orders, no one should reenter until everything reasonably possible has been done to ensure that there is no bomb on the premises.

FIRES

From a security/loss-prevention perspective, using fire-retardant materials in building and furnishing properties and installing sprinklers and smoke detectors, as discussed in Chapter 2, can help minimize if not actually prevent losses attributable to fires. Nevertheless, they can still occur. Fires can be caused by exploding bombs, and they can be deliberately set (arson). They can also be caused by acts of nature, accidents, or negligence. Notwithstanding fire-resistant construction and other preventive measures, waiting until a fire occurs before deciding what to do is unwise. The need for planning and preparation includes, but is not limited to, staff training and involvement.

First, when any fire is detected a speedy response is essential if it is to be extinguished with minimal loss and disruption. Therefore, a cardinal rule in dealing with fires, regardless of their size, is to call the fire department immediately. That a fire is contained and seems small enough for employees to put out does not excuse a failure to call the fire department. Notification is preferred by fire departments even if small fires have already been extinguished before the apparatus arrives.

Next, despite including standpipe in construction plans and specifications, having fire hose, and using fire-retardant building materials and room furnishings, there are standards having the full force and effect of law, promulgated by the United States Department of Labor's Occupational Safety and Health Agency (OSHA), that require that fire extinguishers and emergency lights be available. However, the types of extinguishers chosen are left to the discretion of the person with the overall management responsibility for a given facility.

Three things should be kept in mind with respect to implementing the extinguisher requirement: choosing the types of extinguishers, clearly marking their locations, and ensuring that employees know how to use them properly. Of the three principal types of extinguishers, only one is multipurpose. It can be used to fight all types of fires, whether they are electrical, grease, solids or liquids, soft goods or hard. Therefore, as a practical matter the best choice would be the multipurpose one since it eliminates the need to decide quickly whether or not a particular extinguisher can be used to fight a small fire. As an example, water should never be used to try to extinguish an electrical fire.

Some extinguishers are kept in receptacles, recessed in walls, in which hose is also stored. Their only drawbacks are that the receptacles are recessed for aesthetic reasons, and they are in colors that blend with the surrounding walls. While we shall discuss training employees in the use of extinguishers, a guest encountering a small fire might want to try to put it out with an extinguisher, providing that one can be located quickly. Consequently, thought should be given to identifying fire hose and extinguisher receptacles through the use of inoffensive but contrasting colors.

In other cases extinguishers are mounted on walls. Obviously, these are easier for both employees and guests to see. However, if wall-mounted extinguishers are preferred, close attention should be paid to the height at which they are hung. The size and weight of the kinds of extinguishers usually found in commercial buildings, hotels included, are such that mounting them either too high or too low can pose a problem for someone who needs to use one.

Although on rare occasions a guest might try to put out a small fire with an extinguisher, an employer is more likely to be involved. For this reason, a select number of employees from each department and shift should be trained, and periodically retrained, in the proper use of fire extinguishers. Since, as we already have said, time is of the essence in fighting fires of any size, precious minutes are lost if persons have to stop and read the instructions on an extinguisher before they can use it. Almost without exception, fire departments will gladly assist in the training effort.

Earlier in this chapter we discussed the need to be able to quickly identify guests who have physical impairments and might need help in an emergency evacuation. Particularly important, in a fire there is a dual threat to their safety—the fire itself and smoke inhalation. Therefore, there must be a way to identify impaired guests so that proper help can be provided. In addition, employees charged with giving help also should have some idea as to the nature of a guest's disability. Then they will know if more than one person, or possibly special equipment, will be needed to safely and quickly remove the guest from the premises.

Notwithstanding plans, deciding on how evacuations will be ordered and what routes are to be used, and training a number of employees in the proper use of fire extinguishers, the usefulness of periodic fire drills should not be overlooked. Preceded by information assuring guests that they are *only* drills, they provide a chance to test the various systems that would be used if an actual evacuation was in order. Beyond that, except for employees who are directly assisting guests, drills can provide management with information about how long it takes employees to evacuate and report to their designated assembly areas.

If drills are to be held and employees are to participate, two things are worth remembering. They should be told that if an alarm sounds as part of a drill and they are actually serving guests (as in an outlet), they are not to evacuate unless ordered to do so. However, there is good reason for not telling members of the staff who would be expected to participate that it is just a drill. Time is of the essence in responding to a fire and effecting an evacuation. Knowing that evacuation is part of a drill and not a response to an actual event, people tend to wait for friends, stop to pick up one or two personal items, or move at a rather leisurely pace. When this happens, general managers cannot get a reasonable approximation of the time needed for employees to evacuate and report to their department areas.

NATURAL DISASTERS

Acts of nature can trigger emergency conditions, and the results can often be disastrous. However, in terms of loss prevention, those most likely to be encountered offer innkeepers far better opportunities for planning and preparing than other incidents, largely because of two factors.

First, despite the suddenness with which natural acts can occur, location (geographically speaking) makes it easier to distinguish between real probabilities as opposed to mere possibilities. For instance, an explosion could happen anywhere, regardless of location, but only certain areas are vulnerable to severe earthquakes. Second, as noted before, modern science and technology, can make it easier to develop a response to acts of nature.

Based on the foregoing, the real question is, how do innkeepers react? Do they, or those charged with the protection of lives and property, consider these eventualities well ahead of time, or do they simply wait until the act strikes—or is so close to striking that a state of borderline panic results?

Of course, even the best of analytical skills and the closest monitoring of weather forecasts cannot compensate for or take into account other related matters. Although competing with each other, people in the lodging industry also tend to cooperate or help each other in a crisis. Ordinarily, this spirit, plus good networking among general managers, means Hotel B will do its best to accommodate guests displaced by a fire at Hotel A. However, unless caused by a bolt of lightning during a thunderstorm, fires are not natural acts. Furthermore, when acts of nature do strike, they can cut a wide swath. Consequently, reliance on competitors for help when victimized by natural disasters is unwise since those usually most willing to cooperate may be equally affected.

In addition, when acts of nature do strike, hotels and motels may encounter different but unique problems even though they themselves may not be directly affected. The impact of a natural act, such as an ice storm, blizzard, hurricane, typhoon, tornado, or an earthquake, on the surrounding community may leave some people temporarily displaced or stranded.

Such events impose a moral oglibation (in addition to contributing to good public relations) on properties that have not suffered to help by providing food and shelter for those in need. Thus, in the event of a natural disaster—assuming the inn itself is unharmed—from a security/loss-prevention perspective, there is a need to simultaneously protect the property's best interests and take care of those for whom temporary refuge is provided.

Balancing the need to serve both objectives is not always easy. General managers may have to do more than analyze the situation; they may also have to make some hard decisions. Analytically speaking, two things have to be considered. One is the projected duration of the event. A weather forecast from a reasonably reliable agency, such as the United States Weather Service, indicating the anticipated length and severity of the problem will obviously influence what may have to be done. For instance, no matter the severity of a hurricane and the need for cleanup, once it has passed there is no real reason for third parties to remain on the premises. On the other hand, the need for cleanup after a blizzard of equal duration may prompt government to impose strict limitations on any appreciable movement of traffic on streets or highways.

From the foregoing it becomes clear that the second consideration will involve the number of persons who may be affected by conditions and to whom some help may have to be given. They may include registered guests, employees, and third parties seeking refuge. A forecast projecting a lengthy, severe, and potentially disastrous act of nature, as opposed to a relatively brief and moderate one, can pose vastly different problems.

In this regard, for innkeepers to be good Samaritans is one thing; to be realists is another. Neither they nor their security managers can afford to ignore the fact that the longer a sizeable number of people are confined in a relatively small space, the greater the risk of troublesome incidents. Therefore, unless hotels take steps to prevent such crowding, assets could be damaged or lost, and people could be injured.

Let us first consider ways to prevent loss to the inn. Properties with security personnel are well advised to either initiate or increase the frequency of patrols. Those without a security staff should seriously consider using other employees, such as the bell staff and members of the engineering and housekeeping departments, for that purpose. The temporary use of contract personnel under these circumstances has drawbacks, largely due to their lack of familiarity with the property, an essential part of the loss-prevention effort.

Patrols should cover all back-of-the-house areas to ensure that persons other than employees are kept out. Otherwise, there is the risk that third parties may enter, and if they do, their mere presence can interfere with operations. However inadvertently, their presence can be more than merely disruptive; it may lead to damage to assets and, of even greater import, to injuries to both employees and themselves.

Hallways have to be patrolled to prevent persons who are not registered guests from having access to rooms. Stairwells also have to be covered to prevent third parties from using them as a way of getting to guest room floors or possibly even starting a fire. In addition, they must be kept absolutely clear to make certain that they would be available for use should a need arise to evacuate the property.

All hotels have rest rooms that are available for use by people who are not necessarily registered guests. They are a potential source of loss even under normal conditions, and the risk is increased when a hotel provides temporary shelter to third parties. Paper towels in toilets cannot be flushed down, and a backup can cause damage. That damage can become greater when a well-meaning (or annoyed) person tries to do something about the situation. An empty soap dispenser may prompt someone who is angry to pull it off the wall. As a result, these facilities must also be inspected when patrols are made.

Both the lobby and function rooms open to the public in response to a natural disaster should be included in patrol rounds to minimize the risk of damage to furniture and furnishings. To allow people the use of these spaces is one thing, but to tolerate actions that can result in breakage to or soilage of assets is another. To expect that everyone to whom help is being provided will be so appreciative of the inn's efforts that they would not possibly misbehave is a naive assumption that can prove costly.

Aside from the possible damage to or loss of assets, confining a substantial number of people in relatively limited space for an extended period of time can also increase the risk of injuries to people. People miss their privacy, and the abnormal conditions in which they find themselves can cause tempers to flare. Not only can emotional outbursts result in damage to an inn's property, but in some cases they can also pose a threat to the safety and well-being of the staff, registered guests, and others for whom shelter is being provided.

Innkeepers obviously cannot control peoples' tempers, but they can initiate action to avoid aggravating the problem. A significant step is to close those outlets that serve only beverages and secure their bar stock. Another is to stop serving all alcoholic beverages even in outlets where food is available. This admitted, albeit temporary, loss of revenue must be weighed against losses that otherwise may be incurred and that could be far more costly.

In this respect, despite some loss of income, stopping the sale of alcoholic beverages is not without its benefits. This action lessens the risk of violence on the part of those confined. In doing so it also decreases the risk of losses due to damaged or destroyed assets in those parts of the hotel to which people other than registered guests have access. Another benefit is that instead of focusing on the lobby outlets, and function rooms, security personnel are free to patrol other parts of the hotel where assets may be damaged, rooms broken into, and registered guests disturbed if not actually victimized. No less important is its defense role in a lawsuit alleging that a plaintiff's injuries were due to the property's failure to exercise care by continuing to serve alcohol during what was a tense and trying time, claiming that it should have foreseen that personal safety was at risk.

CIVIL DISTURBANCES

Civil disturbances, like natural disasters, can result in damage to or the loss of assets and have an impact on guests and staff. However, they are different in that while the lodging industry often goes out of its way to open its doors to accommodate victims of natural disasters, prudence dictates that access to the property via those same doors must be controlled when the threat of a civil disturbance is present.

Under some circumstances the activities accompanying a civil disturbance may be limited to sidewalks and streets adjacent to the hotel; in others there may be an actual or attempted invasion of the property. Regardless, as is the case with so many natural events that now lend themselves to forecasting, the possibility also exists that at times general and other senior managers may be able to reasonably anticipate that an inn will be the focal point of a civil disturbance. The genesis of the disturbance could be either a controversial organization's presence at the hotel or a labor problem. In any case, whatever the cause, a civil disturbance can affect reputation, among other things, if an inn is unprepared to deal with the situation.

The sales department's role was discussed in Chapter 3 and also, in connection with planning for conventions and large groups, in Chapter 4. We emphasized how important it is for the sales staff to keep the matter of security in mind and to work closely with whoever is in charge of loss prevention. However, their need for cooperation and good communication is even greater when they are booking space for organizations that are known to be controversial and whose very presence is likely to attract people in opposition.

The decision to sell or not sell rooms and function space to organizations in this category is one to be made not by the security manager but by the sales director and general manager. They have to consider the risk that such a group's presence could prompt a disturbance that would have an impact on both operations and other guests. However, once a decision is made to accommodate such an organization, the security manager should be told immediately and given complete data relative to the dates, activities planned, function and other rooms sold, and the number of participants expected. At the same time, since bookings of this kind usually are made well in advance in order to ensure that accommodations will be available and participants can plan to attend, there is ample opportunity for the hotel to also plan ahead and be prepared for the organization's arrival. To wait until the participants arrive to see whether or not there is an adverse reaction before making plans is unwise.

The subject of public safety liaison will be discussed in detail in Chapter 7. In the interim between the booking and the function, whenever a sale has been made to a group whose presence may result in a civil disturbance, the appropriate law enforcement agencies should be contacted. Good relations with the latter will allow the hotel to benefit from intelligence information they collect relative to any disturbances that may be planned by opposing organizations. This initial contact also alerts them to the fact that their help may well be needed in order to minimize a disturbance's impact on the inn's operations and guests.

To reduce the risk of interruption to operations and inconvenience for guests, among the plans to be made in anticipation of the group's arrival are those for controlled access to the property. These controls have to apply to the receipt of deliveries as well as to the admission of employees and both registered and newly arriving guests.

If deliveries are interfered with, operations cannot help but be affected. For instance, imagine the impact on food and beverage outlets; being unable to serve guests in outlets or at catered functions means lost revenue. Even other services, such as housekeeping and laundry, may suffer if vendors cannot make timely delivery of needed supplies, and no one wants to stay at a hotel where clean bed linens and towels are unavailable. Among other things, a property's reputation also becomes a casualty.

The police can help clear, and keep clear, public ways leading to the receiving dock. However, the hotel is responsible for making certain that only authorized delivery personnel are allowed to enter the dock area. If there is a security department but a security officer is not regularly assigned to the receiving dock, one can be posted to that area for this purpose on a temporary basis; otherwise, thought should be given to the use of contract security personnel for the duration of the disturbance. Alternatively, this task can be assigned to the cost controller. Since it is likely that the person in this job knows the drivers who regularly deliver to the inn better than anyone else on the staff, he or she can be very effective. Developing a timetable indicating the approximate times when and from whom deliveries can be expected is also helpful.

Although there may be an occasional exception, as a rule employees enter and leave the property by using an "employees' entrance." In some cases employees have coded identification cards to gain access; they record their arrivals and departures by inserting the cards in card readers. One of the many benefits to be derived by using card readers in general is the ability to program them so that cardholders' access can be restricted to both certain hours of the day and days of the week. This feature becomes an additional benefit in controlling access if there is a civil disturbance.

At other properties it is not unusual to find timekeepers on duty. It is their job to either clock employees in and out or at least make sure that each person punches his or her own arrival and departure times. In either case, while timekeepers should be required to check whatever form of employee identification is used (as discussed in Chapter 3) as part of a standard employee arrival and departure procedure, their doing so takes on added significance when access has to be controlled because of a civil disturbance affecting the hotel. However, if neither card readers nor timekeepers are used, it may be necessary to have security personnel verify employment and control access. Not unlike the situation at the receiving dock, this is a proper posting if the inn has its own security department; if it does not, the temporary use of contract security officers should certainly be considered.

A far greater risk of demonstrators entering the premises exists when they use, or try to use, those entrances normally available to registered and newly arriving guests. Should they succeed in gaining entrance, assets may be damaged, operations interrupted, and guests inconvenienced or harassed. Since the disturbance may be relatively short-lived, the impact on revenues may be equally short-lived, but the impact on the hotel's reputation may be long-term. Therefore, while access to the receiving dock and the employee entrance must be controlled, it is even more important to control public access.

While not an absolute, properties that can accommodate large organizations usually have more than one entrance for use by guests and the general public, the security implications of which were discussed in Chapter 2. However, if but a single entrance is normally used, it will have to be monitored; if more than one is normally accessible, the total number has to be taken into account whether a civil disturbance exists or is threatened.

Consequently, an important first step in protecting the inn, its assets, guests, and employees is to restrict access to a single—probably the main—entrance for the duration of the disturbance in order to minimize the risk of demonstrators getting in. In preventing unauthorized access to the premises, care must be taken to avoid any measures that would interfere with or prevent the use of other doors should there be an emergency requiring an evacuation.

Limiting access to a single entrance rather than multiple doors is comparable to replacing a sieve with a funnel; there now is one hole instead of many. In other words, this action by itself is insufficient since it will not prevent unauthorized persons from entering.

Limited access has to be supplemented with the use of security personnel, but even they cannot absolutely guarantee that demonstrators will be prevented from getting in. However, with front office support their presence can go a long way in reducing the risk. This support is essential because one cannot safely rely on someone's appearance in deciding to permit or deny access. Using a person's looks as the criterion for entry can be more than foolhardy since not allowing a legitimate guest to enter can be insulting and embarrassing to that person as well as damaging to the hotel.

Authorization for registered guests at properties using electronic locks can be authenticated by asking them to show their card keys. Since the latter are convenient to carry, guests almost always keep them on their persons whether leaving their rooms or the property, so producing them is seldom a problem. This frequently is true even if standard keys are used, providing that they are not tagged.

The decision-making process becomes somewhat more complex where standard, tagged keys are still given to guests. Because of their relative bulk, guests often drop them off at the front desk, especially when leaving the hotel. Consequently, if it is at all feasible, security personnel assigned to controlling access should be provided with an alphabetical listing of all registered guests. They also should be given a list of persons who have reservations and who are expected to arrive on any given day during an ongoing disturbance.

Most difficult is deciding whether to allow or refuse admission to a person who is neither a registered guest nor someone with a reservation but who wants to be served in one of the inn's outlets. Whatever the decision, conceivably it could be the wrong one since it depends entirely on a security officer's judgment. In this case, taking into account an individual's appearance and behavior, as well as whether the request is for a party of one or more, cannot be avoided. If the security officer reacts favorably to the person's looks and behavior, only one person or a very small party is involved, and the request seems to be legitimate, it may well be in the hotel's best interest to take a calculated risk and grant permission to enter. If possible, having a security officer or member of the bell staff escort the person (or party) to the specified outlet would be an additional safeguard.

To this point we have focused on peaceful civil disturbances, but do not be blind to the possibility that a peaceful one could turn violent. Some demonstrators may be inclined to violence, or perhaps the disturbance is the result of a strike resulting from a labor dispute. It would be naive to deny that in some cities lodging industry unions are among the most militant. Therefore, the risk of violence in any civil disturbance, including a strike, cannot be ignored; instead, it calls for special consideration.

As long as participants in a disturbance or strike make no effort to enter the hotel, the latter's primary concern is with the possible inconvenience to guests and staff. During civil disturbances of any appreciable size, the sidewalks and streets around a hotel are usually patrolled by police. Their presence may be required because of a statute or a local ordinance or simply because public safety depends on the unimpeded flow of pedestrian and vehicular traffic. Therefore, the police will monitor activities outside the inn. If the demonstration is strike related, limits, of which the police are also aware, are imposed by law on the activities of picketing strikers.

Hotel management is confronted with a far more serious situation when demonstrators or strikers succeed in entering a property; at this point they are trespassing. There may not have been any violence associated with their entrance, yet while their presence may be peaceful, it is disruptive and cannot be tolerated. The question is, how to get them to leave?

The preferable approach, which may not succeed, is to identify the leaders, diplomatically tell them they are trespassing, and ask them to leave. If they willingly depart, management can breathe a sigh of relief; if they refuse, forcible ejection may become necessary. This portends at least some resistance, and if it becomes violent, injuries to people and damage to assets can result.

Happily, the times when force may be needed to evict demonstrators (or strikers) from the premises are relatively rare; but should the occasion arise, prudence dictates that it is best to turn the matter over to the police even if a property has its own security organization. This serves a dual purpose, one of which is directly related to at least minimizing, if not actually preventing, losses.

The vast majority of security officers are not trained to deal with incidents in which they are called upon to use force. It is safe to say that guests injured, however inadvertently, by security officers who are trying to remove demonstrators will most likely sue the inn. If a demonstrator is injured by an excessive use of force, the risk of a suit for damages is real. That the injured party was a trespasser does not automatically eliminate the possibility of liability. Even if covered by insurance, the hotel still suffers the loss of its deductible if a plaintiff succeeds, and despite the insurer's defense, the inn still may want to be represented by its own attorneys. This expense adds to its loss. Then, too, suppose a security officer is injured in the process. It makes no difference whether the injury was due to a lack of training or a demonstrator's resistance, the officer will file a workmen's compensation claim.

The police, on the other hand, are not only trained to deal with incidents that may require the use of force, but they also have access to the resources needed to effect the removal of demonstrators in a reasonably short time with minimal disruption. A party injured by the police may sue the hotel, but ordinarily the action will not lie. If an injured party alleges that an excessive amount of force was used, the claim would be against the city, not the inn. Compensation claims for police officers' injuries would be filed with their department, not the property. Therefore, under these conditions the risks of litigation and liability can be greatly reduced by making a timely call for police assistance.

In addition, to further safeguard against the risk of litigation and liability, it is imperative that when management asks for police help and the latter arrive, it limits its involvement to explaining the situation and what it hopes can be done. Thereafter, the police must be allowed to perform their duties under their own supervisors and according to their training and departmental policies. If hotel management in any way interferes—or even appears to interfere—with what the police propose to do or do, injured parties could sue the hotel, charging that the police were merely acting as the property's agents rather than independently. A showing that management exercised any control over the police may find the hotel liable. Therefore, interference serves only to defeat the very purpose of seeking police help in the first place.

TERRORISM

Generally speaking, hotels are not terrorists' primary targets, but neither is it safe to say that hotels are never the victims of terrorist organizations. Consequently, the relative rarity with which they are victimized can lead to complacency and a complete absence of any plans or preparations for dealing with an attack. Terrorist attacks almost invariably are sudden, unexpected events that result in damage to property and possibly injury or death to persons; therefore, they require an immediate response. They certainly satisfy the definition for disasters, and plans and preparations for dealing with them should be made accordingly.

Despite the similarities, there are also differences between terrorist activities and the types of disasters that are more likely to occur. Understanding the differences is important. As a rule, most disasters with which the lodging industry has to deal stem from acts of nature or from human negligence or accidents that cause fires. Earlier in this chapter we noted that between management's carefully analyzing probabilities versus possibilities and a combination of science and modern technology, it is now possible to forecast natural disasters with a reasonable degree of accuracy. Sprinkler systems, smoke detectors, and fire retardant construction materials and room furnishings can reduce the risk of loss of life or property when fires occur. However, the lodging industry cannot rely solely on these or comparable measures with respect to forecasting terrorist activity or target selection. For any possible help in this respect, good contacts with local and federal government agencies are needed.

Not all terrorist organizations have the same professed reasons for their existence. They may be motivated by perceived or real political, social, economic, or religious injustices. Targets are chosen to get the public's attention, but not necessarily for the same reasons. In most cases they will be selected because in the terrorists' minds they represent, either directly or indirectly, the instruments of government, business, industry, or religion thought to be responsible for the alleged injustices. The objective is to bring government down or intimidate authority or create enough fear to force capitulation to their demands in whole or in part.

They also need money with which to carry out their programs; thus extortion may be a primary reason for their choosing certain targets. In any case, maximum impact and publicity are considered essential. With respect to maximum impact they look for targets that are "soft," but since those occupied by government tend to be considered "hard," they turn their attention to more vulnerable places, such as hotels. Despite the fact that guests and staff are usually wholly innocent, the inherent nature of lodging industry operations makes hotels vulnerable, and as a result, innkeepers dare not take it for granted that they are immune from target selection.

Examples may be helpful. In one case political terrorists in northern Spain, actively engaged in extortion, kidnapping, and assassination, had become accustomed to seeking asylum in France. However, a point was reached when France decided not only to stop this practice but also to return the terrorists to Spain. To show their displeasure with the French government, they bombed a Madrid hotel in which the French government had an interest. There were casualties in addition to significant damage to the property.

In another, explosions occurred at two California hotels, part of a major chain that, in turn, was a subsidiary of a multinational conglomerate. Of all the latter's holdings, the two hotels were chosen because they were considered to be the softest targets. The reason for their being targeted was a group's opposition to the conglomerate's involvement in Chilean politics. The explosions caused no deaths or injuries at either location, and property damage was slight. However, when hotels are targeted by terrorists, even if their insurance covers bodily injury and property damage, the mere fact that they were targets creates an uncertainty in the traveling public's mind that may be reflected in at least a temporary decrease in occupancy.

We have already noted that the reactions to terrorism are similar to the actions taken in response to any disaster. The difficulty that is of concern is trying to prevent, or at least minimize, the impact. Finding a solution is made even harder by the nature of terrorist activity, the underlying reasons for and unpredictability of such behavior, and a willingness to both injure or kill people and destroy property. Innkeepers, however, are not entirely without any defense.

The answer lies in the innkeepers' ability to collect and analyze intelligence and to maintain good relations with the police and those federal agencies that are aware of and follow terrorist organizations' activities. In Chapter 4, and earlier in this chapter, we discussed factors that sales personnel should keep in mind when booking space for large groups or organizations in order to prevent or at least minimize the potential for losses. Reducing the risk of becoming a terrorist target is equally important.

Suppose a well-known, perfectly legitimate organization, such as Planned Parenthood, has booked space. Among other things it advocates a woman's freedom of choice with respect to abortion. It is a well-known fact that some people strongly disagree, as is their right. That they may elect to demonstrate or try to disrupt the meeting is not, by itself, terrorism. However, in some situations abortion opponents have gone beyond demonstrations; they have knowingly killed or threatened to kill abortion providers. This is terrorism.

From the standpoint of intelligence and analysis, it's impossible to predict when a possibly controversial organization may want to meet at a particular property. Therefore, hotel management—and security department heads in particular—need to be aware of both organizations that may attract terrorists and groups that participate in terrorist activity. In addition, if a possibly controversial organization does book space, management should contact both the police and the appropriate federal agencies to request any information they may have regarding a possible terrorist reaction. This also serves to alert them so that they can be prepared if, in their opinion, the threat of violence is real. In other words, hotels need not avoid doing business with organizations that may be controversial, but they need to be well prepared to deal with opponents' possibly violent reactions.

SUMMARY

While security and risk management departments are both dedicated to preventing losses, each approaches its mission differently. Security tries to prevent all forms of loss, yet knowing that some are inevitable, its secondary goal is to keep the dollar amount of the latter as low as possible. These twin objectives also mandate security's involvement in plans and preparations for dealing with emergencies and disasters. Risk management's role is to provide protection against losses, including those that might be caused by security operations, through the medium of insurance.

In planning and preparing for a proper response in case of an emergency or disaster, the security/loss-prevention effort has to focus on a wide range of incidents that can result in the loss of life or assets and injuries to guests and staff. Plans mean that employees will know what to do if an incident occurs, as well as what to do and how they can be accounted for if evacuation is necessary. Preparations involve having available the resources needed to respond. Fires, acts of nature, civil disturbances, or possibly even terrorist activities can result in losses.

While by definition emergencies and disasters are sudden, unanticipated events that require immediate responses in some cases, such as acts of nature, forecasting can help with preparations. Many other situations, such as bomb threats or acts of terrorism, cannot be predicted. Nevertheless, by weighing probabilities against possibilities, training the staff, and establishing priorities in terms of resources, meaningful programs can be designed to deal with many of these occurrences. If a natural disaster occurs and a hotel opens its doors for the benefit of its neighbors or others in the community, additional precautions may be called for in order to minimize the risk of damage to or the loss of assets or of injuries to people.

Innkeepers should not hesitate to seek help from local public safety agencies when there are incidents that its own security staff cannot handle without outside assistance. An example would be a bomb threat when a possible search of the premises by the police would still require at least some employee involvement. Certainly police help will be needed if a civil disturbance (or strike) escalates, or threatens to escalate, to a point where force may be needed to either keep access to the property clear or to eject demonstrators from the premises.

From the standpoint of prevention, therefore, much can be done on the basis of careful analysis and flexibility in both planning and preparing a response. This does not alter the fact that the most difficult problem arises when the possibility of terrorist activity exists. There are limits to what can be done in the way of preventive action, but the importance of good communication and relations with police and appropriate federal agencies, as well as an inn's own ability to collect and analyze intelligence, cannot be overemphasized. If an act of terrorism does occur, the response is the same as in any other disaster.

REVIEW QUESTIONS

1. What is meant by the deductible in an insurance policy?
2. How do security/loss prevention and risk management differ?
3. Is there a need to have insurance coverage for security operations?
4. Can acts of nature be forecast?
5. Do audible alarms by themselves provide sufficient notice of an evacuation?
6. How can staff be accounted for if evacuation occurs?
7. Who should decide whether or not to evacuate a property?
8. What is a bomb threat checklist?
9. Why should police assistance be requested if demonstrators in a civil disturbance are to be removed from the premises?
10. Why are hotels not necessarily immune from acts of terrorism?

CHAPTER 6

LEGAL CONSIDERATIONS
IN PREVENTING LOSSES

On March 4, 1933, in his first inaugural address as president of the United States, Franklin Delano Roosevelt said, "The only thing we have to fear is fear itself." Today hoteliers find themselves troubled with fears of their own. One is the need to remain profitable in an increasingly competitive environment; the other is the fear of being sued and of the adverse publicity that may accompany litigation.

With regard to profitability, even major chains have been acquired by real estate investment trusts. Notwithstanding retention of their previous names for identification purposes, in reality the number of chain operations has decreased as ownership consolidation has increased. Distasteful as this may be, especially to operators of single properties and owners of small chains, it merely indicates that the lodging industry is not much different from other industries. Acquisitions and consolidation have become a part of today's highly competitive business world.

At the same time, the risk of being sued has become increasingly worrisome. Over the last several years service industries, particularly lodging and retailing, have had to deal with shrinking profits attributable not only to competition but also to increased litigation. In part this is a price they pay for their obvious dependence on and exposure to public use, coupled with the fact that we live in a highly litigious society.

People who feel that they have been wronged are almost encouraged to sue by some lawyers' advertisements that, despite existing controls, imply that retention of those lawyers will assure a judgment in favor of the plaintiff. Add to this the unconscionably large awards granted in some cases. Even when juries find for defendant hotels, the cost of their defense cuts into profits. Furthermore, depending on the basis for the suit and the extent to which it is covered by the news media, the hotel's reputation may suffer and indirectly contribute to an additional loss of profit.

On occasion these realities, plus the fear that the Congress of the United States will act if the industry does not, have prompted some industry leaders to advocate establishing industry-wide security standards. Considering the many variables that exist among properties, however, it becomes evident that developing meaningful standards is virtually impossible even for chains. In reality, one cannot formulate effective security/loss-prevention programs without factoring in the location, size, types of guests catered to, staff size, and the overall nature of each facility's operations.

Does this mean that innkeepers are completely at the mercy of disgruntled guests and overzealous lawyers? Is there any way in which they can prevent all risk of litigation? As a practical matter, the answer to both questions is *no*. Nevertheless, there are ways in which some lawsuits can be avoided, just as there are some ways in which the extent of damages awarded to successful plaintiffs can be mitigated. To the extent that any litigation can be avoided or damages mitigated, hotels benefit.

First, it is important to understand that there is no single or simple way to deal with these concerns. Multiple factors have to be taken into account; some of them are not within a property's control, while some of them are. Obviously, a disgruntled guest's decision to sue or not is beyond an inn's control. If a case goes to trial, the same is true of the outcome. Remember, too, that claims are not necessarily limited to personal injury; they also may be for the loss of or damage to guests' property. Even when a plaintiff's claim is a hazard covered by a defendant property's insurance, the decision to settle or go to court may rest entirely with the insurer.

If an out-of-court settlement is not reached and a trial is held, the reasonableness of an inn's security in any given situation is to be the determinant with regard to liability. Reasonableness supposedly is determined objectively in light of all of the facts. While this is true in theory, in reality what is reasonable is what a jury says it is. In some instances juries may be inclined to see the guest/plaintiff as David pitted against the hotel/defendant's Goliath. These are some of the realities that innkeepers must face.

Nevertheless, some things within a property's control can be done to either prevent lawsuits or mitigate damages. What are they? One is the effective use of physical security, covered in detail in Chapter 2. Peepholes and chains on guest room doors, the proper types of locks installed, key controls (where keys still are used), good lighting, appropriate use of closed-circuit television, clearly marked evacuation routes, the availability of safe-deposit boxes, and the use of fire-retardant materials are among the things that can be done to protect both guests and innkeepers.

For example, suppose a guest alleges having been assaulted and robbed. A claim is filed; the case goes to trial. In its defense the inn proves that each guest room door has both a peephole and door chain. Under cross-examination the guest admits that neither was used; the door was opened in response to a knock. Under the circumstances the inn's security measures were reasonable; the plaintiff's behavior was not.

Sole reliance on physical security as a defense is insufficient. When guests allege some form of injury or loss, the human element as a factor cannot be ignored. Either personal injury or the loss or theft of personal property may fall into those categories of offenses that can be crimes, torts, or both. The former are defined as offenses against the state; the latter, as offenses against persons. Injured parties can elect to file a criminal complaint, a civil action in tort, or both.

Except for the most egregious offenses, for which guests may choose to pursue matters both criminally and civilly, the preference is to sue in tort—

and with good reason. First, in a criminal case the plaintiff is the state, not the victim. If a defendant is found guilty and fined, the money goes to the state rather than the victim. If in a civil suit the judgment is for the plaintiff, it is the latter who is entitled to the sum on which the jury has agreed. Second, the standard of proof needed for a conviction in a criminal case is higher than that required for a judgment in a civil matter. Convictions in criminal cases mandate proof beyond a reasonable doubt; only a preponderance of the evidence is needed to win in civil court.

Consequently, if guests sue in tort a lower standard of proof is required in order to win, and they are the ones who benefit from any monetary award. Furthermore, if they win they need not worry about the defendant being judgment-proof since in all probability the property is insured. What they need to prove is that the inn owed them a duty to do or not to do something, that duty was breached, and as a result they suffered some form of injury or loss.

From this definition of a tort it is obvious that what an inn's staff does or does not do in relation to caring for guests can trigger a lawsuit, and it is equally obvious that these are matters largely within management's control. Key elements are the role of the human resources department, including the training given to all employees in doing their jobs and relating to guests and the quality and effectiveness of supervision. Although these subjects were discussed in Chapters 3 and 4, primarily from an operating point of view, they need further consideration from a legal perspective.

All guests and their personal property have some degree of exposure to an inn's employees. That exposure may be direct or indirect, depending on any given employee's specific duties. Allegations of theft from rooms or a guest's illness resulting from something prepared in the kitchen, tend to implicate members of the staff. Occasionally, guests may allege that they were assaulted by employees. Therefore, should a guest choose to sue for any of these reasons, in all likelihood one count in the complaint will be negligent hiring by the inn. In theft or assault cases, character is an issue; in cases of illness, the health of food service employees may be in question.

Be assured that under these circumstances plaintiff's lawyer, either on a motion for discovery, during depositions, or at trial, will want to know all about the property's preemployment procedures, including physical examinations. The risk of liability is markedly increased, and the defense is greatly weakened, if there is proof that an employee was involved in the loss or injury and that the defendant does little or nothing in the way of screening.

Hoteliers who are willing to accept inadequate or nonexistent preemployment screening are shortsighted. No matter the job involved, it is not in a property's best interest for its human resources department to merely shuffle papers or do a cursory examination of applications. Some will protest meaningful preemployment procedures, physical examinations included, saying the expense cannot be justified since so many lodging industry jobs either are or border on the menial. That the cost of a single award to a plaintiff may far exceed the cost of adequate screening is ignored. They forget that even if insured the deductible itself may cost them more than would an acceptable preemployment screening program.

Next is the adequacy of training, which should include instruction on what employees should both do and not do in terms of dealing with guests. This goes beyond the traditional concept of being hospitable. As noted in Chapters 3 and 4, there are things that virtually every employee, whether directly or indirectly involved with guests, should be doing not only to make the latter feel comfortable but also to reduce the risk of problems that might lead to litigation.

Among them are specifically asking registering guests if they want to use a safe-deposit box, making note of those who might need help in an emergency requiring evacuation, and if asked about the city, providing information about parts best avoided. How the laundry handles guests' garments not only in terms of washing and dry-cleaning but also in finding items inadvertently left in them by guests, as well as housekeeping's exposure to guest property, need to be addressed as part of staff training. Room assignments for women guests and the offer of escorts to and from parking facilities can also help avoid lawsuits or at least help in an inn's defense. No less important, employees must understand that if problems with a lawsuit potential do arise, they make no commitments in the hotel's behalf; obligating a property rests exclusively with its senior management.

The value of even the best training can quickly be lost without oversight to ensure implementation. This means an adequate level of supervision. Without resorting to needless legalese, it may be helpful to understand the process from two different views. One is the way in which lawsuits are initiated; the other, the nature of the employee-employer relationship.

With respect to the process of initiation, in criminal cases the plaintiff is the state, not the victim. Cases go forward on the basis of either a grand jury indictment or an information filed with the court by a prosecutor. In either event, each offense with which a person is charged, and which the prosecution has to prove for a conviction, must be set forth. In civil cases the aggrieved party is the plaintiff. Defendants are served with a summons and complaint, the latter enumerating each alleged grievance upon which the suit is based. Consequently, depending on the incident involved in a civil suit against a hotel, it is conceivable that a plaintiff/guest might include in the complaint counts for negligent hiring, negligent supervision, and possibly even for negligent retention of an employee, depending on that person's work history.

The employee-employer relationship has to be understood because it bears on the question of liability. In this regard, the laws of the fifty United States and of many other countries recognize certain underlying principles. They are based on the doctrines of master and servant, principal and agent, and *respondeat superior*. The latter term means that the master is responsible for the servant's acts. Practically speaking, the key difference between master and servant and principal and agent revolves around discretion. In the former, the master is in complete control; in the latter, the agent has some discretion in terms of performance.

To illustrate, a housekeeper has virtually no discretion insofar as job performance is concerned. The specific rooms to be serviced and the way in which they are to be serviced are prescribed by management. Thus from a legal perspective, housekeepers are "servants", and the general manager is the "master." In contrast, department heads are the general manager's "agents" since they have to be allowed some discretion in order to do their jobs. However, in neither case is the superior relieved of responsibility for the subordinate's acts, even if that responsibility is only indirect and leads to an employer's vicarious liability insofar as the law is concerned.

Nevertheless, employers will not necessarily be liable, either directly or indirectly, in every case in which the underlying issue is an employee's conduct. Here, two separate and distinct factors need to be considered. One deals with the very nature of the employee's job and the relationship between the job and the act complained of; the other has to do with the question of foreseeability on the employer's part.

Insofar as a legal defense is concerned, the job-incident relationship is critically important. Ordinarily, evidence showing that the employee's behavior was beyond the scope of that person's employment would relieve the employer of liability. In other words, the employee's actions were not in furtherance of the employer's business or in its best interest; they served only to satisfy the employee. Notwithstanding this defense, depending on the nature of the plaintiff/guest's grievance, the question of a defendant's liability may also hinge on whether the employee's conduct could reasonably have been foreseen. In other words, could management reasonably have anticipated the employee's aberrant behavior? Once again, the answer to this question often lies in what was known about the individual prior to being employed and what that person's conduct was after joining the staff.

As an example, suppose a woman guest was assaulted in her room by a room service waiter and sues the hotel. In no way did the assault benefit the inn; to the contrary, it was harmful and certainly not within the scope of the waiter's employment. However, during discovery proceedings preceding trial, the victim's lawyer learns that (a) the hotel did nothing in the way of a background check; or (b) the waiter had a record of similar behavior in a previous job but was hired nonetheless; or (c) he had no such record, but although female co-workers at the inn had complained about his conduct toward them, their complaints were ignored. In this case foreseeability might well be an issue; counts of negligent hiring and supervision undoubtedly would be included, and possibly even negligent retention.

These are not the only circumstances under which questions of foreseeability may become an issue, and if they do, the only thing that counts is the defendant/hotel's position. In other words, it is what this particular property does to protect its guests and staff that counts, not what competitors do or do not do. This necessitates looking beyond operations per se; such things as a property's location, its history of incidents, the nature of its activities, the kind of guests it attracts, and the type of staff it employs all need to be taken into account.

In some respects good, but legally permissible relations with local police departments can be helpful. They can provide information not only about crime statistics for the area in which the property is located but also about the types of offenses committed. The data can be useful for advising guests about places best avoided and certainly for making plans for the protection of guests, employees, and the inn's assets.

The inn's history of incidents affecting guests and staff should be more than a record of things that have happened; it should be a working tool. Aside from neighborhood, incidents that do occur may be related to the nature of both the activities and types of guests attracted to an inn. Thus the person responsible for security/loss prevention should know how often and precisely where incidents have occurred in order to plan a course of action to prevent, or at the very least reduce, the problem's scope and magnitude. If it appears that guests or employees were victimized in ways similar to previous incidents, they no doubt will argue that what happened should have been anticipated and that preventive measures should have been taken.

One source of possible litigation, too often ignored, is the way in which security personnel, where employed, do their jobs. Key factors in any lawsuit based on security officers' behavior or job performance are a security department's size and the quality, training, and supervision of its personnel. In a case in which security personnel are provided by a contract agency instead of being proprietary, the written agreement between the hotel and the contract agency can be critically important. The extent of an inn's liaison with public safety agencies can also have a bearing on the subject. However, since these matters will be fully discussed in Chapter 7, we now turn our attention to another area concerning the law vis-à-vis loss prevention.

Thus far we have looked at the risk of loss from the law's perspective based on incidents that for the most part could be classified as crimes, torts, or both. However, it would be wrong to assume that efforts to reduce the risk of litigation—or to have an effective defense if sued—are limited to matters of that kind. In fact, it is possible that some claims could result from deficiencies in a property's safety program.

Guests injured because of real or perceived unsafe conditions are likely to sue; employees will file workmen's compensation claims or, depending on the circumstances surrounding their injuries, may elect to sue or appeal a compensation board's decision. Since guests stay a relatively short time while employees are present long-term, the risk of some form of personal injury claim is obviously greater with respect to the latter. Therefore, providing for the safety of both guests and staff is important.

Inasmuch as there is no monetary limit on the amount for which an allegedly injured guest can sue, as compared to what a workmen's compensation board might award, let us consider guest safety first. To some extent this subject was discussed in Chapter 5 relative to plans and preparations for unsafe conditions that can be caused by acts of nature. However, other existing or potentially unsafe conditions may exist that call for action; what is covered under this umbrella should be all-inclusive. In reducing the risk of safety-related problems, every member of the staff has a role to play. What that role is should be clearly defined in the training given to every employee.

To illustrate this point with a few examples may be helpful. For instance, suppose a carpet in a corridor or a room is torn. Besides adversely affecting a hotel's reputation, an even greater concern is that it can cause someone to trip and fall and hurt themselves. Therefore, when such an unsafe condition is detected by an employee, it should be reported promptly to housekeeping and given a high priority for repair. A damaged piece of furniture could result in someone's being injured; it should be replaced, or at the very least removed, without delay. Emergency lights, illuminated exit signs, and fire extinguishers should be tested or inspected regularly to ensure that they are in good working order. These are matters that can affect the safety of both guests and employees.

Additional concerns about employee safety are at issue. If they are ignored and employees are injured, the number of workmen's compensation claims filed will increase, and so will the premiums paid for mandated coverage. Furthermore, the Williams-Steiger Occupational Safety and Health Act was enacted into law by the United States Congress in 1970[1] for the purpose of ensuring that employees are provided with a safe and healthful workplace. States may have their own programs if they satisfy the criteria established for approval by the federal government.

Whether administered by the United States Department of Labor or a particular state, the standards prescribed have the force and effect of law. As a result, if any employee's injuries are sufficiently serious, or if there is a death, compliance officers from either the federal or state occupational safety and health agency will descend on the property. In the event that safety standards were violated, they will issue citations; depending on he circumstances, civil and/or criminal action also may be taken by the government against the employer.

These laws make it obvious that proper training of employees in how to do their jobs is critically important. No less important is the condition of the equipment with which employees work. Equipment must be in good condition and, where appropriate, must also have suitable safeguards. To further protect themselves and prevent losses, innkeepers need to make certain that employees are properly supervised with respect to complying with the hotel's safety policies.

As a matter of fact, federal and state agencies responsible for compliance with government-mandated safety standards acknowledge that employees as well as employers have an obligation to try to prevent occupational injuries and deaths. They recognize that some employees' injuries are caused by their own carelessness. However, this also makes it incumbent on employers, and it is in their own best interest, to be able to show that when employees fail to comply with the safety program they are disciplined.

SUMMARY

Innkeepers worry about lawsuits that can be costly both financially and in terms of impact on reputation. This concern is understandable, given the combination of a litigious society encouraged to sue by lawyers' advertising and the size of juries awards to successful plaintiffs. While guests who allege that they have been the victims of some form of criminal activity often have the option of filing a criminal complaint, a civil action, or both, they tend to pursue the matter civilly since in these cases they, not the state, benefit from a favorable judgment.

It is this fear, along with concern about possible government intervention, that from time to time prompts the lodging industry to ignore the variables encountered with respect to individual properties and speak about adopting so-called "industry standards." Such discussion ignores reality. The many variables found at individual properties in terms of size, location, types of guests attracted, and incident histories suggest that in actuality the adoption of standards, from a legal perspective, could prove to be more of a burden than a boon. In civil litigation, juries decide what is reasonable or foreseeable. If an inn's security is at issue, reliance on certain standards if an individual property's characteristics realistically prevent application could result in a judgment of such magnitude as to possibly result in bankruptcy or even force closure.

Concerns about lawsuits are legitimate, and litigation cannot be totally discounted as a business consideration. It is immaterial whether the basis is a guest's lawsuit for damage to or loss of property or for personal injury resulting from an assault or otherwise unsafe condition. Other possibilities are losses attributable to injuries sustained by employees that result in their filing workmen's compensation claims, or citations accompanied by penalties that are issued by occupational safety and health compliance officers. The fact remains that while it is impossible to prevent all forms of legal action, it is possible to prevent some and to be able to mitigate damages in many others.

In most cases when legal action is formally initiated, plaintiffs' lawyers will want to do two things: One is to depose persons who, in their opinion, can provide meaningful information about the incident that is the basis of the lawsuit; the other is to file motions with the court for discovery in order to gain pretrial access to documentation related to defendants' practices in relation to the incident.

One can be assured that if employees allegedly were involved in any way, whether in connection with a guest-related matter or their own appeal of a workmen's compensation board's decision, among the documentation most likely to be sought will be data about the human resources department's practices. Depending on the circumstances in any given situation, lawyers may be particularly interested in how applicants are screened and how those hired are trained, supervised, and even disciplined.

Unfortunately, the cliche "penny wise and pound foolish" too often can be applied to employers who either ignore the long-term benefits of applicant screening and employee training, supervision, and discipline when necessary, or tend to rely on insurance coverage as their loss-prevention vehicle. They forget that the amount awarded to a successful plaintiff may far exceed what it would have cost for suitable precautions to have been taken both before and after hiring. Remember, while a properly selected and trained staff cannot prevent all lawsuits (and losses), it can help prevent many; in cases where legal action cannot be prevented, it can be invaluable in mitigating damages.

REVIEW QUESTIONS

1. What factors have increased the risk of legal action being taken against hotels and motels?

2. If legal action is taken, is the risk of a monetary loss the lodging industry's only concern?

3. Why are industry-wide security standards not viable?

4. What factors militate against adopting such standards?

5. Is it possible to avoid all forms of legal action?

6. Do guests sue only in cases where they claim personal injury, or can they also sue for damage to or the loss of personal property?

7. If a case goes to trial, who actually decides whether or not a defendant inn's actions were reasonable?

8. Is reliance solely on physical security sufficient for the prevention of losses?

9. Under what circumstances might employees take legal action against their employers?

10. What is the relationship between loss prevention and the preemployment screening of applicants and the training, supervision, and discipline of employees?

ENDNOTES

1. 29 U.S.C. 657

CHAPTER 7

THE SECURITY DEPARTMENT'S ROLE

While the point has been made from the outset that not every property necessarily needs to have a full-fledged security department, no hotel or motel can ignore the need for a security/loss-prevention program. Recognizing the need for profitability one has to allow for the fact that the size of some inns does not justify employing a full-time staff dedicated exclusively to security. Although the decision whether or not to have such a department rests with owners or their general managers, the fact remains that with or without a department, optimum benefits are realized only if the security/loss-prevention program is fully integrated into all aspects of a property's operations.

Even at smaller properties, where full-time security personnel may not be needed, security/loss prevention calls for two things. Both have already been examined. One was discussed in detail in Chapter 3. With or without a security department, all department heads at all properties have roles to play in preventing losses and protecting assets. Furthermore, physical security, needs, as well as the need for policies and procedures to guide department heads in how to prevent or at least minimize losses, require hoteliers to assign responsibility for the security/loss-prevention program to someone at management level. There must be a focal point for whatever is to be done to protect the inn's assets.

Of course, many properties can justify having full-time security organizations. In these cases more is involved than simply deciding that having them is in the inns' best interests. Many questions have to be answered, but to be assured that they are answered correctly and in those interests, both general managers and those who hope to become general managers need to have at least some understanding of what is involved.

General managers and their executive assistant or resident managers, exposed as they are to the many facets of hotel administration and operations as they rise through the ranks, are ever mindful of the need to be profitable and protect assets. They appreciate the relationship between these needs and the workings of an inn's various departments, but even if they have worked at hotels with security departments, they often have not had a meaningful relationship with the security/loss-prevention function.

Without this relationship, the results will be less than satisfactory. Over- or understaffing and failure to fully integrate security/loss prevention into all phases of operations can be costly. Although the responsibility for a security department's daily activities properly rests with the department head, general managers are ultimately responsible for everything that occurs at their properties. Consequently, they should have at least enough familiarity with a security department's role and operations to avoid becoming the captives of their security managers. For general managers to understand the department's organization, to whom its manager should report, whether to use proprietary or contract personnel, and how it should function operationally are essential.

THE SECURITY DEPARTMENT'S COMPOSITION

At the outset four different but related things have to be considered with regard to the security department's composition:

a. The selection of the department head;
b. To whom he or she should report;
c. Department size; and
d. Whether the staff should be proprietary or contract.

Selecting the Department Head

In choosing a department head, the importance of fully integrating security/loss prevention into all phases of operations for optimum benefits has been emphasized throughout the text. Thus it is essential that a security manager learn how a particular hotel's various departments function. Therefore, whether the security officers themselves are proprietary or contract, the department head should be the inn's employee for three reasons.

First, integration makes it necessary for the security manager to understand how all the other departments function, yet the heads of those departments should not discuss the hotel's business with an outsider. To do so is obviously unwise, but if contract services are used, having a person assigned by the agency as the department head means accepting either a risk of disclosure or a less than optimally effective program. Regarding the risk factor, there is nothing to prevent that person from being transferred, even to a competing property.

Second, do not underestimate the importance of loyalty. Again, if contract services are used and the manager is someone assigned by the agency, that person's first loyalty is to his or her employer rather than to the hotel. Consequently, if an agency elects to move a manager to another customer site, there is a break in the continuity of the inn's loss-prevention program irrespective of the level of its effectiveness.

Third, along with the question of loyalty is the matter of a conflict of interest or the appearance of a conflict. Whether it is the lodging industry or contract security agencies, all organizations that sell services understandably seek ways to increase sales. In addition to providing security officers, many agencies also offer undercover investigative services and hi-tech systems. As a result, there is the risk that an agency-provided security manager will urge an owner or general manager to add security personnel, use investigators, or lease or buy hi-tech equipment even if not actually needed.

Agreeing that the security/loss-prevention department head should be an employee is one thing; selecting the right person for the job is another. The candidate should understand security's role in loss prevention in the lodging industry. With the operative word being "prevention," recognizing that there is a difference between the word's use in policing and in security is imperative. To law enforcement personnel, prevention means the speedy identification, apprehension, and punishment of wrongdoers. As has been pointed out throughout the text, from security's perspective it means actually preventing incidents from occurring in the first place and minimizing the value of losses that are inevitable; these goals are most easily accomplished when security is fully integrated into all aspects of operations.

Understanding this distinction is, or should be, an important consideration in choosing the department head. The notion held by some general and human resources managers that police or experienced investigators are the sine qua non for security managers is misleading. While it is true that meaningful liaison with the appropriate public safety agencies is essential, that is not a security manager's primary responsibility. The latter's first duty is to the inn, and it includes the ability to work with rather than alienate both coworkers and guests, a skill that is too often lacking in those who move from policing careers directly into the private sector.

Police departments are quasi-military organizations in terms of rank and discipline. When given orders their personnel are expected to obey without question. Although they must deal with the general public, this obedience to orders tends to carry over, and persons who question police officers or hesitate to comply with their instructions are often arrested. Consequently, security managers who expect unquestioned compliance with their instructions on the part of coworkers and guests can cause labor relations problems with the former and both public relations and possibly legal ones with the latter. This does not mean that all police personnel are unqualified for private-sector work. Instead, their experience should be considered neither a plus nor a minus; each applicant's qualifications must be examined in their entirety.

What, then, should be considered in weighing a candidate's qualifications? The person should have good general managerial skills and the ability to make decisions in order to run an efficient, cost-effective program. In addition, he or she must be able to communicate easily with people at all levels, both orally and in writing. Good human relations skills are imperative. Otherwise, the security manager will not be able to gain the support of executive management and other department heads, earn the trust and cooperation of the staff in general, and deal effectively with guests.

To Whom Should the Security Manager Report?

This may seem to be a simple question; its answer is not. Although security managers are responsible for designing and implementing loss-prevention programs, as well as overseeing compliance, in reality success is achieved only when three goals are reached. One, everyone has to understand that security is considered important. Two, the security manager is neither an enemy nor intent on taking over the jobs of other department heads. Three, the greatest benefits will be derived only from a team effort in which all employees actively participate.

Reaching the third goal depends largely on success in achieving the first two. To whom the security manager reports is one measure of the program's importance. Whether or not a formal table of organization exists, the security manager should be at the same level as all other department heads. If they report directly to the general manager and attend and participate in the latter's staff meetings, so should the security manager; if only some have this direct reporting line, the security manager should be among them.

This positioning serves three purposes, the first two of which we now consider. First, it obviously sends a signal to everyone that the general manager considers security an important function. Second, at staff meetings it encourages not only an open and free discussion of everyone's security/loss-prevention concerns but also a more collegial environment. The latter minimizes the fear other department heads may have of the security manager's intentions vis-à-vis their operations. From this the team approach to loss prevention follows more easily.

The third reason for the security manager to report to the general manager is to provide the former with direct access when needed but without becoming a burden to the latter. We already noted that as a security manager a person's experience and ability to make decisions are important factors. Security managers are hired because they are responsible and able to perform their duties with little direct supervision. Thus the need for access to a general manager should be very infrequent, but when it is, time can be of the essence. The inherent nature of the security/loss-prevention function is such that on the rare occasion when a decision is needed only the general manager can make it (or the executive assistant or resident manager in his or her absence), the security manager should not have to go through intermediate levels to get the authority to proceed. Such an unwarranted delay conceivably could be costly and, in retrospect, hard to justify.

The Security Department's Size

The answer to the question of how many security officers should constitute the department is not a simple one, but it is one that needs to be carefully considered not only by security managers but also by general as well as executive assistant or resident managers. They need to avoid the pitfall of either overstaffing or understaffing. One can be needlessly expensive; the other can leave the property unprepared for possibly foreseeable events.

Realistically, department size has to be based entirely on the needs of a particular property, not on those of its competitors. For instance, two hotels may have the same number of rooms and may even be located in comparable neighborhoods, but these similarities do not automatically mean their security needs are the same.

Of course, the number of rooms and the neighborhood have to be taken into account in calculating a security department's optimal size. However, they are only two of several factors. Among other things to be considered are the types of guests and functions attracted to the hotel, the ease with which the public can enter and leave, other physical security considerations, and the presence or absence of a garage or other parking facilities. Consequently, in determining size these various issues are best dealt with collectively rather than individually.

Chapter 2 discussed ways in which using physical security can be used to protect inns. It can also be used to reduce the number of security officers needed, given the right conditions. To illustrate, a combination of electronic controls and card readers can be used effectively for employee arrivals and departures without requiring a security officer's presence, but unless someone monitors the systems to ensure proper use, their value is markedly reduced. Thus a first step in deciding on size is to determine the extent to which physical security can be used in lieu of security officers. But remember, although the number of security posts may be reduced, the need for some staff will remain.

Next, distinguish between those posts that have to be staffed full-time, including patrol rounds, and those that require only limited coverage. As an example, a security control room or monitoring center must be staffed at all times, while a receiving dock does not; patrol rounds are a constant, but the day shift may need fewer officers than the other two because of generally increased movement by guests and the presence of housekeepers on the floors. In some cases it may even be possible to cover one or more posts with part-time officers; why pay someone for a 35- or 40-hour week if a post requires only 20 hours a week for ample protection?

Other factors, such as time off between shifts, at least 48 consecutive hours off at the end of each work week, and the number of hours worked per shift, must also be taken into account. While covering one post around the clock in theory calls for 4.3 security officers, reliance on this formula is one of those pitfalls that can result in either over- or understaffing. A more practical approach in terms of both ensuring proper coverage yet allowing for time off is to chart out the 21 shifts (three per day for a seven-day week) in relation to each post to be covered, then fill in the blanks. The result is an easily understood visual duty roster for reference by both security officers and the department head.

Overstaffing can usually be attributed to one of three things: (1) security managers who are bureaucrats and weigh their own importance against the size of their organizations and budgets instead of their accomplishments; (2) those who see security officers as the *only* way to prevent problems from arising; and (3) those who feel that the department must have a large enough staff to be able to cope with all situations without a need for anyone to work overtime. Understaffing most often can be traced to (1) general managers (or comptrollers) who do not appreciate what security/loss prevention can contribute to profits and are unwilling to provide adequate financial resources and (2) security managers who either lack the ability to justify their requests for financing and willingly acquiesce to or submit minimal budget proposals to impress their general managers. Security managers who themselves are responsible for either over- or understaffing evidence a lack of good managerial skills.

Properly charting shifts and posts serves a dual purpose; it helps ensure both adequate coverage and time off for security officers. Normally, however, it makes no provision for either vacations or emergencies. Nevertheless, since department heads have to manage their human and financial resources, they must be prepared to provide for the inn's continued protection without incurring excessive overtime expenses when employees take vacations or when emergencies arise. As a rule this can be done with managed overtime.

Just what is "managed overtime"? Some overtime, like some losses, is inevitable; the aim is to keep it to a minimum. Practically speaking, managed overtime is less expensive than simply increasing a department's size to avoid paying overtime. It can also be helpful by giving security officers a chance to increase their earnings. The need for overtime arises most often to ensure coverage for vacationing staff and to cope with emergencies.

Let's illustrate the point with regard to vacations. A newly hired security manager was confronted with a problem during his first year. The hotel had a generous vacation policy, no limit on the number of vacation days that could be accumulated, and unionized security officers, many of whom were long-time employees. Furthermore, his predecessor had granted whatever time was requested, whenever it was asked for. Naturally, the cost of vacation coverage soared.

Examining prior years' budget playbacks showed that most of these charges were incurred during the summer months. This prompted certain changes in the way vacations were taken and resulted in a marked reduction in the cost of coverage. Neither any of the security officers nor the union were alienated once they realized that everyone would benefit.

First, it was made clear to the staff that vacation time was not limited to the period between Memorial Day and Labor Day; it extended from January 1 through December 31. Next, the number of weeks that could be taken at one time would be limited, but more than one vacation could be taken during the year. Last, security officers would submit their first, second, and third choices for each vacation with the understanding that if there were no conflicts, first choices would be granted. If conflicts did exist, they would be resolved on the basis of seniority.

There are two ways in which emergency coverage can mean overtime. The first is the type of emergency or disaster discussed in Chapter 5. Under those conditions trying to manage overtime verges on the impossible. The best interests of properties confronted with those situations mandate coverage regardless of the overtime involved. The second is the number of times when a security officer fails to report for duty. Obviously, if any officer does this habitually, the reasons need to be carefully examined. Can the cost of continuously paying overtime to cover for this person be justified? In most cases it cannot be, and termination is warranted.

However, on occasion conscientious, reliable employees are confronted with personal emergencies that may prevent them from coming to work. The definition of an emergency as a sudden, unforeseen situation that requires an immediate response applies equally to those that may be caused by personal needs, but the post of a security officer absent for such a reason still has to be covered. If a security manager feels that under such circumstances coverage is unnecessary, a general manager needs to ask why funds are being expended for the position in the first place. That aside, among the most common personal emergencies are illness or a death in a family.

While overtime cannot be avoided in these cases, its management takes on a different meaning; it is also easier to administer. As we have said, when some overtime can be justified, it gives security officers a chance to add to their earnings. It can also be a morale booster, but only when the opportunities are distributed in ways that are fair and that do not compromise the overall loss-prevention program.

There are two parts to being fair. One consists of identifying those who are willing to work overtime when the occasion arises. The other is keeping a record of each officer's overtime so that over time everyone's chances are as equal as possible.

To avoid compromising the program requires the staff to be alert and able to respond to whatever incidents may arise while they are on duty, whether monitoring security systems, making patrol rounds, or working at fixed posts. People tend to be less alert and take longer to respond, no matter what their jobs, as their time at work lengthens. Security officers are no exception. Whether their normal work days are eight or twelve hours, their efficiency will be markedly decreased and risks to the hotel increased if they are asked to work an additional tour of duty to cover for someone's absence. In these cases it is advisable to split the coverage. Although it is no panacea, having an officer on duty extend his or her shift by an additional half a shift and then have another come in half a shift earlier than usual is better for both the officers and the hotel than having someone work a double shift.

The number of security officers employed will have a bearing on the number of supervisors needed. Only those managers interested in developing bureaucracies rather than in the department's accomplishments will contend that the number of officers assigned to each shift should be a factor. Security personnel, like other employees, need supervision. Since supervisors are part of the management team, except for experience their qualifications should be similar to those previously outlined for security managers.

Realistically, hiring a supervisor to oversee the work of five or more security officers on a shift is one thing. However, if there are only two or three, it is an expense that can hardly be justified. This does not mean supervision is unnecessary; rather, it can possibly be provided in other ways. In earlier chapters the point was made that in those cases where inns cannot justify full-time security managers, let alone full-time security departments, there nevertheless must be a member of management to whom the responsibility for loss prevention is assigned. This same principle can be applied when security department shifts are minimally staffed even if there is a full-time security manager. In other words, have night managers responsible for generally overseeing the property's second and third shifts also supervise the security officers.

The computer age has not eliminated the need for reports, record keeping, written instructions to security department personnel, security policies and procedures for the entire hotel staff, memoranda, and letters. Consequently, the department manager and supervisory staff (where there is one), must have secretarial and clerical support. However, this should not represent a significant increase in department size since, as a rule, both functions can be handled by one person.

Contract versus Proprietary Security Personnel

Although the justification for a hotel's hiring its own security/loss-prevention manager has already been discussed, the question of whether to hire its own security officers or use contract agency personnel must be considered in terms of a department's composition. There are pros and cons for the use of each, with cost, quality, and the inn's protection in case of litigation among the most important factors.

The argument that contract services are less expensive is not always true; geography can be a factor. In some places, but not all, the hourly rate for quality contract services may be at parity with the combined hourly wage plus fringes for proprietary personnel. However, to decide solely on the basis of cost can be risky and may prove to be far more expensive in the long run. Consequently, without minimizing the importance of cost, quality of service and the property's protection against possible lawsuits (and their attendant expenses) deserve even more attention.

A proprietary staff's quality will be examined in relation to how it is recruited, trained, and supervised, but for now we shall consider both quality and the legal ramifications of using agency personnel. Historically, most security managers have preferred proprietary security officers based on legitimate concerns about contract agencies. Many of those objections were, and in some cases still are, valid; they can also be dealt with.

In all fairness, the problems that arose or that still arise can be traced to the way in which an agency's services are retained. Today most concerns can be disposed of by combining a good contract with the choice of a reliable agency. Using purchase orders for a certain number of security-officer hours at an agreed-upon rate is wholly unsatisfactory. Purchase orders have neither meaningful terms nor conditions covering the quality of the service to be provided or the hotel's protection should a lawsuit be filed on the basis of a security officer's actions. What is needed is a written agreement.

There are two kinds of contracts for agency services: an agreement prepared by the agency or one prepared by the customer's lawyers. For no particular reason, other than possibly saving a legal fee, the inclination is to accept the former, notwithstanding the fact that lawyers who prepare contracts understandably write them in ways that most likely will be favorably interpreted for their clients' or employers' benefit.

A contract consists of an offer of goods or services by one party, acceptance by another, and the passage of consideration (something of value) between them. While an offer and acceptance presume a meeting of the minds, as well as good faith on the part of both parties, disagreements can and do arise. When they do, the parties can try to resolve the matter amicably, but if they cannot, they end up in court where the written agreement becomes the key to the solution.

Contracts prepared in behalf of agencies tend to be relatively brief and less detailed than those prepared in behalf of their customers. They will focus mainly on the nature and cost of the service. In contrast, customer-prepared contracts can be expected to be considerably longer, and they will take other issues into consideration. For instance, to properly and adequately cover both the quality of the services contracted for and the hotel's protection, among the subjects to be included are the requirements relative to the types of personnel to be assigned, uniforms, training, equipment, supervision, insurance, protection against litigation precipitated by the conduct of agency employees, possibly confidentiality, and the submission and payment of invoices.

There should be no hesitation about asking agencies to sign contracts prepared by an inn's attorneys. Reliable agencies should not have problems in satisfying the agreement's terms and conditions, and since they, like other businesses, need customers to be profitable, few if any will balk at this request. Beware of an agency that insists it will sign only its own contract form.

For those electing to use contract services, a condition precedent to the signing stage is the selection of a reliable agency. A number of factors need to be considered in an agency's evaluation; among them are the owners' experience in the security/loss-prevention field, time in business, reputation, size, financial stability, and pay and promotion policies.

Agencies must be licensed by the state(s) in which they do business, and it is not uncommon to find the licensing procedure covered under statutes pertaining to private investigators. For the most part the statutes set a minimum age for applicants, require them to be of good moral character and have no past convictions for felonies or serious misdemeanors, call for some investigative experience, and require them to be able to post a bond.

Judging by these requirements, it is evident that the experience, if any, called for in order to get a license and offer contract security services is not in security/loss prevention; it is much closer to policing. That is not what innkeepers need or should want. Only agencies whose owners are truly prevention oriented, rather than those to whom prevention means detection, apprehension, and punishment, should be asked to submit proposals.

The length of time that an agency has been in business is important since it has a bearing on reputation and financial stability. To illustrate this point, a chain took over the management of a property in a relatively small community and decided to use an agency for its security department. The inn's size and location did not warrant hiring its own security manager; instead the responsibility was assigned to the rooms division manager who asked for the corporate security director's help in selecting an agency.

The latter learned that there were four agencies, all local, in town; the nearest city with nationally known agencies was seventy miles away. The corporate security director and the inn's general and rooms division managers agreed that using a local agency would be better for community relations and that it also would shorten the agency management's response time in an emergency. The corporate security director contacted the sheriff, whom he knew, for any information that could be provided about the four firms.

The sheriff suggested one, his primary reason being that it, unlike its competitors, had at least been doing business in the town for five years.

An agency's reputation is obviously important. Certainly, inquiry should be made of the references it provides, but the investigation should not be limited to them since it is highly unlikely that the names of dissatisfied accounts will be given. Contacting the local Better Business Bureau and checking civil court records for any possible lawsuits or liens against the agency can prove helpful.

Size is a factor with regard to an agency's ability to satisfy an individual customer's needs. In other words, although an agency enjoys an excellent reputation, does it have the personnel resources to staff that particular hotel? When asking references about performance, also ask about the number of security officers assigned to their facilities. For instance, despite glowing reports about service and management's responsiveness, the references' staffing needs may require far fewer officers. This factor has to be taken into account as part of the decision-making process. Unless an agency can give assurance that an adequate number of officers can be provided, it should not be chosen.

Failure to consider an agency's financial stability can be risky. From a security/loss-prevention standpoint, the last thing a general or security manager needs is to learn that security officers have not come to work because they have not been paid by the agency, or its insurance policies have been cancelled for nonpayment of premiums, or the government has attached its bank accounts for nonpayment of taxes. A reliable, reputable agency desirous of getting a potential customer's business will willingly provide a copy of its most current financial statement.

The same is true of an agency's willingness to make known its pay and promotion policies, information that should be of interest to any prospective user of its services. Pay and promotion have a bearing on both the kinds of people hired and their retention. Security officers are usually paid by the hour, and some agencies pay their personnel no more than the minimum wage set by law. Ordinarily, this is no inducement for the best people to join those agencies. Keeping in mind the need for security officers to be able to relate to both guests and employees, pay is a factor to be considered in terms of the types of security officers who may be assigned to a property.

In addition to pay, opportunities for promotion can have a bearing not only on the kinds of people willing to work for an agency but also on the quality of the service provided. The relatively high turnover rate at some agencies often means that promotions are based on seniority rather than ability. This policy will ensure loyalty on the part of those responsible for overseeing agency personnel assigned to a customer. However, loyalty does not equate with competence, and the security staff's competence is important in preventing losses and maintaining good labor and guest relations. Therefore, to the extent that contracts with agencies call for any supervision of those assigned to properties, general and security managers need to know on what basis agency employees are promoted and what supervisory personnel are paid.

While many of the reservations about agency use can be overcome through the medium of detailed, well-written contracts, admittedly there are some things that no contract can cover. As a result, after weighing all the factors, including cost, some innkeepers prefer to do their own staffing. If they elect to do so, they need to pay particular attention to certain factors.

In the final analysis the success of any truly effective security program depends on its ability to prevent losses or at least to minimize their scope and magnitude, but in reality it also hinges largely on security officers' attitudes. The latter are significant since an important aspect of loss prevention involves being able to get the cooperation and good will of those who are either the victims of losses or able to help prevent them.

Consequently, over and above the ability to have good relations with guests and coworkers, lodging industry security officers' personalities and attitudes are especially important. Healthy attitudes are needed, and they are derived from good pay, good working conditions, and recognition when a job is done well. These, in turn, contribute to a sense of pride in the job and loyalty to the employer. Obviously, loyalty cannot be incorporated into any agency's contract.

Because personality and loyalty play a prominent role in the way security personnel, and consequently the loss-prevention effort, are perceived by guests and other employees, care must be exercised in choosing members of the security staff. Concern with this issue is often a factor in deciding whether or not to use proprietary security officers.

If a security officer is to be an inn's employee, the task of setting standards for employment and the responsibility for careful screening should be shared by the department manager and human resources. Thus the selection process rests exclusively with the employer, who does not have to rely on an agency to screen, select, and assign its employees.

If contract services are to be used, it is only right that as the employer the agency should do the screening, selecting, and assigning of its staff. However, as the customer a hotel can still have input with respect to the security officers assigned to it. The contract can provide both that the hotel has the right to reject any agency employee sent to it and that it can at any time ask for the removal of an assigned security officer. Therefore, if the main reason for a proprietary staff is concern with contract officers' personalities and their attitudes, these contractual safeguards are helpful.

RECRUITING, TRAINING, AND SUPERVISING SECURITY PERSONNEL

Chapter 6 discussed legal considerations in loss prevention and noted the importance of carefully screening, training, and supervising the property's staff. Not doing so can increase the risk of a suit alleging negligent hiring, supervision, or retention based on an employee's behavior. This need for care is heightened where security personnel are concerned. By virtue of their jobs they are the employees most likely to have some form of physical contact with either guests or other members of the staff.

The risk of liability exists whether security officers are the inn's or an agency's employees. As noted in Chapter 6, employers are liable for the acts of employees that fall within the scope of their employment; the mere fact that security officers work for an agency does not automatically relieve a customer of liability. Therefore, no matter whether a property uses its own or agency security personnel, both general and security managers need to be aware of and take an interest in their selection, training, and supervision.

Recruiting

When security officers are recruited, the careful screening and selection of viable applicants can either contribute to or help minimize the effects of the loss-prevention effort. It is during the screening process that the prospective employer can gain insight into a person's personality, attitude, reliability, and overall fitness for a job.

Here, differences exist between agency and proprietary security officers. True, if the former are used, customers understandably have no control over the methods employed to recruit and screen, but this does not have to mean that customers are at the agency's mercy. A provision in the contract can stipulate that upon request the customer is to have access to background information on any officers to be assigned to it. By the same token, if a proprietary staff is preferred, the inn controls the entire process as long as it doesn't violate any provisions of either federal or state employment laws. The race, creed, sex, religious beliefs, age, and country of national origin of an applicant are immaterial; also, disabled persons could possibly fill certain jobs.

A first step in the process is recognizing that security personnel for any service industry have a unique role to play. In their work for hotels and retail stores, doing their jobs with courtesy, consideration, and the ability to relate to people is especially important. The criteria used to recruit and screen people for security positions should include those qualities.

In looking for the best-qualified people, some consider people with police experience or, in some cases, even moonlighting police officers as the "best qualified" due to their having been screened and knowing the law, how to investigate, and how to deal with people. Moonlighters also have authority and can help promote good relations with the police department. Beware of those who advocate this position. They are either unaware of or prefer to ignore the possible pitfalls. A qualified police officer is not necessarily the best-qualified security officer, nor are past or present police personnel in the latter role able to immunize their employers against lawsuits and their attendant costs.

First is the difference in approach. Policing focuses on crime prevention. That entails identifying, arresting, and punishing criminals to prevent them from committing further crimes; presumably, it also serves to deter others from pursuing criminal careers. Security's role is to prevent crime, but it also wants to prevent a number of other incidents that cause losses. To do this it focuses on identifying conditions that can lead to losses, so that preventive action can be taken ahead of time.

True, police officers know the law and have authority. Nevertheless, at times the line separating their roles as police and security officers can be a fine one. On more than one occasion, employers using police personnel as security officers have found themselves in court. In their dealings with third parties, the question to be decided is whether they were acting in the public interest as police officers or as security officers for the primary benefit of their private employers. In either case, and regardless of the outcome, the very need to go to court is a form of loss in itself.

The argument that police officers and, consequently, their private sector employers benefit from the officers' experience in dealing with people is a specious one. Great are the differences between the kinds of people with whom they most likely have contact as police officers and those to whom they must relate as hotel security officers. Understandably, the stress and personal danger confronting them are such that they often have no room for courtesy or diplomacy, but a lack of courtesy and diplomacy on the part of a hotel security officer is inexcusable.

People who are not criminals but who feel mistreated by the police may grumble. They even may file complaints. Unless their treatment is so egregious as to justify suing the department and being awarded a judgment, the principal damage is to the department's reputation. A security officer's failure to be diplomatic or courteous does more than tarnish an inn's reputation. Even minor incidents can be costly if offended guests avoid future stays at the property and urge friends to do the same—a point worth illustrating.

A block of rooms had been reserved at a 350-room chain-managed hotel for out-of-town guests attending a wedding. Upon returning to their rooms from an afternoon event, two couples reported the apparent theft of some jewelry to the front desk. They were told that the property's only security officer, a moonlighting police officer, would contact them when he came to work for the 4 P.M. to midnight shift. The security officer met with the victims as promised, but afterwards both parties were dissatisfied with their treatment and expressed their feelings to the other guests. Their dissatisfaction was largely due to the way in which they had been questioned about their losses. They said that although they were the victims, they had been made to feel as if they were the suspects, and they vowed to never again stay at any of the chain's properties.

This incident indicates that on occasion there is a need for an investigation. In addition, there also is a need for effective liaison with police agencies. However, both matters will be discussed later in this chapter, the former under training and the latter under public safety liaison.

Training

Some of the fifty United States have passed laws mandating training for security personnel. From time to time members of the United States Congress try to pass laws for the same purpose; that they have not succeeded does not mean that they will not renew their attempts. At both the state and federal levels, the basis for their action has been the need for security officers to interface with the general public while performing what they perceive to be a public safety or quasi-public service.

Legislation aside, the fact is that having properly trained security personnel is a loss-prevention measure in itself. A well-trained security staff can do its job more effectively and efficiently with less need for direct supervision or discipline. Two other important benefits also are derived. Properly trained and supervised security officers are less likely to create or find themselves in situations that might lead to lawsuits being filed. Training also can help defend a hotel's position, and in case of an adverse decision it may well help mitigate damages.

Despite this, too many security officers are either inadequately trained or not trained at all. This most often is the case when general managers—and in some cases even security managers—do not really understand the security department's role in preventing losses, or else they consider security officers' work as being wholly devoid of any complexity or risk. After all, what is so complicated about patrolling, or monitoring closed-circuit television and alarm systems? Those who think this way make no allowance for contacts that can occur among security officers, guests, and employees and the problems that can arise when untrained officers do not act in the inn's best interests.

Devising and implementing an effective training program is an important part of a security manager's job. Training should be given to all new hires, but not limited to that one time. There should be periodic in-service training to refresh security employees' memories and keep them abreast of any new developments or changes in the loss-prevention program.

Keeping records of all training is important. If the conduct of security personnel is at issue in a lawsuit, rest assured that during the pretrial discovery process, and again at trial, the plaintiff's lawyer will seek information about the nature, adequacy, and frequency of training. Consequently, the quality of the training and of the records can either help or hurt the inn's defense. They also can have a bearing on the amount of damages if a plaintiff gets a judgment.

All training must be designed to ensure that the inn's best interests will be served. This means that instruction must be given not only on what the security staff is to do in any given situation but also on what is *not* to do. Without the latter there is a risk of lawsuits being filed by complaining guests who allege that security officers with whom they had contact made statements, or offered to do something for the guest, that the guest now feels binds the property.

Training must obviously cover the duties and responsibilities of the security staff. Security officers must know what they are expected to do (their duties) and, equally important, that they will be held accountable (responsible) for doing their jobs effectively, efficiently, and courteously. They must also be given to understand that they have whatever authority they need to get the work done but that there are limits to their authority. Excesses in this respect are inexcusable; they can also prove to be a source of needless expense and embarrassment. At the same time, it is unfair to hold someone accountable for performing a particular job while denying them the authority needed to do it.

Supervision

The interface that takes place between security personnel on one hand and guests and employees on the other is accompanied by certain risks that can be costly and embarrassing. Effective supervision is one way of reducing those risks, even though, to a degree, they are inherent in security operations. To achieve this involves, among other things, good interpersonal, human relations, and communication skills on the part of both the department head and the supervisory staff.

Nowhere are these skills more evident than when it becomes necessary to discipline someone. Many managers and supervisors find the need to discipline subordinates distasteful, primarily due to their tendency to associate discipline with punishment as meted out to errant police or military personnel. Although discipline must also be maintained in the private sector, relying mainly on punishment for that purpose can be self-defeating. A punished employee may lose interest in the job, perform poorly, and show his or her resentment by an act of vandalism or even by violence against the person administering the punishment. This is not to say that on occasion an individual's conduct merits punishment, which can range from loss of pay to suspension and even to termination in the most egregious cases.

The need to discipline arises most often when employees make mistakes. This is something of which we all (managers and supervisors included) can be guilty from time to time. In truth, the very mistakes that may suggest a need for discipline frequently are more the result of a supervisor's failure to communicate clearly than of a subordinate's willful misconduct. Consequently, since making mistakes is a human frailty, good managers and supervisors will use discipline as a teaching tool, appointing themselves as the teachers.

Of course, discipline is not the sole or necessarily most important aspect of supervision. Among the many things that managers and supervisors have to do to be effective is to keep their subordinates informed by providing them with information that pertains to their work; at the same time, they must ensure that they, in turn, are kept informed with respect to any out-of-the-ordinary conditions or incidents that could result in a loss of assets. This is as it should be. However, the principle also applies to those same managers and supervisors who, unfortunately, do not always keep *their* superiors informed. They tend to theorize that, having been hired for their security expertise, they are largely autonomous.

General managers who tolerate, even encourage, a laissez-faire attitude on the part of their security managers may rue the day. Certainly, neither they nor their executive assistant or resident managers should be burdened with information or reports of a routine nature, but just as it is imperative that security officers and supervisors keep their superiors informed of all unusual incidents that can affect the hotel, so should a security manager be required to let his or her superiors know of such occurrences.

Nevertheless, in order to avoid the occasional pitfalls, general managers need to remember certain things. The better part of any meaningful, integrated, loss-prevention program is based on a combination of good general management, communications, and human relations skills, a basic understanding of what security is really all about, and a high degree of common sense. Therefore, although not security experts, general managers, as the persons responsible for the success or failure of their properties, should not be cowed by security managers whose proposals may not always be in the hotel's best interests.

One of the hardest things for general managers to do will be to strike, then maintain, a balanced approach. This means avoiding being too casual on one hand or trying to micromanage the security department on the other.

The former can encourage security managers to feel they have a degree of independence not enjoyed by their peers. In contrast, micromanagement can cause them to let things that need attention pass in favor of letting their general managers do what should be done. Obviously, neither will provide the sought-after benefits of an effective security/loss-prevention program.

It is important for general managers to be kept informed, but none should have to spend time or effort looking at security-related minutia of no real import to an inn's profitability, guest or labor relations, or reputation. Such things as that security officers reported for duty and made their rounds, housekeeping was told about a torn carpet, or engineering was asked to fix a lock do not have the kind of impact to justify being reported to a general manager. Certainly the opposite is true if a guest alleges a robbery or assault, if a fire, suicide, or homicide have occurred, or if an employee has been seriously hurt. Is there a best solution to these potentially vexing problems? Yes. The security manager should be told just what sorts of things the general manager wants promptly reported, what other kinds of data are to be routinely submitted, and the frequency with which that information is to be made available.

UNIFORMS AND EQUIPMENT

The choice of uniforms should be compatible with the environment in which security officers work; it should also take into consideration the impact on guests. Guests do not want to be frightened; they want to feel safe and comfortable in their surroundings. However, should the need for security assistance arise, they also want to be able to identify members of the security staff with relative ease. Security officers in police-type uniforms, with all of the accoutrements normally associated with policing, are easily identified. They also tend to convey the impression that if an inn finds it necessary to have a private police force it must have serious security problems. Not only can this frighten guests, but it also does not project the most desirable image.

Dressing the security staff in color-coordinated uniforms consisting of blazers, slacks (skirts optional for female members), and shirts and ties (blouses and scarves for women) is much more consistent with the hospitality industry's environment and desired image. Name plates, together with the hotel's logo and the word "security" on the breast pocket, provide identification for the benefit of both guests and employees, yet there is nothing about them to frighten people or suggest an abundance of problems.

The economics of buying versus renting uniforms should be considered. Buying uniforms is an investment, and it can be a sizeable one for properties where climatic conditions necessitate uniform changes from season to season. With staff turnover, not uncommon among rank-and-file security officers, there can be a buildup of inventory when departing employees' sizes and those of their replacements differ so much that alterations cannot be made. As for security officers' general appearance, a hotel's laundry can ensure that uniforms are always clean and pressed, and housekeeping can make minor repairs should they be needed.

As far as equipment is concerned, standard items, such as flashlights for those working at night or patrolling darkened areas, and suitable outerwear for those whose duties may require them to be outdoors in winter or in rainy weather are obviously necessary. It is also worthwhile to provide notebooks and pens so that officers have no excuse for not recording conditions in need of attention or incidents to which they responded.

From the property's and the security staff's points of view, two-way radio communication is invaluable. The resulting flexibility when a security control center and officers on post can speak directly with each other may well mean that a smaller staff can still provide the desired level of protection. Furthermore, being able to move personnel quickly to an incident scene and allow officers to keep the control center informed both enroute and upon arrival saves time. This, in turn, can help speed up help for an injured or otherwise distressed party, or to send additional personnel to assist the first responding security officer. For the same reasons, resort properties with extensive acreage might find it advisable to have a patrol vehicle.

A controversial issue where equipment is concerned is whether or not to give security officers weapons of any sort. In reality, the need for doing so is more than questionable; it is hard to justify. Issuing weapons in the form of handguns to security officers is fraught with danger to both persons and the hotel. Therefore, the practical considerations involved must be carefully evaluated before deciding to make this kind of investment.

That persons are licensed, or eligible for a license, to carry firearms does not automatically mean they are properly trained in their use. Completing a course in firearms safety before getting a license is required in some states. But it is just that—a course in safely handling a weapon; it is not a guarantee that the user can hit a target at which the weapon is aimed.

One important factor is cost. Aside from buying the guns, ammunition is needed for training and issue. From time to time more will have to be bought so security officers can periodically requalify in the weapon's use; a onetime qualification is wholly inadequate. Next is the cost of additional insurance to cover the property against any claim that might be filed due to a weapon's deliberate or accidental discharge.

Suppose an armed third party in the lobby is posing a threat to guests and employees alike. An armed security officer, having been made aware of what is going on, approaches. He or she hopes to prevent anything more

Lobby, The Lenox Hotel–Boston

from happening. The mere fact that the security officer is also armed is perceived by that person as a threat. Unless that person is suicidal, the greatest concern now is self-preservation and escape, possibly feeling that there are two choices: a shoot-out in which someone is injured or killed or taking hostages as a bargaining chip. If anything even remotely like this situation could occur, does arming security officers outweigh the risks to innocent people, liability, and bad publicity?

Not insignificant is the risk that a security officer trying to cope with an unruly person might rely less on human relations and communication skills and more on his or her weapon. Without question, people sometimes get out of hand and have to be dealt with, but a premature use of force is not the solution. Using force should be a last resort, and if it seems to be necessary because calm, quiet conversation has not defused matters, the hotel is best advised to call the police instead of relying on an armed security officer.

Considering the costs and risks of arming hotel security officers in relation to the few times when they might need to resort to a gun—so rare as to be virtually nonexistent—the liabilities outweigh whatever remote benefits might be derived. All these factors must be evaluated as part of the

Chapter 7   The Security Department's Role

227

decision-making process when considering whether or not to arm the security staff.

DUTIES AND RESPONSIBILITIES

A security department's overall duties and responsibilities really are, or should be, determined by general managers. This does not mean becoming involved with the minutiae of individual security officers' work; rather, they define the manager's role. That, in turn, enables the manager to define the staff's role. What general managers prescribe in this regard is a reflection not only of their understanding of the benefits to be derived from effective security/loss-prevention programs, but it is also evidence of their confidence in their security managers.

As in any organization, duties and responsibilities will vary from place to place and from job to job; the higher the position, the greater they are. However, as noted before, no matter what the position is, one cannot be assigned tasks and held accountable for their performance without also having the necessary authority to act.

Security managers are obviously assigned the greatest number of duties and responsibilities. While they prepare their budgets, oversee the department's operations, develop and ensure compliance with security policies and procedures, and do those things normally considered to be managerial functions, they also should serve as in-house consultants on loss prevention to their general managers and other department heads. Otherwise, the ultimate goal of an integrated loss-prevention program, as described throughout this text, cannot be achieved.

To be effective, loss-prevention programs must be proactive rather than reactive. In their consulting roles security managers have to meet with their peers, learn how each department operates, and see if there are ways in which, by working together, the loss potential can be reduced, if not eliminated. This is the key to a meaningful security program.

Inevitably, incidents resulting in losses of one sort or another will sometimes occur. It then becomes the security manager's duty to investigate, but whether working with other department heads as consultants or conducting an investigation, a security manager must not lose sight of the fact that the goal is loss prevention. Consequently, in both capacities he or she must focus on conditions that either allowed or could allow something to happen to the hotel's detriment and then take reasonable steps to change those conditions. Of course, some people, be they employees or guests, will always be willing to gamble if they think they can win. Thus it is by changing the conditions, rather than focusing on who caused the loss, that the greatest benefits are realized.

Security officers' duties and responsibilities obviously are not as broad as those of their managers. They will vary depending on the nature of an officer's assignment. Here are three basic principles, more or less generic, with which all members of hotel management should be familiar;

1. To protect and conserve the employer's tangible and intangible assets to the best of their ability. Protection and conservation equal loss prevention, and security officers are in a position to help prevent four of the five sources of loss. They can help prevent crime, waste, accidents, and unethical behavior, but rarely will they be able to prevent mistakes.

2. To protect all persons—including both guests and employees—who are lawfully on the premises, as well as their property if it is lawfully on the premises.

3. To be of all possible assistance to those lawfully on the premises so long as doing so is consistent with the security department's basic mission.

While one hopes that no member of the security staff will engage in activities that will directly or indirectly contribute to losses, it would be naive to say it cannot happen. The risks can be minimized when security managers and supervisory personnel set a good example and provide effective supervision. However, of all of the possible sources of loss, the most subtle of the lot, and the one that requires particular attention, is the matter of ethics. Unethical behavior, or the appearance of unethical behavior, must be avoided. Regrettably, security managers can be as guilty of ethical lapses as their subordinates, and even if there is no measurable loss in dollars and cents, such breaches can be costly.

Two scenarios help illustrate this point, one at the manager level, the other involving security officers. Virtually all states have some restrictions on public access to criminal history information. Security managers who use personal police contacts or complimentary meals to get information to which they are not entitled are doing more than skirting the law—they are engaging in unethical behavior. If discovered, it may involve a fine, if provided for by the criminal history statute. It also can be a source of bad publicity and embarrassment if it becomes known to the news media.

With respect to security officers, unless prohibited by a union contract, policies calling for a search of employees' parcels when they leave work are not uncommon. Certainly there is no constitutional prohibition against searches by private persons, but the way in which those searches are conducted can be unethical.

Any evidence of discrimination in searching based on an employee's race, creed, color, sex, religious beliefs, or country of national origin is both unethical and intolerable. Unlike the security manager's breach of ethics cited in the preceding paragraph, there may be no fine and little risk of adverse publicity or embarrassment, but that does not mean there is no cost or loss to the hotel. Discrimination has an impact on employee morale; it can trigger anything ranging from a loss of productivity to acts of vandalism or a possible job action, all of which can be costly in either direct or indirect terms.

Consequently, the duties and responsibilities of all security department personnel at all levels have to be clearly defined. In addition, they have to be monitored in order to make certain that while the staff focuses on preventing losses that can be attributed to others, it does not engage in activities of its own that are inimical to the property's best interests.

RECORDS AND COMMUNICATIONS

Virtually all department heads keep records and have some form of communication. This being the case, one might well ask why general managers should take a special interest in those records related to security and loss prevention. The question has several answers, all of which are important both because of the useful information that they can (or should) provide and because of their potential use in case of litigation.

Security managers should advise their general managers of all significant incidents as soon as they possibly can. In some cases they may do so almost simultaneously with the occurrence; in others, immediately thereafter. However, the general managers also need to know about the status of the loss-prevention program with regard to matters that are not necessarily significant. Just as other department heads report on their respective operations, so should security managers report on loss-prevention matters at prescribed intervals.

To be able to manage their departments effectively and provide activity reports requires security managers to develop and maintain good records that document operations and can be used as working tools. Of course, the kinds of records will vary from property to property, but all should include data on such things as security posts left uncovered due to absences; dates, times, and kinds of training for each staff member; number and types of security incidents reported; value of lost or stolen property reported; number of investigations conducted and value of lost or stolen property recovered; number of times police or fire department help was needed; number of contacts with guests; and number of duty-related contacts with employees. The data, in synopsized form, should be submitted to general managers regularly. This information also can help general managers weigh a security department's budget request against its reported work load.

Records must be factual, detailed, and up to date if they are to be useful as working tools for the department's benefit and as the basis for general managers' reports. Furthermore, they can be important to a hotel's insurer who responds to a claim based on a security-related issue, and they most likely will have to be produced for plaintiffs' lawyers during pretrial discovery proceedings.

Earlier we took note of potential legal ramifications due to the unique nature of security operations and their possible impact on guests and employees. Therefore, in addition to its records, the importance of a department's communications should not be overlooked.

Security managers are agents as well as employees. As a result, unless their actions are clearly beyond the scope of their employment, what they say or do not say, whether orally or in writing, may be binding on the property. Therefore, they must be made to understand that whether they are instructing security officers, speaking with guests or employees, or writing to a third party, all job-related oral and written communications must be carefully thought out and carefully worded. Otherwise they may well become the basis for a lawsuit.

COOPERATION WITH OTHER DEPARTMENTS

Merely wishing for an integrated loss-prevention program and the benefits that one brings will not make these things happen. Such results will be achieved only if security managers can rely on the close cooperation of other department heads, and vice versa. For this to happen, much will depend on a combination of their professional skills, personalities, and above all, the leadership provided by their general managers.

There is a cliché about not being able to see the forest for the trees; it can apply to department heads. On occasion they are so close to a situation that they do not readily see possible loopholes in their operations. Security managers' professional training and experience often enables them to identify potential problems and sources of losses, but only if they first understand how any given department functions.

Human nature being what it is, unless the foundation is laid it is inadvisable for security managers to simply start asking questions of their peers. Other department heads may see this as an encroachment upon their own areas of responsibility, and their answers can be less than candid and not especially cordial. One important step in overcoming this attitude requires a display of leadership on the part of the general manager. He or she must make two points clear to the other managers. One, the security manager is

authorized to meet with them and ask questions about their respective operations. Two, this is no reflection on them or their ability; it is simply taking
advantage of the security manager's experience in preventing losses and thus
benefiting the property.

Despite this display of leadership and explanation, a security manager's
personality and experience are critically important. Security managers still
have to establish their own relationships with individual department heads.
It is here that personality can be a factor. To demand answers to questions or
to give the impression that they are superior to or more knowledgeable than
their peers will not elicit the cooperation needed to prevent losses. Among
other things the various department heads must be assured that security
managers have no preconceived ideas, nor do they feel obligated to find anything wrong; in fact, they would prefer not to. They simply are trying to learn
so that they can make useful contributions to the hotel's operations.

In addition, the security manager demonstrates professionalism when
he or she not only identifies potential problem areas or sources of loss but
comes up with ideas about how to deal with the issues. To be effective, security managers must be willing to share their thoughts about possible corrective actions rather than arbitrarily trying to impose them. Solving what they
see as purely a security problem may in fact create a more severe operating
one. By freely expressing their respective concerns and ideas about what to
do, two managers can probably reach a solution that will satisfy the needs of
both. The ability to achieve an agreement then becomes more than a sign of
cooperation; it is a first step in implementing whatever changes are needed.
Truly professional security managers are much more interested in avoiding
problems and preventing losses than in who gets credit for corrections made;
the results will speak for themselves, and their handiwork will be recognized.

PUBLIC SAFETY LIAISON

Normally, among a security manager's duties is liaison with public safety
agencies. Not only is developing and maintaining good working relationships with both the fire and police departments advisable, but it also is something that should be done before a need arises for help in dealing with a fire
or a crime. Liaison is best done at the level of those in command of the units
whose territories include the hotel, such as the appropriate fire department
battalion chief and commander of the police precinct or district, not with the
fire and police commissioners.

The work of both agencies is important, but from a loss-prevention
point of view, the fire department relationship is the more helpful since it can
serve several purposes. As an example, inviting departmental representatives

to periodically visit and inspect the property can be useful in preventing fires. Their training, plus their not being at the hotel on a daily basis, may result in their seeing potential sources of fires that employees, accustomed to their surroundings, may be inclined to overlook.

Another benefit of these visits is the opportunity for the fire department to familiarize itself with the inn's design, layout, storage facilities, and especially the location of departments that might be the most likely places for fires to start. This information can help the fire department keep losses down since it would be able to respond to an alarm more quickly and efficiently.

In discussing fires in Chapter 5, we noted the importance of having at least some employees trained in the proper use of fire extinguishers. They need to know more than how to empty the contents; they need to learn which kind of extinguisher to use and where to point the nozzle, depending on the type of fire. By and large, if the relationship between the hotel and the fire department is a good one, the latter will be more than happy to either provide or help provide that training.

As for the police, since theirs is largely a reactive function there is usually less need to ask for their help. For the most part, their contribution to the hotel's loss-prevention effort will be minimal. Nevertheless, good police liaison is necessary and is one of a security manager's proper functions.

However, this relationship, unlike that with the fire department, may need closer oversight on the general manager's part. One of the several goals of an effective security program, cited repeatedly throughout the text, is to prevent unethical behavior, and it would be naive to deny that on occasion an ethical question may arise.

While by no means universal, the risk tends to be greatest when security managers either are former law enforcement personnel or think of themselves as part of the law enforcement community. Fostered by a desire for good relations and perhaps even encouraged by general managers, they will often offer free meals to the "cops on the beat." Such favors may seem harmless enough, yet they can violate a police department's regulations with respect to the acceptance of any form of gratuity. This behavior can be embarrassing and costly to both the hotel and the officers involved.

There is even greater concern when ethical, or at least questionable, issues arise not because of free meals or coffee but because other kinds of favors are involved. For example, security managers might ask the police for information to which, by law, private persons are not entitled; or they might attempt to ingratiate themselves with the police by acceding to requests from the latter that are inimical to their employers' best interests.

A few examples to help illustrate these points from a hotel's perspective may be useful. Asking for police help if a crime has been committed is certainly proper. So is arranging for a paid police detail if a major function is likely to cause a major traffic problem, or if the presence of celebrity guests requires crowd control outside the hotel. On the other hand, to ask the police for a person's criminal history, knowing that by that state's laws hotels do not qualify for access to this kind of information, is unethical. Furthermore, it can result in a fine, bad publicity, and embarrassment if found out.

Then there are requests from, rather than to, the police. Care in dealing with these issues is no less important. Again, examples may be helpful in understanding the possible impact on a property if security managers fail to first consider their obligation to their employers. Perhaps one of the best illustrations is how comparable situations were handled differently by two corporate security directors, both with similar backgrounds, working for major chains.

Case Number 1

In the absence of a security manager, the general manager of a motor hotel on New York City's West Side was asked by drug enforcement agents if he would compliment a suite and another room so they could monitor a significant narcotics transaction that they proposed to arrange, following which they would make an arrest. Before committing himself, the general manager called the corporate security director for guidance. The latter approved the request without asking any questions.

As the agents moved in to make an arrest, shots were exchanged, resulting in the death of an agent and a guest who happened to be passing by the room where the transaction took place. Not only were others injured, but the trauma also caused another guest to have a heart attack, from which he later died. To the news media this story warranted continuing special attention based on the incident itself and the guests' lawsuits that followed. In addition to the expenses related to the litigation and losses attributable to the judgments awarded the plaintiffs, the incident embarrassed the hotel; people wondered if it would be safe to stay at that property.

Case Number 2

The only real initial difference between this case and the preceding one lay in its location; this was a hotel near the Los Angeles International Airport. However, the greatest difference was that this time the corporate security director asked questions of the agents instead of simply agreeing that their request for complimentary rooms be honored. He wanted to know if (a) the confidential informant acting on the agents' behalf would be wearing a transmitter, (b) the transaction would be recorded, (c) the agents had reason to believe the drug dealer would be armed, and (d) they knew if he would be using his own automobile or a taxi.

The answer to all four questions was "yes." Knowing that they would have the recorded transaction for evidentiary purposes, and being aware of the New York City incident, the security director said he would approve their request on condition that the arrest would be deferred until the dealer was in the act of entering either his car or a taxi. The agents refused to accept the offer. Their request for space was denied; risk to the property was avoided.

It is evident that effective liaison with public safety agencies is important. It can be especially helpful with regard to fire departments. However, effective liaison and an ethically questionable relationship are not the same. This is a distinction that general managers need to appreciate. In the final analysis, everyone benefits when security managers, as well as the public safety officials with whom they occasionally will need to have contact, mutually recognize the importance of ethical behavior in their dealings.

SUMMARY

Not all hotels and motels need or can justify having fully staffed security departments, but for many having one is another form of insurance insofar as preventing losses is concerned. In some cases owners will make the decision; in others those managers responsible for the hotel's success and profitability will decide.

Well-managed security departments contribute, albeit indirectly for the most part, to preventing losses and thus to increasing profits; poorly managed ones can add to losses. As a result, it is for their own benefit that general managers should have some understanding of security operations. If they do not, they risk becoming captives of their security managers and agreeing to whatever the latter want, regardless of whether the results will be in the hotel's best interests.

Optimal benefits are derived when security/loss-prevention programs are integrated into all phases of hotel operations. The key to success in this respect lies in the careful choice of a security manager, a clear definition of that person's authorized role to ensure the cooperation of other department heads, and equally clear evidence of the general manager's support by having the security manager report directly to him or her.

Despite these precautions, the possible impact of the loss-prevention program on profits, as well as on guest and employee relations, suggests the advisability of learning something about the department's actual operations. Questions of the department's size, whether to employ a proprietary or contract staff, and how to recruit for the former have to be answered. That training and supervision cost money should not blind management to the potential for much greater expenses and bad publicity if untrained or inadequately trained and supervised security officers' behavior leads to litigation.

A hotel's image, especially guests' first impressions, are important. Consequently, the selection of uniforms and equipment issued to security officers need to be carefully chosen because of the message they convey to both guests and employees. Some kinds of equipment, such as two-way radios, are a good investment; weapons are not. Giving security officers weapons does more than reflect adversely on image; it is also costly in many ways.

In broad terms general managers define the duties and responsibilities of all departments, security included, but the individual department heads refine and implement them. To satisfy themselves that the program is working as it should and simultaneously make certain that security managers do not inadvertently create needless problems, general managers should obtain regular reports on the departments' activities. In the event that security managers are authorized to communicate in writing with guests, it may be prudent for general managers or their executive assistant or resident managers to review those letters before they are mailed. This can reduce the risk that something might be said that could be construed to obligate the hotel.

That successful loss-prevention programs require the cooperation of all department heads is obvious. However, there also needs to be effective liaison with public safety agencies. This is especially true of fire departments. Their help in preventing fires and training employees in the proper use of fire extinguishers can be invaluable. A need for police help tends to be infrequent and more limited. Nevertheless, good liaison with them, although it can be ethically more sensitive, is also important. Any impropriety or appearance of impropriety can prove costly in various ways and must be avoided.

REVIEW QUESTIONS

1. What factors need to be taken into account when deciding on a security department's size?

2. Why is it in a hotel's best interest to have the security manager report directly to the general manager?

3. What role do general managers play in ensuring that the loss-prevention program is integrated into all aspects of operations?

4. Why is it important to have close cooperation between security managers and other department heads?

5. If contract services are to be used instead of a proprietary staff, what information should be obtained from agencies as part of the selection process?

6. What risks does a hotel take if it fails to provide proper training and supervision for its security officers?
7. State the reasons why arming security officers is inadvisable.
8. Who really decides on a security department's duties and responsibilities?
9. What purpose should security department records serve?
10. Of the public safety agencies, which one is in the best position to contribute to loss prevention?

SAMPLE CONTRACT FOR SECURITY AGENCY SERVICES

THIS AGREEMENT NO. _____ dated this _____ day of _____, 20 ___, by and between XYZ Corporation with its principal office at _____ (hereinafter referred to as the Vendor), and ABC, a _____ Corporation located at _____ (hereinafter referred to as ABC). WHEREAS VENDOR is in the business of providing guard services for business concerns and hotels and desires to supply such services to ABC; and WHEREAS ABC desires to make use of such services under the terms and conditions set forth herein;

NOW, THEREFORE, in consideration of the mutual covenants specified herein, the parties hereto agree as follows:

Article I: Agreement Term

The term of this Agreement will be Twelve (12) months beginning on the date first written above and continuing thereafter in full force and effect unless and until either party gives the other ninety (90) days prior written notice of termination. Upon termination both parties agree to continue honoring their respective obligations hereunder for the ninety (90) day notice period or such shorter period of time as may be mutually agreed upon.

In no event will ABC's liability for payment hereunder extend beyond the number of guard hours actually provided by Vendor under the terms of this Agreement.

Article II: Employment

A. Vendor shall employ all persons necessary to perform its obligations hereunder according to the terms of this Agreement and ABC's requirements, which may be modified by ABC at any time, and Vendor will be solely and exclusively responsible for all acts or omissions by its employees.

B. Vendor shall not discriminate against any applicant for employment or employee on the basis of race, creed, sex, color, country of national origin, religion, or age, in violation of any federal or state laws or local ordinances.

C. No former ABC employees shall be assigned to ABC without ABC's prior written consent.

D. Guards will be solely the employees of Vendor and not ABC, and Vendor shall pay all of their salaries and related expenses, including but not necessarily limited to all taxes and employees' contributions.

E. Vendor agrees that all services provided by it and through its employees under the terms of this Agreement will be performed by qualified, careful, efficient personnel in strict conformity with the best practices and according to standards that ABC may from time to time prescribe. Vendor also agrees that it will remove from service any employee(s) if asked to do so by ABC with or without cause.

F. All personnel employed by Vendor will be covered by a fidelity bond, the amount and terms and conditions of which are acceptable to ABC, and a copy of said bond shall be provided to ABC prior to the effective date of this Agreement.

G. ABC agrees that it will not make an offer of employment to any employee(s) of Vendor without having first obtained written approval to do so.

Article III: Guard Qualifications

A. All guards assigned to ABC will meet the minimum standards set forth below, the only exception(s) being guards on temporary assignment. For the purpose of this Vendor, any assignment of less than one week's duration will be considered temporary. ABC reserves the right through its authorized agent(s) to waive any requirements set forth herein, but only in writing and in individual cases. In no event is any waiver in any particular case to be construed as revising that standard as it applies to other guards.

B. Before assigning any of its personnel to ABC, Vendor will do the following with respect to each such employee:

1. Conduct as complete a background investigation of that person as is legally permissible, complying with all laws relating to the making of investigative reports and the disclosure of their contents.

2. Verify that the person is a high school graduate or has the equivalent of a high school education.

3. Verify that the person has no record of criminal convictions, minor traffic violations excepted.

4. Determine that the person has not had any credit difficulties within the past three (3) years.

5. Certify the following for each employee:

   a. That the person is in good mental health, and has no physical defects or abnormalities that would interfere with complete performance of all guard duties.

   b. That the person has binocular vision correctable to 20/20, is able to distinguish standard colors, and has normal hearing without the use of hearing aids.

   c. That the person's weight is in proportion to his or her height.

   d. That the person is capable of performing duties that may require moderate to arduous physical exertion including, but not necessarily limited to, standing or walking for an entire tour of duty, climbing stairs and ladders, lifting and carrying objects weighing up to fifty (50) pounds, running, and acts of physical self-defense.

6. Provide ABC with a copy of the medical certification for each person as evidence of the fact that that person meets the prescribed minimum physical standards.

7. Certify to ABC in writing that a thorough background investigation of that person has been completed, and that the qualifications set forth herein have been complied with.

C. Vendor will maintain the employment applications, or copies thereof, of all of its personnel assigned to ABC under the terms of this Agreement, in Vendor's office located at _____, and made available for review by ABC upon request for a period of three (3) years following that person's last appearance at ABC whether permanent or temporary.

D. Vendor also will maintain at that office, or at some other location acceptable to ABC, records of all training and all disciplinary action provided or taken by it with respect to each of its employees assigned to ABC in the performance of this Agreement, and they shall be made available for ABC's review upon request.

E. ABC reserves the right to review the employment application and/or resume, and to interview every person that Vendor proposes to assign to it. The final decision regarding an individual's acceptability for assignment to ABC will rest with ABC. Vendor understands that if the parties hereto agree to the assignment of supervisory personnel to ABC, those proposed for such assignment shall have had not less than three (3) years of increasingly responsible duties as guards.

F. Notwithstanding any of the foregoing, nothing in this Article or this Agreement is to be construed to imply employment of any guards by ABC, and guards shall be solely the responsibility of Vendor.

Article IV: Guard Assignments

A. Hours and Posts to be covered are as per Exhibit "B," which is attached hereto and made a part hereof. Vendor agrees that no guards assigned by it to ABC will be permitted to work in excess of twelve (12) hours in any given twenty-four (24) hour period, or more than sixty (60) hours in any given week, and each guard will be off duty not less than twenty-four (24) consecutive hours in each work week. For the purposes of this Agreement, the work week will begin at 12:01 A.M., Sunday, and end at 12 midnight the following Saturday. The provisions of this paragraph relative to time off may be waived only by ABC's authorized representative, and in writing.

B. A schedule of guard assignments in conformity with ABC's requirements will be submitted to ABC not less than seven (7) days before its implementation.

C. Guards assigned to ABC will remain at ABC for a period of one (1) year or the remaining term of this Agreement, whichever first occurs, unless (1) the guard's employment is terminated, (2) ABC agrees to the guard's prior transfer, (3) the guard is promoted by Vendor and no such position exists at ABC, or (4) the guard requests transfer.

D. In no event will Vendor assign to ABC a guard who has been removed from any other assignment for cause.

E. If it becomes necessary at any time for Vendor to provide guards for special duty it will be compensated for those special duty hours at the unit rate hereinafter set forth.

F. In an emergency Vendor may be required to provide up to two times the number of guards normally assigned to ABC under the terms of this Agreement. In all such cases the unit rate hereinafter agreed upon will prevail, but ABC will reimburse Vendor for the actual cost of expenses incurred in providing such services that are in excess of those incurred in regularly furnishing guards to ABC under the terms of this Agreement, including premium wages, additional administration, and overhead, provided, however, that the total payment to Vendor will not exceed 150% of the unit rates times the number of emergency guard hours actually worked.

Note: Properties that from time to time key officials of the United States Government, or of governments for whom the United States Government provides protection, should include the following additional paragraph:

G. Inasmuch as certain guards assigned to ABC may have to be given a security clearance by the United States Government, Vendor agrees that it will assign only personnel eligible for such clearances, and in the event that any guard assigned by it to ABC is denied clearance, that guard will be replaced immediately by one who can be cleared at no cost to ABC.

Article V: Uniforms and Equipment

A. Vendor will provide each of its guards with all uniforms, equipment, including flashlights, and related materials as specified by ABC necessary for the performance of their duties. ABC will furnish all fire-fighting equipment.

B. THE USE OR CARRYING OF WEAPONS, FIREARMS INCLUDED, ON ABC PREMISES IS PROHIBITED. Weapons may not be stored on ABC premises unless first approved in writing by ABC's General Manager, or his or her designee, which approval will state specifically the terms and conditions under which such storage will be allowed by Vendor's employees.

C. At all times while on duty, each guard will wear or otherwise display such form of identification badge as will be provided by ABC.

D. Immediately upon termination of any guard assigned to ABC, regardless of reason, Vendor shall immediately notify ABC in writing of the termination and reasons therefor, and it also will immediately recover and return to ABC the identification originally issued to that guard. If for any reason the ABC issued identification is not available, Vendor will submit in writing to ABC its explanation as to why the identification cannot be returned, and the efforts made by it for recovery.

Article VI: Training and Supervision

A. In addition to whatever general training Vendor provides to all of its guards, it also will provide, prior to assignment to ABC, a minimum of forty (40) hours of training covering the subjects set forth below unless such requirement is waived in writing by ABC, or temporary guards as previously defined herein are used in unusual circumstances.

B. The subjects to be covered in training will include, but not necessarily be limited to, the following:

1. Legal restrictions on arrests, searches, and seizures.
2. Detection, reporting, and control of fires; the use of portable fire-fighting equipment; the control of fire suppression systems; and the use of emergency breathing apparatus.
3. Appearance, attitude, and conduct as may be set forth in ABC's Guard Manual or otherwise prescribed by ABC's authorized representative(s).
4. General application of patrol routines, activities, and report writing.
5. Guest, employee, and other human and public relations.
6. Controlling access to and exit from the premises.
7. Controlling the movement of ABC's assets, and of other property for whose protection ABC may be responsible, while on the premises.
8. Riot, strike, and emergency procedures.

9. Other topics selected from among those listed in ABC's Guard Manual or prescribed by ABC's authorized representatives.

C. Upon first reporting for duty at ABC, each newly assigned guard will be given a minimum of sixteen (16) hours of "on-the-job" training, and Vendor will not charge ABC for the services of any guard until all training required under the terms of this Agreement, including on-the-job training, has been completed to ABC's satisfaction.

D. Vendor also will give each guard assigned to ABC a minimum of eight (8) hours of refresher or in-service training once every six (6) months.

E. Vendor will provide at least twice weekly, at random times to cover all shifts on a regular basis, unannounced inspections of each post to which its guards are assigned by one of its nonresident supervisors.

F. Vendor agrees to remove and replace any guard from assignment at ABC (1) if such employee is not properly performing his or her duties, or (2) upon request of ABC.

G. Vendor agrees that it will not knowingly hire or assign to ABC any person who is or has been assigned, whether on a temporary or a permanent basis, to any entity that is a business competitor of ABC.

Article VII: Guard Responsibilities

A. Unless otherwise specifically instructed in writing by ABC's authorized representative, guards will be responsible for all aspects of protection, including, but not necessarily limited to, the following: monitoring shipping and receiving dock activities; guarding the premises against fire, flood, burglary, theft, breaking and entering, pilferage, acts of vandalism, damage to or the destruction of property; preventing malicious injury to persons; and allowing only authorized persons to enter the premises. They will make regular tours of the property, report immediately all violations of fire and safety regulations, and when instructed to do so they will control traffic on and in all ABC-owned roadways and parking areas. Guards also will carry out such special written instructions as may from time to time be issued to them by ABC's authorized representative(s).

B. Upon completing a tour of duty each guard will submit a written report to ABC's designated representative covering all activities, including details of all unusual or hazardous conditions encountered during such tour. Any guard who discovers an emergency condition will report it immediately, in person, by two-way radio, telephone, or by alarm, whichever is most appropriate, and will confirm both the discovery and action taken in response thereto in the written report submitted at the conclusion of his or her tour of duty.

C. Guards are prohibited from making arrests, detaining persons, or swearing out complaints on behalf of ABC without the express written consent of ABC's General Manager or his or her designee. In the event that a guard witnesses a crime being committed in his or her presence, on ABC premises, it will be reported immediately to either ABC's Security Manager or the ABC manager then in charge of security, if one is then on duty, and if not, to the guard's Contractor supervisor, and if the ABC representative or guard's supervisor, as the case may be, is of the opinion that immediate action is required, the ABC representative or guard's supervisor may notify the police directly with notification immediately thereafter to both ABC's Security Manager or representative and ABC's General Manager or his or her designee.

Article VIII: Liability/Indemnification

A. Vendor will indemnify and hold ABC, its directors, agents, employees, and representatives, harmless against all loss and liability resulting from personal injury or death to its own employees or others, property damage, assault, false arrest and false imprisonment, slander, defamation of character, negligence, or any other cause arising out of or in connection with the services to be provided hereunder irrespective of whether performed on ABC's premises or elsewhere.

B. In the event a claim is made against ABC, its directors, agents, employees, or representatives, for which Vendor has undertaken to indemnify ABC, ABC or its legal representative will promptly notify Vendor in writing of such claim or lawsuit arising out of or in connection with the services provided under the terms of this Agreement, will forward to Vendor all related documents, and Vendor then will defend the case at its own expense. However, ABC reserves the right to be represented by counsel of its own choice, and at its own expense, at any proceeding or settlement discussions related thereto.

C. Vendor will procure and maintain a minimum of the following insurance:
   1. Workmen's Compensation Insurance as prescribed by the laws of   and Employer's Liability Insurance with a limit of $100,000.00.
   2. Comprehensive Automobile Liability Insurance, including Automobile Non-Ownership Liability, with limits of $1,000,000.00 for bodily injury or death of each person; $1,000,000.00 for bodily injury or death for each occurrence; and $1,000,000.00 for property damage in each occurrence.
   3. Comprehensive General Liability Insurance, including contractual liability, broad form property damage, and personal injury liability, with a combined $2,000,000.00 bodily injury and property damage limit in each occurrence.
   4. Employee Dishonesty Insurance with a limit of $1,000,000.00 per loss.

D. Within two (2) working days of this Agreement's execution, Vendor will furnish ABC with a Certificate of Insurance as evidence that the required coverage is in effect, and that ABC has been named as an additional insured under both the Comprehensive General Liability and Automobile Insurance policies.

E. Each of the insurance policies referred to above will include a provision that it may not be cancelled without thirty (30) days' prior written notice to ABC of such cancellation.

F. Nothing in this Article will be deemed to limit Vendor's responsibility to the amounts stated above, or under any other provisions of this Agreement.

Article IX: Payment

A. The services to be performed hereunder will be billable on an hourly basis at the rates shown on Exhibit A, attached hereto and made a part hereof (billable rate). All of the rates set forth in Exhibit A, with the sole exception described in paragraph B of this Article, will be in full force and effect for the duration of this Agreement, and they will include all of Vendor's profit, overhead, guard and supervisory salaries, administrative expenses, and all other costs related to the performance of this Agreement. The billable rate will apply to all guard services provided irrespective of the date or time of day when such services are to be performed. ABC will not be subject to any overtime or premium billings for additional hours or holiday rates except as provided for in paragraph B, below.

B. In the event that ABC, with less than twenty-four (24) hours' prior notice to Vendor, requests additional hours of unscheduled service, Vendor will make every reasonable effort to provide such service to ABC without any charge for overtime. However, if the additional hours of service can be provided only with overtime, Vendor will advise ABC of that fact, the overtime rate that it will have to charge, and the number of hours to which it will apply.

C. Not until authorization has been received from ABC's Purchasing Manager, or his or her designee, will Vendor provide such additional hours of service, and the additional cost of the overtime will be paid by ABC within thirty (30) days from the receipt of a separate invoice referencing an ABC Purchase Order for the stated amount.

D. Vendor will maintain complete, clear, and accurate records of all guard assignments, hours of work performed by each, and actual direct labor hourly rates incurred in the performance of this Agreement. ABC reserves the right to inspect and audit, during regular business hours, Vendor's business records as they relate to the services rendered under this Agreement. Vendor agrees to make such records available either at ABC, or at one of Vendor's locations within a twenty-five (25) mile radius of ABC, and to retain all such records for a period of not less than three (3) years from the date of completion of this Agreement.

E. Vendor will submit for payment one (1) invoice supported by all documentation required by ABC for the verification of the billing on a weekly basis for the preceding month, except that any overtime authorized by ABC, as set forth in this Article, will be invoiced separately against an ABC authorized Purchase Order.

F. If ABC disputes the billing, in whole or in part, it will process promptly for payment the undisputed portion thereof, and it will confer with Vendor relative to the disputed portion. ABC is not obligated to make any payment until the billing and documentation therefor are submitted in a form acceptable to it.

G. Within thirty (30) days following the receipt of a valid invoice and its supporting documentation ABC will remit payment.

H. Vendor will be responsible for all sales, use, or other taxes, if any, applicable to the work.

I. If, in ABC's opinion, guard rates should be reduced to conform to any reductions in minimum wages, Vendor agrees to renegotiate its billing rates.

J. Vendor warrants that the billable rate charged ABC hereunder is as low as the Vendor charges any client purchasing such services in the same or greater quantity under similar terms and conditions, and in the event Vendor grants any other client a lower rate for the same quantity of services under similar terms and conditions during the term hereof, then ABC's price shall be adjusted for the balance of the term to reflect the lower rate.

Article X: Default

A. If Vendor fails to perform any of the services called for by this Agreement, or if any proceeding is filed by or against it in bankruptcy or insolvency, or an assignment is made by it for the benefit of its creditors, or if there is a transfer of proprietary interest, and such condition or conditions are not remedied to ABC's reasonable satisfaction within fourteen (14) calendar days following written notice thereof given by ABC, ABC may without any liability immediately terminate all or any part of this Agreement by written or telegraphic notice to Vendor and seek similar services elsewhere.

B. If, during the term of this Agreement, Vendor for any reason is unable or unwilling to furnish ABC the number of guards required for the protection of the site covered thereby, ABC may contract with another guard service of its choice, at the then prevailing rate, for such additional or replacement services as it may require.

C. In such an event Vendor will be responsible for all damages and expenses incurred by ABC prior to the replacement of such services, as well as for all additional expenses incurred by ABC above and beyond the rates set forth in this Agreement for the protection of the site covered thereby.

D. ABC agrees to make every reasonable effort to pay all properly submitted and documented Vendor's invoices within thirty (30) days of their receipt. In the event that Vendor has not been paid within that time, provided Vendor has submitted correct and documented invoices and has otherwise complied with its obligations hereunder, it then may issue a written demand for payment to ABC, and if within fifteen (15) days of the receipt of such a demand by ABC Vendor still has not received payment, it then may notify ABC in writing of its intention to terminate this Agreement forty-five (45) days following ABC's receipt of such notice.

Article XI: Confidentiality

A. All information obtained by Vendor from ABC in connection with this Agreement, its performance, or for any other reason, is received by Vendor in confidence, remains the property of ABC, and will be used by Vendor only to the extent necessary for the performance of this Agreement.

B. All such ABC information and property will be returned to it upon the expiration, termination, or cancellation of this Agreement, or at any time that ABC requests its return.

C. Vendor agrees that it will not disclose to others, advertise, or publish the fact that it is performing or has performed any service or work for ABC, whether under the terms of this Agreement or otherwise, unless it is expressly authorized to do so in writing by ABC. It also agrees that all information, data, results, analyses, and reports received, collected, developed, prepared or written by it, its employees, representatives, or agents in the performance of this Agreement will be maintained in confidence without restriction as to time, that disclosure will be made only to ABC, and that no such information or material will be used by it for any purpose other than the completion of its obligation to ABC.

D. Vendor agrees that the provisions of this Article XI will survive the expiration, termination, or cancellation of this Agreement.

Article XII: ABC-Furnished Documentation

A. ABC will prepare written instructions, including a Guard Manual where deemed appropriate, setting forth specifically the days and hours of the week when guards are to be on duty, the number of guards required and the duties that they are to perform, and the location of guard rooms, and it will furnish guard logs. All materials provided by ABC, including, but not necessarily limited to, Guard Manuals, post orders, copies of ABC's Security and Safety Policies and Procedures, and of ABC's telephone directory, will not be reproduced by Vendor or distributed to any of its personnel other than those working at ABC or on its premises, and all such materials must be returned to ABC immediately upon the completion of this Agreement, its prior termination, or at any other time that ABC requests their return.

B. ABC may modify or revise these materials at any time upon twenty-four (24) hours' prior notification to Vendor.

C. All guards will be required to sign in and out in the guard log provided by ABC.

D. If requested by ABC, Vendor agrees to assist with the preparation of written materials for guards, such as post orders, manuals, etc., at no additional charge to ABC.

Article XIII: General Provisions

A. This Agreement and any amendments hereto will be governed by the laws of the State of   . If any provision contravenes such law, it will be deemed to have been deleted, but no such deletion will in any way affect any of the other portions of this Agreement.

B. This Agreement, and all exhibits referenced herein, or attached hereto and made a part hereof, constitute the entire understanding between Vendor and supersede all prior oral or written communications, agreements, representations, statements, negotiations, and undertakings relating to the subject matter hereof.

C. No representation, promise, waiver, modification, or amendment will be binding on either party unless made in writing and signed by an authorized representative of each.

D. ABC's failure to insist upon, or enforce in any instance, strict performance by Vendor of any part of this Agreement, or to exercise any of the rights herein conferred upon or reserved by it, will not be construed as a waiver or relinquishment by ABC to any extent of its right to assert or rely upon such terms or rights on any future occasion.

E. All notices required to be given by either party under the terms of this Agreement must be sent by Registered or Certified Mail, Return Receipt Requested, and addressed to:

ABC Hotel
Street Address
Anytown, USA
ATTN: Purchasing Manager

VENDOR: _____

ATTN: _____

F. Neither this Agreement nor any interest hereunder may be assigned, in whole or in part, by either party without the prior written consent of the other, and any such attempted assignment will be null and void.

G. Vendor agrees that without having first obtained ABC's written consent it will neither disclose to any person or persons outside of its employ, nor use for any purpose other than the performance of this Agreement, any information pertaining to ABC or ABC's affairs, including the contents of this Agreement.

IN WITNESS WHEREOF the parties hereto have caused this Agreement to be executed in duplicate by their duly authorized representatives as of the day and year first written above.

ACCEPTED: ACCEPTED:

_____   ABC HOTEL

BY: _____   BY: _____

TITLE: _____   TITLE: _____

Chapter 8

International Operations

For all practical purposes major hotel chains can be described as multinational since, regardless of ownership, they are involved with properties in more than one country. They may own some or they may have contracts to manage others for their owners. In either case, it is not unusual for them to promote members of individual properties' management staffs as one way to retain competent managers. As a result, the latter are often required to relocate.

To illustrate, there is the story of one person employed by a chain. An executive assistant at a hotel in Venezuela, he was promoted to general manager and then transferred to Puerto Rico before being assigned as general manager of a larger property in Jamaica. From Jamaica he moved to Hawaii to oversee the construction of a new hotel, of which he became general manager when the project was completed.

Since the principles enunciated in Chapters 1 through 7 are valid no matter where hotels and motels are located, one might ask, why a separate chapter on international operations? The answer is that while the fundamentals of sound security/loss prevention are the same everywhere, local conditions may have a bearing on program implementation.

In many countries no major obstacles will interfere with the adoption of meaningful loss-prevention measures. In others the problems may be of such magnitude that overcoming them is so difficult as to verge on the impossible. The latter conditions are more likely to exist in, but are not necessarily limited to, countries where the government itself, frequently in the person of a self-perpetuating head of state, is the owner. Profit, efficiency, and guest comfort are important; but staying in power is more so, and it governs what is or is not permissible Therefore, general managers new to a country who want to upgrade an existing security effort or start an effective loss-prevention program should familiarize themselves with local restrictions before acting. They should do so regardless of whether the chain owns the hotel or is only managing it. This advice also applies to physical security considerations as well as to the security department, assuming there is one.

For instance, security-conscious managers know that certain methods and equipment can help prevent losses and simultaneously contribute to a more efficient but smaller security staff. However, where international properties are concerned, knowing this is not enough. Before deciding on possible implementation, answers are needed to questions of cost, availability, service, and government approval.

For example, a manager might want to use closed-circuit television or to install a computerized access-control system. Closed-circuit television might be available, desirable, and acceptable to the government. However, if the combined cost of the equipment and import duties would far exceed the wages paid for additional security officers, it may not be a good investment. As for computerized access control, it might be affordable, but it would be a poor investment unless the vendor has a local service office to effect repairs if problems should arise.

As previously noted, it is important to recognize the government's role before proceeding with changes. Even if cost, availability, and service are not major factors, getting government approval may be. The government of a South American country limited ownership of a particular camera, used to make photo identification badges, to government agencies; private owner-ship or use was prohibited. Although the government had an interest in the hotel, the latter could not issue its employees the corporate-wide photo iden-tification badge.

The size of the security staff at a Middle Eastern hotel could have been reduced by a third, and its efficiency improved, if its officers had been equipped with two-way radios. The longtime head of state, always afraid of a possible coup, decreed that no private organization or person could use, let alone own, two-way radios. Although he owned the property and had it managed by a chain, it fell under the "private" category and was not exempt from the government's edict.

For management of international operations to try to put into effect and implement meaningful changes to prevent losses and improve profits can be even more challenging and difficult where security departments are con-cerned. While this is not universally true, it is more likely to occur in coun-tries where the government, either as an entity or in the person of a seemingly perpetual head of state, either owns or has a major interest in the hotel. Notwithstanding a management contract with a reputable chain, when these conditions exist the owner may well dictate who will be the security manager and what will be at least some of the security department's duties.

Two examples illustrate the extent to which this can happen. At the pre-viously mentioned Middle Eastern property owned by the country's ruler, neither the managing corporation nor the general manager had any say in the choice of the security director. The government ordered the appointment of an army officer to be assigned for a specified tour of duty. With very few exceptions, he got his instructions from the owner via the army's high com-mand. He alone determined the security staff's duties and responsibilities. Corporate and local management wanted to have the benefits of an inte-grated loss-prevention program, but their extremely limited control over the security director, plus his personality and demeanor, made implementation impossible. The security officers were civilians whose principal job was to pa-trol the building and its grounds, and to bar anyone from entering whose ap-pearance might be offensive to the country's customs and mores. In reality they were nothing more than a private police force commanded by an army colonel and subject to military discipline.

The other property, also owned by a head of state, was in the East Indies. Like the hotel in the preceding paragraph, management had no say in the choice of a security manager. The only difference in this respect was that instead of his being an army officer, he was a major in the National Police assigned for a three-year tour of duty. In addition, a slightly lower-ranking member of the same department was posted as the security manager's second in command. Like his Middle Eastern counterpart, he alone decided what the security department's duties and responsibilities would be but with even less input from the managing corporation or general manager.

Again, the security officers were civilians. In some ways their role was similar to that of the officers at the Middle Eastern hotel, but in others security's job was more pervasive. Here, security officers on patrol carried a report form on which they recorded everything that they saw or heard while making rounds. This was required whether guests or employees were involved.

This owner was paranoid. He had two major interests: One was self-preservation; the other was making as much profit from the hotel as possible. He was afraid of ideas that he did not originate, including those based on an integrated approach to loss prevention. As much as the managing corporation and general manager wanted to integrate security into all phases of operations, the atmosphere was not conducive to such a program. Since the general manager and a majority of the department heads were European, the owner felt they could not be trusted. To test his suspicions, he directed the security manager to focus on what they did and said. In obedience to these orders, the security manager installed recording devices in at least some of the managers' offices.

National government interference is not the only issue that can arise where security staffing is concerned. There can be problems at the local level even where no ownership or other direct financial interest in a hotel exists. This was the situation encountered at a Central American property managed under the terms of a contract.

The hotel was not large enough to justify employing a full-time security manager, but it was big and busy enough to warrant having a small number of security officers. Its high occupancy was due primarily to the presence of several American manufacturing plants that also reduced the number of unemployed in this city of more than 250,000 people. Given the very small labor pool from which to recruit security officers and the need for them to be able to read and write, the only logical solution seemed to be the use of contract agency officers. This was the course followed by both the city's other hotels and the manufacturing plants.

In this case, the only contract agency in the area was owned and operated by the local chief of police. Left without a choice, the hotel entered into an agreement for the use of his agency's services. Shortly thereafter a problem arose; one of the security officers was caught stealing from a guest's room. The matter was reported to the police chief, who openly functioned as the agency's manager as well. He would not remove the officer from the hotel, refused to take a complaint filed jointly by the guest and hotel, and said that if the hotel insisted on pursuing the matter, he would cancel the contract and leave the hotel without protection or any recourse.

SUMMARY

The need for sound security and loss-prevention programs is no less in international operations than it is in those hotels and motels located in the United States. Knowledgeable and security-conscious management personnel appreciate their many benefits. However, no matter how good and worthy of implementation ideas may be, nothing is gained if they cannot be put into practice. Thus general managers subject to overseas assignments need to learn what will and will not be feasible concerning program development in the places to which they are to be sent.

Although there may be some obstacles to implementing meaningful programs in the United States, for the most part they are not insurmountable. To a large extent the same can be said of hotels and motels in North America, western Europe, and some countries in the so-called Pacific Rim. The difficulties facing hoteliers in some other countries may be so great as to virtually stop progress in terms of preventing losses.

In some countries, especially with respect to physical security, there may be practical problems that could be overcome, but the cost would be prohibitive. In others, cost might not be a factor, but facilities to properly service the equipment would not be available. The government also may restrict or prohibit the use of certain kinds of security equipment.

The problems may be more difficult and, if not impossible, certainly harder to overcome in matters relating to having a security department in countries where heads of state both fear a loss of power and either own or have a financial interest in a hotel. The degree of government interference may actually prevent the managing corporation or general manager from instituting a loss-prevention program that would benefit operations and the profit picture. It is conceivable that the person in charge of security will be arbitrarily imposed on the hotel and that he will take his instructions from the government, not from the general manager.

REVIEW QUESTIONS

1. From the standpoint of implementing a security/loss-prevention program, does it make any difference whether a chain owns the hotel or merely manages it under contract?

2. Why is it important for management personnel assigned to a foreign country for the first time to familiarize themselves with local conditions vis-à-vis security?

3. Do the underlying principles of security and loss prevention have application to international operations? If they do, what are the two main factors that can affect their adoption?

4. Should cost be the primary determinant in looking for ways in which to use physical security? If not, what other factors need to be considered?

5. What may motivate a hotel owner who also is the head of state to insist on appointing a person of his choice as security manager?

6. Is the government's appointment of the security manager likely to be an asset or a liability with respect to the general manager's efforts to integrate the loss-prevention program?

7. Under what circumstances might it be possible to have integration despite the security manager's being a government appointee?

8. Do the international operating problems encountered relative to security exist in all countries other than the United States?

INDEX